Performance Interventions

Series Editors: **Elaine Aston**, University of Lancaster, and **Bryan Reynolds**, University of California, Irvine

Performance Interventions is a series of monographs and essay collections on theatre, performance, and visual culture that share an underlying commitment to the radical and political potential of the arts in our contemporary moment, or give consideration to performance and to visual culture from the past deemed crucial to a social and political present. *Performance Interventions* moves transversally across artistic and ideological boundaries to publish work that promotes dialogue between practitioners and academics, and interactions between performance communities, educational institutions, and academic disciplines.

Titles include:

Alan Ackerman and Martin Puchner (*editors*)
AGAINST THEATRE
Creative Destructions on the Modernist Stage

Elaine Aston and Geraldine Harris (*editors*)
FEMINIST FUTURES?
Theatre, Performance, Theory

Maaike Bleeker
VISUALITY IN THE THEATRE
The Locus of Looking

Clare Finburgh and Carl Lavery (*editors*)
CONTEMPORARY FRENCH THEATRE AND PERFORMANCE

James Frieze
NAMING THEATRE
Demonstrative Diagnosis in Performance

Lynette Goddard
STAGING BLACK FEMINISMS
Identity, Politics, Performance

Alison Forsyth and Chris Megson (*editors*)
GET REAL: DOCUMENTARY THEATRE PAST AND PRESENT

Leslie Hill and Helen Paris (*editors*)
PERFORMANCE AND PLACE

D.J. Hopkins, Shelley Orr and Kim Solga
PERFORMANCE AND THE CITY

Amelia Howe Kritzer
POLITICAL THEATRE IN POST-THATCHER BRITAIN
New Writing: 1995–2005

Marcela Kostihová
SHAKESPEARE IN TRANSITION
Political Appropriations in the Post-Communist Czech Republic

Jon McKenzie, Heike Roms and C. J. W.-L. Wee (*editors*)
CONTESTING PERFORMANCE
Emerging Sites of Research

Jennifer Parker-Starbuck
CYBORG THEATRE
Corporeal/Technological Intersections in Multimedia Performance

Ramón H. Rivera-Servera and Harvey Young
PERFORMANCE IN THE BORDERLANDS

Mike Sell (*editor*)
AVANT-GARDE PERFORMANCE AND MATERIAL EXCHANGE
Vectors of the Radical

Melissa Sihra (*editor*)
WOMEN IN IRISH DRAMA
A Century of Authorship and Representation

Brian Singleton
MASCULINITIES AND THE CONTEMPORARY IRISH THEATRE

Performance Interventions
Series Standing Order ISBN 978–1–4039–4443–6 Hardback
978–1–4039–4444–3 Paperback
(*outside North America only*)

You can receive future titles in this series as they are published by placing a standing order. Please contact your bookseller or, in case of difficulty, write to us at the address below with your name and address, the title of the series and the ISBN quoted above.

Customer Services Department, Macmillan Distribution Ltd, Houndmills, Basingstoke, Hampshire RG21 6XS, England

Contemporary French Theatre and Performance

Edited by

Clare Finburgh
(Senior Lecturer in Modern Drama)

and

Carl Lavery
(Senior Lecturer in Drama, Theatre and Performance)

Liberté • Égalité • Fraternité
RÉPUBLIQUE FRANÇAISE

This book is supported by the French Ministry of Foreign Affairs, as part of the Burgess programme run by the Cultural Department of the French Embassy in London. (www.frenchbooknews.com)

First published 2011 by
PALGRAVE MACMILLAN

Palgrave Macmillan in the UK is an imprint of Macmillan Publishers Limited,
registered in England, company number 785998, of Houndmills, Basingstoke,
Hampshire RG21 6XS.

Palgrave Macmillan in the US is a division of St Martin's Press LLC,
175 Fifth Avenue, New York, NY 10010.

Palgrave Macmillan is the global academic imprint of the above companies
and has companies and representatives throughout the world.

Palgrave® and Macmillan® are registered trademarks in the United States,
the United Kingdom, Europe and other countries.

ISBN 978–0–230–58051–0   hardback

This book is printed on paper suitable for recycling and made from fully
managed and sustained forest sources. Logging, pulping and manufacturing
processes are expected to conform to the environmental regulations of the
country of origin.

A catalogue record for this book is available from the British Library.

Library of Congress Cataloging-in-Publication Data

Contemporary French theatre and performance / edited by Clare Finburgh
    and Carl Lavery.
        p. cm.
    Includes index.
    Summary: "This is the first book to explore the relationship between
experimental theatre and performance making in France. Reflecting the
recent return to aesthetics and politics in French theory, it focuses on
how a variety of theatre and performance practitioners use their art work
to contest reality as it is currently configured in France" — Provided by
publisher.
        ISBN 978–0–230–58051–0 (hardback)
    1. Experimental theater—France.   2. Theater—France—History—21st
    century. I. Finburgh, Clare. II. Lavery, Carl, 1969–
    PN2635.2.C66 2011
    792.0944'09051—dc22   2011001640

10   9   8   7   6   5   4   3   2   1
20 19 18 17 16 15 14 13 12 11

Printed and bound in Great Britain by
CPI Antony Rowe, Chippenham and Eastbourne

To Immanuel, Inez, Raphael and Saul

Contents

List of Illustrations

Acknowledgements

We have endeavoured, where possible, to use respected translations in this volume. When this was neither possible nor appropriate, we either asked contributors to provide their own translations, or translated texts ourselves with the support of Dominic Glynn and Cathy Piquemal. We adopted the same principle with respect to titles of plays, performances and texts. On all occasions, the date in brackets refers to the original French publication, and not to the English translation. The meaning of titles that remain in the French original are, we trust, self-evident. Finally, we have tried to engage the chapters in a dialogue with each other by making use of extensive cross-references and editors' notes. Some of the editors' notes are for the benefit of an Anglophone audience and provide information on key figures, terms and events in France.

We gratefully acknowledge permission to edit and reprint sections from an essay by Michel Corvin, 'L'Esprit du lieu', *Théâtre/Public*, 183 (2006), 36–44.; and sections of a document by Clare Finburgh, 'External and Internal Dramaturgies', *Contemporary Theatre Review*, 20:2 (2010), 206–19 (http://www.informaworld.com). We would also like to thank the contributors and companies who supplied images for the volume. This book owes much to the translation, linguistic and organizational skills of Dominic Glynn at Exeter College, Oxford University and Cathy Piquemal, the Publications and Research Officer at Aberystwyth University. Their help has been immense. Thanks must also go to the French Ministry of Foreign Affairs for the generous Burgess Grant, which helped to subsidize the translation work.

This volume would not have been possible without the support of the Institut Français, who provided a Burgess Grant for translation fees. In difficult economic times, Aberystwyth University and the Department of Theatre, Film and Television (TFTS) went beyond the call of duty and financed translation costs, supplied administrative support and funded a research trip to Paris in 2009. We are indebted to Professors Adrian Kear and Lynn Pykett.

We would like to mention the colleagues and friends who commented on extracts from the book and helped to source images. These include: Anne-Françoise Benhamou, Christophe Brault, Joseph Danan, Andrew Filmer, Reuben Knutson, Noëlle Renaude, Mike Pearson, Bruno

Tackels, David Williams and Ralph Yarrow. For a number of personal reasons, some good, some bad, this book has taken longer than it should have. We would like to acknowledge the patience and forbearance of our contributors and to express our gratitude to Elaine Aston and Bryan Reynolds, the Series Editors, for letting us get on with it, and to Paula Kennedy and Benjamin Doyle at Palgrave Macmillan for being supportive and alleviating the inevitable stress.

As ever, we would like to thank our partners and families for supplying the necessary child-care and giving us the endless support needed to bring this project to a close.

Notes on Contributors

Elaine Aston is Professor of Contemporary Performance at Lancaster University, UK, where she teaches and researches feminist theatre, theory and performance, a field in which she is widely published. Her authored studies include *An Introduction to Feminism and Theatre* (1994); *Caryl Churchill* (1997/2001); *Feminist Theatre Practice* (1999) and *Feminist Views on the English Stage* (2003). She has co-edited four volumes of plays by women and, with Janelle Reinelt, co-edited *The Cambridge Companion to Modern British Women Playwrights* (2000). Her most recent publications include *Feminist Futures? Theatre, Performance, Theory*, co-edited with Geraldine Harris (2006); *Performance Practice and Process: Contemporary [Women] Practitioners*, co-authored with Geraldine Harris (2007) and *Staging International Feminisms*, co-edited with Sue-Ellen Case (2007).

David Bradby is Emeritus Professor of Drama and Theatre Studies at Royal Holloway, University of London. He is the author of *Modern French Drama 1940–1990* (1991), *The Theatre of Michel Vinaver* (1993), *Beckett: Waiting for Godot* (2001) and *Mise en Scène: French Theatre Now* (1997, with Annie Sparks). His edited works include *The Paris Jigsaw: Internationalism and the City's Stages* (2002, with Maria M. Delgado) and two volumes of *New French Plays* (1989 and 1998). He has translated and edited two books by Jacques Lecoq: *The Moving Body* (2000) and *Theatre of Movement and Gesture* (2006) as well as plays by Michel Vinaver and Bernard-Marie Koltès. In 1997 the French Government awarded him the title *Chevalier des Arts et Lettres* for services to French theatre. In 2002 he was invited to join a team of French scholars compiling a history of French theatre from the Middle Ages to the present day. This work (assisted by an Arts and Humanities Research Council grant) is now complete and the book *Le Théâtre en France de 1968 à 2000* was published by Honoré Champion (Paris) in 2007. He is general editor of the Cambridge University Press series 'Cambridge Studies in Modern Theatre' and is joint editor (with Maria M. Delgado) of the quarterly journal *Contemporary Theatre Review*.

Robert Cantarella was until March 2010 the Artistic Director of the Centquatre along with Frédéric Fisbach. He is a renowned theatre director, film maker and writer. Prior to his position at the Centrequatre, he was the Artistic Director of the Centre dramatique (CDN) de Dijon-Bourgogne.

Augusto Corrieri is a performance artist, choreographer and writer. Born in Milan, Corrieri first approached performance as a magician and illusionist. In 1999 he moved to England to take a degree in Theatre at Dartington College of Arts, after which he co-founded and worked with Deer Park performance company: their dance-theatre piece *See You Swoon* toured the UK and Europe. In 2004 Augusto joined propeller, a performance and research collective based in Devon, working on ideas of ecology, perception and orientation. Since 2005 he has been developing a solo-led performance practice in the UK, working on how to make spectators critically aware of their place within the construction of a theatre event.

Michel Corvin is Emeritus Professor of Theatre Studies at the Université Paris-III – Sorbonne nouvelle. His many publications focus essentially on the history of dramaturgy, the avant-garde, aesthetics and semiology. His numerous works on these themes include *Petite folie collective, sur le langage dada et surréaliste* (1966, with Copi), *Julien Torma, l'écrivain fantôme* (1972) and *Le Théâtre nouveau en France* (1995). In addition, he has edited the Pléiade edition of Jean Genet's complete theatre (2002), an anthology of European theatre, *De Pinter à Müller* (2007) and the *Dictionnaire encyclopédique du théâtre* (2008). Several of his books and articles are translated into English, notably his biography of Jacques Polieri.

Laura Cull is Lecturer in Performing Arts at Northumbria University in Newcastle, UK. She is editor of *Deleuze and Performance* (2009) and author of a number of articles. She is also Chair of the Performance and Philosophy working group within Performance Studies international, and a member of the SpRoUt collective—a UK-based artists' group.

Bojana Cvejic is a performance theorist, maker and performer. With Jan Ritsema, she has created a number of performances including *TODAYulysse* (2000) and collaborated with Xavier Le Roy, E. Salamon and M. Ingvartsen. She has published articles in *Maska, Frakcija, TkH, Etcetera, Performance Research* and *Radical Philosophy*. She currently teaches contemporary dance and performance in the Department for Media and Culture Studies at Utrecht University.

Chloé Déchery is a French performance artist, writer and researcher based in London. A graduate of the École normale supérieure in France, she is now completing a PhD in Performance Studies at the Université de Nanterre – Paris X . She is also a lecturer and has presented her own work at theatres, interdisciplinary festivals and conferences, published critical articles and is a regular reviewer of performances in London and Paris.

Clare Finburgh is Senior Lecturer in Modern Drama at the University of Essex, UK. She has written on various aspects of twentieth-century and contemporary French and Francophone theatre, notably on Jean Genet, Kateb Yacine, Michel Vinaver, Noëlle Renaude and Valère Novarina. Her essays have appeared in *Theatre Journal, French Forum, French Studies, Research in African Literatures, Yale French Studies, Théâtre/Public* and *Alternatives Théâtrales*. In addition, her translation of Noëlle Renaude's *Par les routes* was staged at the Edinburgh Festival in 2008. She has co-edited a collection of essays entitled *Jean Genet: Performance and Politics* (2006) and is currently completing, with David Bradby, a monograph on *mise-en-scène* innovation in Jean Genet's theatre (Routledge 'Modern and Contemporary Dramatists' series).

Susan Haedicke is Associate Professor in the School of Theatre, Performance and Cultural Policy Studies at the University of Warwick. Previously, she taught in Theatre Departments at the University of Maryland, The George Washington University and the University of Massachusetts/Amherst. She has published extensively on community-based theatre and European street theatre. She is currently writing a book that identifies, analyses and evaluates the distinctive political performance practices of street theatre and explores the concept of public performative art and its role in the urban landscape. She also works as a professional freelance dramaturg in the United States and in France with Friches Théâtre Urbain, a professional street theatre.

Bérénice Hamidi-Kim is a former student of the École normale supérieure, and now teaches at the Université de Lyon 2. Her doctoral thesis was entitled *The Cities of Political Theatre in France from 1989 to 2007*. She has published articles on French theatre in *New Theatre Quarterly* and *Études Théâtrales*.

Jean-Pierre Han is a theatre journalist, Director of the Syndicat professionnel de la critique, and editor-in-chief of *frictions: théâtres-écritures*, a journal that brings together playwrights, directors, critics and philosophers in discussions of contemporary theatre and performance, and their activity in society.

Geraldine (Gerry) Harris is Professor in Theatre Studies at Lancaster University, UK. Her books include *Staging Feminities, Performance and Performativity* (1999), *Beyond Representation: The Politics and Aesthetics of Television Drama* (2006) *Feminist Futures? Theatre Theory, Performance* (co-edited with Elaine Aston, 2006) and *Practice and Process: Contemporary [Women] Practitioners* (co-authored with Elaine Aston, 2007).

Céline Hersant received the highly prestigious *Prix de la chancellerie* for her PhD thesis, entitled *Recyclage et fabrique du texte (Recycling and Fabrication of the Text*, 2006), on the theatres of Daniel Lemahieu, Valère Novarina and Noëlle Renaude. She has published numerous articles and essays on these three authors that have appeared in the journals *Europe* and *Théâtre/Public*, and her essays are included in many collections on Novarina. She teaches at the Université Paris-III–Sorbonne nouvelle.

Carl Lavery teaches theatre and performance at Aberystwyth University. His books include *Jean Genet: Performance and Politics* (2006, with Clare Finburgh and Maria Shevtsova), *Sacred Theatre* (2007, with Ralph Yarrow et al.), *Walking, Writing and Performance: Autobiographical Texts by Deirdre Heddon, Carl Lavery & Phil Smith*, ed. Roberta Mock (2009), *The Politics of Jean Genet's Late Theatre: Spaces of Revolution* (2010) and *'Good Luck Everybody': Lone Twin: Journeys, Performances and Conversations* (2011, with David Williams).

Nigel Stewart is a dance artist and scholar. He has danced for Grace & Danger and Figure Ground, and for the German choreographer Thomas Lehmen, performing in *Clever* (UK tour 2001, 2003) and *Stationen* (Berlin Tanzfest, 2003). He has published many articles and chapters, and co-edited *Performing Nature: Explorations in Ecology and the Arts* (2005). He is a member of the Choreography and Corporealities working group of the International Federation of Theatre Research. He is Senior Lecturer in the Lancaster Institute for the Contemporary Arts.

Éric Vautrin is maître de conférences at the Université de Caen, Basse-Normandie, and Associate Researcher at ARIAS (Atelier de recherche sur l'intermédialité et les arts du spectacle, CNRS / Paris3 / ENS). In addition to a number of journal articles, he has published Claude Régy's archives on DVD, as well as the monograph *Claude Régy* (2008).

Introduction

Clare Finburgh and Carl Lavery

Contemporary French Theatre and Performance is a collection of essays that explores theatre and performance practices taking place in France today. The aim of the volume is to bring to Anglophone readers some knowledge of the innovative but largely unknown developments in the fields of French theatre and performance. This is the first time that these different practices have been discussed in one publication, and the juxtaposition of media enables fruitful parallels and echoes to emerge, indicating both the porosity and the clarity of distinctions between theatre and performance in France. The book is also unique in that contributions are made not only by eminent scholars, but also by directors, playwrights and performance artists from the United Kingdom and France. This variety of backgrounds adds to the richness of perspectives that the volume provides.

Rationale

Most book-length studies of French theatre written in English tend to adopt one of two strategies: either they explore a concentrated area or practice such as playwrighting, *mise en scène* or decentralization, or, conversely, they outline a broad historical survey of the field.[1] As editors of this collection, we have adopted an alternative approach that sits somewhere between the specific and the general. On the one hand, we aim to provide English-speaking readers with a selection of some of the experimental theatre and performance practices occurring in French theatre and performance today; and, on the other hand, we want to reflect on the pressing political questions and aesthetic tendencies that these practices invariably provoke and express. As a consequence of this emphasis, and somewhat inevitably perhaps, we have had to be selective in our choices, and it is important to warn readers that this book does not purport to offer an encyclopaedic guide to contemporary French work and its infrastructures. There are, for instance, no essays on commercial French theatre (*le théâtre privé*), or new circus (*le nouveau cirque*), which the critic Emmanuel Wallon correctly regards as France's most successful export (2008: 91).[2] Nor is there significant discussion of influential state-funded practitioners who have dominated the French stage since the 1960s such as Ariane Mnouchkine, Peter Brook, or Bernard-Marie Koltès.[3] From a performance perspective, we have also omitted to discuss, in detail, the work of French and French-based artists like Sophie Calle, Jeanne-Claude and Christo and Christian Boltanski, who have long been of interest to Anglophone scholars and curators.[4] Similarly, the focus of the volume does not include specific essays dealing with sociological issues in French theatre, although David Bradby, Jean-Pierre Han and Robert Cantarella discuss questions of programming, funding and institutional expectation(s) in their respective contributions.[5]

The editorial rationale for these choices and omissions is threefold. First, we are committed to contemporary practice in its newest forms; second, we are concerned to bring different names to the attention of an Anglophone audience who, in the United Kingdom at least, has little chance of reading about French practice, let alone seeing it;[6] third, we want to assemble a book that contests traditional disciplinary divides in French scholarship between theatre and performance without, for all that, suggesting that they are homogeneous entities. We are confident that this is the first publication in either French or English to approach the field with such a broad-based purview.[7]

With respect to the importance we attach to performance, it might be argued that the collection adopts a specifically Anglophone perspective on French cultural production and thus runs the risk of eradicating difference through an act of cultural imperialism.[8] We hope, however, that such anxiety is unfounded. Not only does this volume contain essays by leading French scholars and practitioners, but there is also a keen desire in France itself to instigate a dialogue between the previously disparate worlds of theatre and performance both in practice and in theory. In 2008, the innovative performance space the Centrequatre, under the creative directorship of Robert Cantarella and Frédéric Fisbach, was opened in the nineteenth *arrondisement* in Paris, with the express intention of 'collapsing the boundaries between the arts' (2009; our translation).[9] Similar experiments have been – and still are – taking place in Paris at the Pavillon in the Musée d'art moderne, the Espace

315 in the Georges Pompidou Centre and the Ménagerie de Verre; in Avignon at the Off festival; in Brest at the Antipodes showcase; in Lyon at Ground Zero and the Demeure du Chaos; and in Marseilles at the Belle de Mai and la Friche.

This impulse amongst curators, programmers, funding bodies and artists to transgress fixed limits and medium specificities is reflected in current academic scholarship, too. The Centquatre publishes its own books and journal (*le Centquatrevue*), and hosts discussions and lectures on architecture, theory and performance; the bilingual magazine *Art Press 2*'s special issue on *Performances contemporaines* (2007–8) seeks to re-evaluate what the term and practice of performance means in France, 'where the available literature is […] lagging a long way behind what the Anglo-American can offer' (Soulier, 2007–8: 31; translation modified); and in 2008–9, the prestigious French journal *Théâtre/Public* ran two volumes on the influence of US performance in France and elsewhere in Europe. Correspondingly, in his most recent publication, Patrice Pavis, one of France's leading theatre scholars, focuses on the work of performance makers such as Guillermo Gómez-Peña, Marina Abramovic and Rimini Protokoll by proffering the hybrid notion of 'la performise' or 'mise-en performance' as a new method of analysis (2007: 43–71). These factors would appear to suggest that our volume, with its interest in theatre *and* performance, is not so much another exercise in Anglo-American 'cultural imperialism', as a timely attempt to enter into dialogue with emergent trends in French theory and practice. The essays published in this volume by Robert Cantarella, the co-director of the Centquatre, and younger French academics such as Chloé Déchery, Bérénice Hamidi-Kim, Céline Hersant and Éric Vautrin, with their focus on points of convergence between performance, experimental play-wrighting, project-based community theatre and poetry, would appear to vindicate this very point.[10] As, indeed, does the contribution of the critic Jean-Pierre Han when he notes that today, 'it is the very definition of theatre that needs to be reformulated' (see p. 80 in this volume).

So what defines this collection?

The impulse for this book is to engage scholars, critics and artists working for the most part in France and the United Kingdom in a creative and critical debate about recent issues and trends in contemporary French theatre and performance. We have invited contributors to take the 'temper of the times', to find out what French theatre and performance artists are doing now and to tease out the wider cultural and social ramifications of their work(s). In response to Han's problematization of the 'standard theatrical survey' (see Chapter 5 in this volume), we

conceive the 'contemporary' as both an historical period (the majority of the essays deal with what has happened in the past decade or
so) and an aesthetico-political concept (a way of grasping how artists
engage with, and seek to move beyond the issues and tensions of the
present).[11] In order to achieve this double objective, we have encouraged contributors to reflect on the current aesthetic and political state
of French theatre and performance in any way they see fit – that is to
say, by mapping distinctive themes or practices; by engaging in detailed
analysis of individual artists and companies; or by reflecting philosophi-
cally on the type of thinking that contemporary work sets in motion.[12]
Whilst not all (though most) of the contributors have taken the invita-
tion to engage directly with politics in their essays, it is telling that all
of them focus on aesthetics, in the extent to which they explore how
the artwork, through its formal and sensual play, reconfigures accepted
ideas of time and space. As we highlight presently in this Introduction,
for us, the radical reappraisal of theatre and performance aesthetics
undertaken by contemporary French artists, and witnessed in many of
our chapters, is in itself politically inflected, since it resists conventional
conceptions of reality, thereby entreating audiences to see, hear, feel
and act differently.

Having, in broad terms, defined 'contemporary', we must now consider what we understand by 'French'. Given France's position as a former
colonial power, French-language theatre and performance span a considerable part of the globe. Lebanese-born Quebecan playwright Wajdi
Mouawad, who was the *artiste associé* at the Avignon Theatre Festival
in 2009, writes in French, and directs his plays with French-speaking
actors; Congolese writer and performer Dieudonné Niangouna, whose
plays have been read at the Comédie-Française (2005), and performed
at the Avignon Theatre Festival, also works through the medium of the
French language. These examples, just two from a great host, illustrate
the extent to which the French language still haunts, or nourishes
(depending on contexts and perspectives) performance and theatre in
France's former colonies. As editors, we chose not to dedicate a 'quota'
of the chapters in this volume to postcolonial Francophone writing.
Notwithstanding, the issues and problems implicit in postcolonial
identity nonetheless emerged in several essays. Bérénice Hamidi-Kim's
chapter discusses in detail the community theatre pieces that arose
from experiences of immigration, the specifically French problems of
'assimilation', and the conflicts that still plague some former French
colonies.[13] In 1958, during the Algerian War of Independence, French
director Jean-Marie Serreau was obliged to stage Algerian writer Kateb

Yacine's play *Le Cadavre encerclé*, which treats the Algerian struggle for sovereignty from France, at the Théâtre Molière in Bruxelles, rather than in France, because of threats from the OAS, an underground far-right organization who opposed Algerian independence through a campaign of bombings and targeted assassinations.[14] In his chapter in this volume, Jean-Pierre Han touches on the difficulty that theatre companies in France still encounter today when attempting to discuss violent episodes from France's colonial past, thereby testifying to the fact that what is understood as 'Frenchness' and French identity are still very much unresolved and problematic both in general, and specifically in the context of theatre and performance. However, while we realize that the word 'French' is a contested term, within the context of this publication it refers almost exclusively to work made by French artists living and working in metropolitan France. Two exceptions are Herman Diephuis, a Dutch choreographer whose dance piece *D'après J.-C.* was staged in France and created in collaboration with French dancers, and Dominique Gonzalez-Foerster whose installation *TH. 2058* was exhibited at Tate Modern in London in 2008–9.

This volume is distinctive from existing books on French theatre owing to the reason that, as well as being directed at an Anglophone readership, it also seeks to appeal to a French one. We endeavour to enable this by asking leading UK-based theatre and performance scholars to think about their own responses to current French work. Our objective here is to demonstrate how UK theatre and performance scholarship differs from its French counterpart in style and methodology, and to set up an implicit contrast between the two.

A cursory glance at the collection suggests that many French scholars – in this case, particularly Michel Corvin and Céline Hersant – tend to invest in a largely structuralist analysis that focuses on microtextual stylistic elements, rather than on macrotextual external factors such as history, society, geography and psychoanalysis. They are less inclined to theorize their insights in overtly political ways, and indeed, often actively reject a political hermeneutic. In this respect, Corvin's and Hersant's approaches are symptomatic of a larger critical trend. Generally, French theatre criticism is considerably more apolitical than its Anglophone counterpart. Since the introduction to France of Russian formalism and structuralism in the 1950s, an aesthetic-semiotic approach to theatre has dominated. Founding works of criticism, notably Étienne Souriau's *Les Deux cent mille situations dramatiques* (1950); Anne Ubersfeld's *Lire le théâtre* (1996); and Patrice Pavis's *Dictionnaire du théâtre* (2002), focus on the discrete formal elements that compose dramatic situations – plot, character, dialogue, didascalia, scenography – rather than on the active part theatre might play in society. However, an important exception to this depoliticized mode of semiotic reading is apparent in the work of Roland Barthes. Inspired by the Berliner Ensemble's visit to Paris (1954), and by Brecht's location of theatre at the heart of the political struggle, Barthes ignited debates around theatre and ideology. Founding the journal *Théâtre Populaire* (1953–64), he continued until the 1980s, with his colleague Bernard Dort, to reflect on the social function of theatre. A political approach to the specifically formal aspects of theatre and performance only subsists today on the margins of French criticism. The group Sans Cible, which comprises directors like Robert Cantarella, Frédéric Fisbach and Gilberte Tsaï, as well as philosophers like Marie-José Mondzain and Myrian Revault d'Allonnes, has published several volumes of their discussions, notably *L'Assemblée théâtrale* (Milin, 2002), *La Représentation* (Milin, 2005) and *Produire la création* (Thomas, 2007), where they specifically discuss the politics of aesthetics.[15]

Hersant's and Corvin's chapters provide detailed readings of the spatial experiments made by French playwrights. Here, space is characterized in terms of crisis and catastrophe, as characters wander melancholically through uncanny landscapes. Hersant insists, however, that, 'by describing space, [these playwrights] do not attempt to talk about the world, or about contemporary issues: they do not include a message'. For her, 'these writers question the very fabric of writing, the way in which a textual object can question or problematize the mechanisms of the stage' (see p. 65 in this volume). According to her argument, one could conclude that contemporary French theatre is characterized solely by its solipsistic obsession with form. Corvin's disavowal of a political reading is less categorical, since he ends his essay by writing, 'It is a decentred theatre where the characters – if they still exist – are blown about, pulled here and there, never finding their centre of gravity. The demon of ubiquity is at work in the modern world and, by extension, in the theatre' (see p. 54 in this volume). Whilst Anglophone criticism certainly has a lot to learn from the kind of meticulously close stylistic and semiotic analysis that dominates French criticism, and that has regrettably all but disappeared in UK and US approaches to the arts, it can nonetheless be fruitful to complement French structuralism with an Anglophone line of enquiry, as we show here.

Though Hersant and Corvin might perhaps deny this point with some vehemence, their detailed readings of the spatial experiments made by French playwrights could possibly be seen in a broader social context, as an expression of and response to a particularly French sense of malaise.

Since the reconstruction of France's cities in the 1950s and 1960s, key French thinkers including Guy Debord, Michel de Certeau and Henri Lefebvre have been involved in a sustained critique of urbanism and the widespread feelings of alienation and *anomie* that it has provoked. The sense of spatial disarray that many in France experienced in the 1950s was amplified by the crisis in social space that followed after the mass migration from Algeria in the wake of Algerian independence in 1962. As Kristen Ross has documented in two key publications (1995, 2002), the irony of the Algerian War was that the very factor that the political Right in France strove to cling on to – *Algérie française* – was in no way abandoned. It simply shifted from North Africa to the Hexagon, as France found itself confronting a new racial reality when tens of thousands of Algerians assumed citizenship rights and moved to the mainland in search of better wages. It is worth repeating, today more than ever, that France remains troubled by the racial and spatial problems that the end of the Algerian War brought into sharp focus. One thinks here of the urban riots that have occurred every autumn since 2005, and of President Sarkozy's intolerant and aggressive policy on immigration, which appears at times to be a concerted attempt to 're-whiten' France (see Susan Haedicke's and Carl Lavery's chapters in this volume).

By placing space, or more accurately its representational crisis, at the forefront of their work, the contemporary French playwrights discussed in this book, like their counterparts in various types of performance and participatory theatre, enable the reader or spectator to rethink what the philosopher Jacques Rancière calls their 'sensible' experience of the world (2006b: 10). It matters little that these artists are not concerned to debate issues such as the disintegration of community and locality explicitly or in any intentional sense, for their meditations on space are designed to enable readers, spectators and critics potentially to arrive at these conclusions themselves.

One final term in our title needs to be clarified: the meaning and usage of the word 'performance'. In English, as research in Performance Studies has demonstrated to the point of exhaustion, a performance can, quite literally, be anything: a theatrical event, a church service, a Balinese ritual, a speech act, a football match, a business activity, a form of management. In French, on the other hand, the noun *la performance* refers specifically (as it does in Spanish and German) to what in English goes by the name of 'performance art'. One of the consequences of what Patrice Pavis describes as the French word's lack of 'elasticity' (Pavis, 2007: 43–5) is that in French academia theatre scholars have tended to write about theatre, whereas art historians have been left alone to deal with performance. While this publication is certainly concerned to contest those disciplinary specialisms, it does, however, remain faithful to the French meaning of *la performance*. That is to say, all of the contributors in this volume are interested in performance as an aesthetic practice, and not as an ethnographic or sociological category.

How might performance and theatre differ?

In the most recent editions of RoseLee Goldberg's *Performance Art: From Futurism to the Present* (2001) and Arnaud Labelle-Rejoux's *L'Acte pour l'art* (2004), performance and experimental theatre are presented as interchangeable entities.[16] In light of this apparent convergence between theatre and performance – a convergence which in theatrical circles is often taken for granted in the United Kingdom – why then does this publication adopt a title, *Contemporary French Theatre and Performance*, that perpetuates what could be seen as a false dichotomy?[17] Surely, it would be less contradictory to call the book *Contemporary French Theatre*, or, failing that, just *Contemporary French Performance*? We have, however, decided to keep both terms in our title, because while theatre and performance practices are indeed often difficult to separate, as many of our contributors and editorial cross-references show, there are nevertheless important compositional differences between them that merit further scrutiny.[18] Arguably, the crux of that difference stems from the very thing that performance, if one agrees with Goldberg's historical account of its genesis and development, was always concerned to reject: the relationship to a specific medium. While it is certainly the case that visual artists and poets interested in performance are keen to root their work in theatrical principles of 'liveness', transience and embodied spectatorship, their engagement with those principles is not of the same order as that undertaken by theatre makers, however experimental. Whereas theatre practitioners, as David Bradby, Michel Corvin, Clare Finburgh and Céline Hersant demonstrate in this volume, might be concerned with subverting dramaturgical notions of plot, language and character, performance makers are usually more interested in exposing or opening up their respective disciplines (for instance, poetry and fine art) to experiences of embodiment and duration. Crucially, the point of this exposure for Bernard Heidsieck, Orlan and Philippe Parreno is not to expand the possibilities of the theatrical medium as it is for, for example, Philippe Minyana, Valère Novarina or Noëlle Renaude. Rather, their goal is to engage spectators in a different spatial and temporal relationship with the materiality of the discrete object in front of them, be that a spoken poem, a living sculpture or site-specific installation. Theatre has no obvious need to escape disciplinary boundaries in this way, since it is already a bastardized medium, grounded in the transience of bodies performing and spectating.

Before proceeding any further with this distinction, it is useful to return to what the US art critic Michael Fried called 'theatricality' in his famous attack on minimalist/literalist art in the journal *Artforum* in 1967. For Fried, the minimalist sculptures of Robert Morris and Tony Smith betray art by depending upon staging or *mise en scène* and by inviting a special complicity with their audience. As Fried notes *à propos* of the 'presence' of literalist art:

> The presence of literalist art [...] is basically a theatrical effect or quality – a kind of stage presence. It is a function, not just of the obtrusiveness and often even aggressiveness of literalist work, but of the special complicity that that work demands from the beholder. Something is said to have presence when it demands that the beholder take it into account, that he take it seriously – and when the fulfilment of that demand consists in simply being aware of it and, so to speak, in acting accordingly. [...] Here the experience of being distanced by the work in question seems crucial: the beholder knows himself to stand in an indeterminate and open-ended – and unexacting – relation as subject to the impassive object on the wall or floor.
>
> (1980: 221)

Unlike colour-field or abstract impressionist painters whose flat canvases refuse to acknowledge the viewer in their exploration of the (spatial) essence of painting, minimalist sculpture, Fried argues, situates the spectator in time. In doing so, it disrupts what he calls the eternity or 'grace' of the work, the process of dematerialization that permits the artwork to transcend its objecthood (ibid.: 239). For Fried, this disruption, a disruption that is inherently temporal and temporalizing, is where the theatricality of minimalism resides:

> The literalist preoccupation with time – more precisely with the duration of the experience – is, I suggest, paradigmatically theatrical: as though theatre confronts the beholder, and thereby isolates him, with the endlessness not just of objecthood, but of time; or as though the sense which, at bottom, theatre addresses is a sense of

temporality, of time passing and to come, simultaneously approaching and receding, as if apprehended in an infinite perspective.

(ibid.: 223)

Regardless of the fact that Fried's dismissive concept of theatricality is
based on theatre's intimate relationship with temporality (the fact that
in theatre things always happen in time), it is crucial to understand
that it does not refer to theatre making *per se*. Rather, theatricality in
Friedian discourse is a *general* aesthetic principle that crosses disciplinary boundaries and places the emphasis on temporality, hybridity
and spectatorship – in Fried's lexicon, this constellation is referred to
derogatorily as 'presence'. If theatricality, somewhat confusingly, is an
attempt to find a vocabulary for what in the 1970s came to be called
performance, and, as such, says little about theatre as a thing in itself, it
seems important, for the sake of accuracy, not to conflate the two. On
the contrary, the scholar must remain attuned to the specific ways in
which theatricality works in theatre *and* performance. In the context of
this book, this means understanding how poets, body artists, installation makers and video artists seek to overcome the spatial limitations of
the page, canvas, plinth and screen and endow their work with a sense
of temporal 'presence'. Equally, it obliges the critic to attend to the ways
in which theatre practitioners reconfigure the linguistic protocols and
dramaturgical landscapes that are unique to what we might term the
'theatrical' stage.

With respect to contemporary dance, the logic of performance is
different, since the focus is not on temporality as such, but rather on
disrupting (via philosophy, theatre or fine art) modern dance's obsession with the kinetic specificity of a moving body. As Bojana Cvejic,
Nigel Stewart and Augusto Corrieri all show in this volume, dance
moves into the field of performance when it consciously avoids issues
to do with technique and athleticism, and instead attempts to become
an alternative form of theatre, sculpture or painting. One last caution:
presence, as we understand it, does not simply refer to the live body of
the artist, as it did in the 1970s and 1980s when artists and theorists re-
appropriated Fried's term for their own purposes; it has been expanded
to include the presence of the spectator and her/his physical relationship to the work, which of course means that mediatized forms, such
as video, cinema and moving-image installations, are now considered
as examples of performance, too.[19] As Carl Lavery shows in his essay
on *cinéma d'exposition* (moving image installations) in this publication,
the spectator is no longer expected simply to look at the work; rather,

s/he is immersed in it, and encouraged to experience the (often slow) passing of time itself.

French theatre today

In a recent collection on contemporary French theatre, theorist Jean-Pierre Ryngaert writes, 'New theatrical poetics [...] abandon the exhausting task of representing the world, whether faithfully or not' (in Féral and Mounsef, 2007: 24). Accounts by critics tend to present French theatre as too recondite, abstracted from the specifics of history and place, and ignoring society and politics. Jean-Pierre Sarrazac goes so far as to describe contemporary French theatre as 'autistic', accusing it of smashing naturalism and, with it, any obvious reference to recognizable social situations (1995: 198; our translation).

The reason why French theatre is so frequently politically neutralized might be attributable to the fact that, typically, it is aesthetically avant-garde. Attacks on the conventions of bourgeois theatre by Brecht and Erwin Piscator in Germany, or by John Osborne and John Arden in Britain, clearly championed class emancipation, or condemned imperialist domination. Contrastingly, when the French theatrical tradition – arguably the most rigid, with its neoclassical insistence on unity and coherence – was contested at the start of the twentieth century, the attack was more obviously formal, rather than political. Alfred Jarry and Roger Vitrac began the onslaught on naturalism at the turn of the twentieth century, which was sustained in the 1950s by writers like Samuel Beckett, Arthur Adamov and Jean Genet, who exploded classical notions of linear action, spatial and temporal coherence, psychological characterization and comprehensible dialogue. The dramaturgically iconoclastic work of these innovators of form has been continued by successive waves of writers who today include, amongst a multitude, Catherine Anne, Michel Azama, Olivier Cadiot, Enzo Cormann, Eugène Durif, Jean-Claude Grumberg, Jean-Luc Lagarce, Philippe Minyana, Valère Novarina, Noëlle Renaude and Michel Vinaver.[20] In their quest to reach the limits of aesthetic innovation, some of these playwrights, most notably Novarina and Renaude, blow apart recognizable theatrical dramaturgy to the point where their plethoric language forms dissolute poetic fragments. Renaude explains that her aim as a playwright is 'to locate theatre beyond its limits, to see if it still holds together, to assess to what point one can speak of theatricality, reality, substance' (2004: 148; our translation). Director Robert Cantarella demonstrates that this emphasis on form rather than narrative or theme characterizes not only contemporary playwrights, but also directors: he advocates a theatrical form distinguished by its 'variations, like those in a fugue: a principle of passage, where motifs disappear, then reappear, meaning that we generate movements, passing phases, rather than a central architecture' (in Milin, 2002: 58; our translation). Theatre for many contemporary playwrights and directors therefore becomes a laboratory for research into formal possibility.

At the same time, the vast variety of styles that contemporary French theatre accommodates must be accounted for. Minyana notes, 'in the 1970s and 1980s people spoke of the absence of playwrights, whereas today there are almost too many' (2008: 116; our translation). Amongst France's great population of contemporary playwrights feature not only formalists, but also those who embrace more classical styles. Bernard-Marie Koltès, arguably the most successful playwright from the second half of the twentieth century, contains his marginal figures within a certain dramatic unity. And most recently, France has witnessed the emergence of a generation of authors, including Fabrice Melquiot and Lancelont Hamelin, who are concerned directly with contemporary social and political issues.

One explanation for the great diversity of themes and styles displayed by contemporary French theatre might be that it is arguably the most internationalist in the world. France has played host to directors, companies, playwrights and theories from around the world since director Jacques Copeau, at the start of the twentieth century, introduced the theories and practices of foreign theatre makers like Constantin Stanislavski or Edward Gordon Craig. Today, festivals across France invite companies from around the world, and contemporary playwrights from a great range of languages, from Norwegian to Hebrew, are translated into French.[21]

The overriding feature that has distinguished French theatre for the past century, and still does, is *form*. Even during the near-revolutionary *événements* of May 1968, when political debate was placed centre-stage in French theatre, questions of form and style prevailed. Politically radical artists like Ariane Mnouchkine, André Benedetto and Armand Gatti not only treated revolutionary subject matter like racism, regionalism or neo-colonialism, but also innovated theatrical aesthetics – the linguistic, corporeal and visual matter with which they made theatre.[22] Benedetto insisted that political radicalism involved subverting not only social conventions, but also theatre's formal conventions: 'We need to break with dominant ideologies at the level of form, of the matter from which production is constructed: the language, the acting, the dramaturgical components' (quoted in Defosse, 1971: 7; our translation).[23] Form and style were thus primary considerations in *all* French theatre then, and still are today, not least in the small but simmering militant theatre tradition.[24]

A formalistic reading of political theatre has therefore existed in France since the 1960s. But what about a political reading of form in theatre? As we have mentioned, many critics describe contemporary French theatre as apolitical, atemporal, aspatial and abstract. We consider, however, that whilst much contemporary French theatre is not explicitly concerned with the political matter of questioning the blind acceptance of material economic and social conditions, it certainly does interrogate the actual means with which these conditions are *represented*.

French performance today

To speak generally. and perhaps too schematically, the expanded field of French performance today is the inheritor of movements and practices that took place in three distinct time periods: the historical avant-garde of the 1920s and 1930s (Dadaism and Surrealism); the neo avant-garde that ran from the 1950s to the early 1970s (which included movements such as New Realism, Fluxus and the Groupe de Recherche Audio-Visuel (GRAV)); and the early queer performances of body artists like Gina Pane, Michel Journiac and Thierry Argullo in the 1970s and 1980s. Within a French landscape, moreover, attention needs to be drawn to the influence of three major figures: Marcel Duchamp, Yves Klein and (arguably most importantly) Guy Debord, all of whom defy neat categorization and periodization. The interrogations launched by Duchamp, Klein and Debord into the nature of artistic value, the status of the art object and the ubiquity of spectacle have encouraged contemporary French artists to use performance as both a form of institutional critique and mode of aesthetic intervention. Ironically, this reference to Duchamp, Klein and Debord discloses a central paradox that appears across this collection of essays. While the artists we have just mentioned, along with others such as Robert Filliou, Jean-Jacques Lebel and Ben Vautier have certainly contributed to expanding the parameters of French performance, it is difficult, if not impossible, to proffer a definition of what French performance actually is – at least not in any ontological or essentialist sense. This is due, in part, to the internationalist nature of performance which, from its earliest days in the Dada cabarets and nightclubs, has perceived itself as a utopian project struggling to discard reactionary notions of national identity. Unlike French theatre with its rootedness in the French language and existing networks of dissemination (the system of National Theatres, for example), French performance has been distributed through an international network of galleries, festivals and exhibitions. As a consequence, French performance has tended to be in dialogue with other artists and movements rather than constituting itself as a separate entity attempting to fulfil a national remit generously funded by the State.

In light of these circumstances, it makes no sense to speak of French performance as a particular and unique mode of art making that would somehow convey or speak for a mythical notion of French identity. Rather, we suggest that it can be more accurately considered as a set of artistic practices that attempts to reflect on, and intervene into, debates between the local and global, and the national and international, as they manifest themselves in a specifically French context. Indeed, as Carl Lavery, Bojana Cvejic and Augusto Corrieri infer in their contributions to this volume, one might even say that context is content, since it is history and politics rather than abstract or transcendent notions of form or medium, which ultimately define the 'Frenchness' of the works in question.

That French performance is a product of what the sociologist Roland Robertson has called 'glocalism' (1995) is apparent in what are arguably today its two defining characteristics: its interest in mediatization and hybridity. In common with performance makers elsewhere in the world, contemporary French artists attempt to address and make us aware of the experiential affects of new visual technologies on bodies and minds, and, at the same time, to blur disciplinary boundaries.[25] Orlan's carnal art, as Elaine Aston argues in this volume, seeks to merge body art with a mediatized *mise en scène* that looks back to the diva tradition of nineteenth-century theatre; Dominique Gonzalez-Foerster's site-specific installations use literature and film as compositional tools; conceptual choreographers like Herman Diephuis, Xavier Le Roy and Jérôme Bel deconstruct dance and transform it into painting, theatre and music; Philippe Parreno uses film to institute new immersive ways of perceiving time; and poetry, as Éric Vautrin describes it, is a soundscape, a theatrical spectacle, a rock concert and/or a type of 'invisible' public intervention. While such aesthetic 'formlessness' has always played a constitutive role in performance's self-conscious attempt to liberate itself from Modernism's concern with the purity of the medium, what is new in the current situation in France is that performance's interest in hybridity and mediatisation is now finally receiving mainstream acceptance by curators, funders, publishers and the general public. Again, though, this is not a development unique to France. Performance has, by and large, lost its oppositional edge and become a relatively mainstream feature in most internationally renowned galleries and exhibitions. In other words, it is accepted everywhere, not just in France.

The politics and aesthetics of contemporary French theatre and performance

Due to the attempts of François Mitterrand's Socialist government to resist (at least in part) the neo-liberal agenda promoted so aggressively by Margaret Thatcher and Ronald Reagan in the United Kingdom and United States, the breakdown in social relations that occurred in the Anglo-American world in the 1980s was delayed in France until the 1990s.[26] As a result, what are seen by some as the distressing effects of neo-liberal economics – deregulation, high unemployment and 'rationalization' – have arguably been more keenly felt. In both artistic and theoretical circles in France, this 'distress' has produced a new enthusiasm for political engagement. This has tended to follow two different paths. With respect specifically to performance, French and French-based artists such as Gonzalez-Foerster, Parreno, Thomas Hirschhorn and Pierre Huyghes have explored a participatory form of art making in which the production of material art objects has been abandoned for a process-based approach stressing the importance of social interaction.[27] According to Nicolas Bourriaud, the influential curator and writer who invented the term 'relational aesthetics', the role of contemporary art is to repair the social bond that has been dissolved by the exponential increase in 'the society of the spectacle' (Debord, 1983) and the 'mass-media imaginary' (Guattari, 2000: 53). In a regulated and disciplinary world where capitalism has appropriated leisure time and public space, Bourriaud argues that human relations have been commodified and commercialized, and individuals transformed into 'extras' (2002: 74–5). For Bourriaud, the politics of contemporary artwork do not lie in supplying utopian solutions, but in activating and enabling new social forms, allowing subjects to (re)discover different ways of being together: '[T]he role of artworks is no longer to form imaginary and utopian realities but to actually be ways of living and models of action within the existing real, whatever the scale chosen by the artist' (ibid.: 13). In concrete terms, this had led to a situation where the art gallery is no longer a place for looking at art objects, but a site for dialogue, conversation and debate. In many ways, the audience is the work, as it is often asked to participate in a social event curated by the artist. One thinks, for instance, of Philippe Parreno's exhibition at Le Consortium in Dijon (1995) where he held a party and invited spectators to *'"occup[y] two hours of time rather than two square metres of space"'* (in ibid.: 32; original italics). Differently from the participatory practices of French theatre in the 1960s and 1970s, the spectator is not encouraged here to take part in a theatrical event scripted in advance and controlled by the performers; rather s/he is free to negotiate with the relational event as s/he deems fit.

Whereas Bourriaud's concept of participation devalue traditional notions of aesthetic experience, positing politics as something that occurs in proximity *to* rather than *in* or *through* the artwork (for instance, in the social relationships it enables), Jacques Rancière, by contrast, argues for the *a priori* political nature of aesthetics. For Rancière, the abandonment of the art object is not only unhelpful, it misses the point.[28] As he argues in a number of publications, the politics of the artwork reside in the latter's capacity for reconfiguring what he refers to as the 'distribution of the sensible' – that is to say, all those sensual images and affective tropes that make up what we know as 'reality' (2006b: 12). In Rancière's thinking, the artwork's necessary relationship with and to sensible experience means that there is no need for the artist to step beyond the aesthetic in her/his quest to emancipate the audience. A more useful strategy is for the artist to produce works of art which provide spectators with the capacity to disidentify with reality as it is currently configured. Or, as Rancière puts it in a recent essay, the politics of the artwork can be measured by how successful they are in transforming spectators into 'active interpreters': 'the effect of the idiom cannot be anticipated. It requires spectators who play the role of active interpreters, who develop their own translation to appropriate "the story" and make it their own story. An emancipated community is a community of narrators and translators' (2009: 22).

While Bourriaud's ideas are discussed in this volume, the majority of the essays focus on what Rancière would see as aesthetic politics. Whether they concentrate on theatre or performance, most of the contributors have been concerned to explain how artists in France have tried to make art objects that provide audiences with different forms of sensible experience. This accounts for why so many of the essays, particularly by English-speaking commentators, have sought to account for their experience by relying on French theorists (Michel de Certeau, Guy Debord, Gilles Deleuze, Jean-Luc Marion, Jean-Luc Nancy and Jacques Rancière). These theorists, albeit in disparate ways, all try to explain how the artwork, in its materiality and sensuality, engages the spectator in alternative processes of thinking, perceiving and being. Indeed, it is arguably here on the terrain of a politics of spectatorship that the convergence between theatre and performance best takes place in France. In both instances, artists are engaged in documenting, critiquing and resisting conventional forms of reality, with the express intention of inviting audiences to experience the world differently. A dominant theme in the book, and one that many authors come back to again and again, is the interest evinced in what one might call 'a politics of perception' – a politics of how voices, images and bodies are perceived as sensual objects in space and time.

Contemporary French theatre makers echo Rancière's sentiments, whether they are conscious of it or not. Each of the chapters on theatre in this volume accounts for the ways in which playwrights concern themselves with interrogating theatrical components at their most basic level: how to represent space, time, language, body, voice. Corvin and Hersant explore sustained experiments with space; Bradby and Laura Cull emphasize the reconfigurations of language and vocality in the directorial practices of several artists. Abandoning conventional representational modes, these artists reject the devalued, bland words and images with which humans and their societies are represented in everyday life. Since mass culture's *raison d'être* is its rapid and ready production and consumption, it has little desire to challenge the consumer's creativity or imagination. Cantarella asks a question, the implied answer to which is affirmative: 'Is it for the "common good" to seek alternative modes of representation to those proposed by the format of television?' (in Milin, 2002: 26; our translation). For contemporary theatre maker Roland Fichet, theatre at its most transgressional 'does not represent a restored world of delivered humans in a renewed society, but it enables spectators to see, hear, understand and speak differently' (in ibid.: 17; our translation).[29] In this book, we therefore understand the deconditioning, or rupture with the representations with which people might unthinkingly construct themselves and their society, to be political. France's aestheticized theatre can therefore be read in terms of its latent humanism, rather than its supposed social abstention.

Reiterating a point we made earlier in this section about the importance of context, it is inevitable that French theatre and performance should seek to question the contemporary significance of the French republican tradition. For some time now, a number of political theorists have highlighted how France, with its Jacobin emphasis on assimilation and sameness, finds it difficult to embrace ideas of difference, be they sexual, ethnic or religious. As Elaine Aston, Bérénice Hamidi-Kim, Susan Haedicke and Nigel Stewart all show in their essays, this leads contemporary performance makers to use national and international forms to question the prejudices and exclusions inherent in French republicanism today. However, the same contributors also draw on the Jacobin revolutionary tradition to think through a progressive and emancipatory trend in French performance that aims to resist the neo-liberal hegemony promoted by UK and US economists and politicians in the name of greater democracy. This politically progressive tendency in French theatre and performance is implicit, too, in the essays by Robert Cantarella, Augusto Corrieri, Laura Cull, Jean-Pierre Han, Bojana Cvejic, Geraldine Harris and Carl Lavery, all of whom outline a politics of equality, grounded in a practice of counter-production. Immediately, one thinks here of David Bradby's typically lucid description of Olivier Py's aesthetic agenda in this volume:

> He [Py] argues that the individual who enjoys a really profound thea-tre experience discovers, *through* that experience, his or her symbiotic link to the wider community. He refuses the debate which starts from political definitions, preferring to start from the real presence of both actor and audience in real time and space, and arguing that any theatre performance which celebrates presence, and touches the individuals in its audience, achieves, through that, the elusive qual-ity of the 'popular'.
>
> (p. 37 in this volume)

Structure of the volume

The French and UK-based contributors to this volume come from diverse backgrounds. Where some are established scholars and thinkers, others base their knowledge on practice-based research and are able to draw their insights from first-hand experience. This diversified approach accounts for the different types of contribution made and methodolo-gies used – something which we, as editors, encouraged in our initial call. In this volume, we relish the fact that the aesthetics and politics of contemporary French theatre and performance are explored from mul-tiple perspectives and in strikingly divergent ways. There are stylistic differences, too. Where many of the essayists invest in the conventions of academic scholarship, others such as Clare Finburgh and Geraldine Harris adopt a more experimental style of writing.

In keeping with the argument in the section 'How Might Theatre and Performance Differ', the book is divided into two sections. Part 1 seeks to assess developments in contemporary French theatre; Part 2 engages with some of the practices in the field of contemporary French performance. However, while this separation is necessary, it is no way intended to preclude dialogue and debate between French theatre and performance, the rationale for which is demonstrated in some shape or form by all of the chapters in this volume.

The section on theatre begins with contributions by two of the field's leading experts, David Bradby (Chapter 1) and Michel Corvin (Chapter 2). The directors Bradby describes resist the preoccupation with the spectacular and image that permeates today's society, instead working with contemporary playwrights who invest in the lyricism of the verbal, rather than the visual. Bradby draws conclusions that echo Rancière's appeal for artists to construct representational means that demand enquiry, rather than the acceptance habitually solicited by dominant media and political discourses. He also raises a question that has been central to French theatre since the 1920s, that of the *théâtre populaire* and the democratization of culture. Back in 1987, David Whitton concluded that the practices of some French directors had become 'intimidatingly intellectual' (1987: 279). Whilst the directors Bradby discusses produce work that is endlessly polysemous and poetic, they still ask themselves how the gap can be closed between a culturally dominant elite and the *non-public*.[30] Bradby focuses on directors, whilst Corvin considers major playwrights, amongst whom he detects a preoccupation with place. Corvin suggests that authors today centrifugally fracture and disorientate space. He suggests that this constitutes a rebellion against a generation of directors – Antoine Vitez, Roger Planchon and Patrice Chéreau, amongst others – who, along with their scenographers, would situate a text in a physical or geographical location appropriate to their own interpretation. Céline Hersant, in Chapter 3, continues this meditation on place, alluding to it as biography and psychology in Philippe Minyana's works; and as unfeasibly vast panoramas filled with detours and deviations in Noëlle Renaude's. Since interior and exterior, proximity and distance dissolve, Hersant concludes, like Corvin, that place in these authors' works ultimately runs no deeper than its linguistic contours. This is particularly evident in Renaude's plays, where typographical layout, almost like an Appollinairian calligramme, in itself carries meaning.

As we have stated, both contemporary French theatre and performance are characterized by their postmodern hybridization of art forms: Corvin notes how playwrights incorporate into their writing the panoramic vistas offered by novelistic and cinematic forms; later in the volume Éric Vautrin, in his essay on performance poetry, discusses the theories and works of Olivier Cadiot who, with Valère Novarina, is both a celebrated playwright and poet. Bradby and Han describe these hybridized playtexts as 'textual material': a raw material stripped of conventional textual reference points such as identifiable time and space, coherent narrative, and realist characterization. In Chapter 4 Clare Finburgh interviews French dramaturgs and a playwright, to ask how this writing might be staged. She, along with Bradby and Corvin, suggests that the hegemonic rule of the director in France has been challenged since the 1990s, since it is not the text that must modify itself in the rehearsal room in order to accommodate the actors, but the actors that must evolve their practices to accommodate the text.

In spite of the accession in France of a Socialist government in 1981, theatre's public sector, especially since the 1990s, has become increasingly subject to neo-liberal economics and to pressures to produce marketable entertainment. Ensembles have gradually dissolved; rehearsal periods have been reduced; self-reflexive work-in-progress, vital for artistic advancement, has been eroded. Jean-Pierre Han's and Robert Cantarella's essays (Chapters 5 and 6 respectively) reflect on the conditions for theatre and performance making today. For Han, one of France's foremost theatre critics, the most successful artists conform to prevailing trends for visually arresting, deliberately provocative productions, in order to appeal to programmers. Mentioning directors and playwrights that Bradby, Corvin and Hersant discuss, Han concludes, nonetheless, by applauding the efforts of a minority of artists who refuse conformity, and push boundaries, whether these be aesthetic or political. Cantarella, a prominent director in France for over two decades, discusses further the limitations encountered by French theatre makers, highlighting the importance attributed to the end product, namely the production, rather than to exploration and reflection. This hierarchization underpins the entire theatrical apparatus, from theatre architecture, to funding decisions, to critical reception. His first-hand experience of these constraints informed his dreams for the Centquatre, Paris's vast cultural complex that opened in 2008 under his direction: it has created a space that brings down the walls between the conception, construction, production and performance of artworks. Intriguingly, if not unsurprisingly, Cantarella's desire for a theatre of research has much in common with corresponding experiments in conceptual French dance, where choreographers such as Jérôme Bel and Xavier Le Roy reject the tyranny of the 'signature' and interrogate the very concept of what a dancing body is actually meant to be or do. For Canterella, as well as for the choreographers we have mentioned, the point is to refuse the polished *objet d'art* or masterpiece for an experimental and exploratory process.

Laura Cull's essay provides a valuable counterpoint, in both focus and style, to the essays just mentioned. Where they concentrate on texts and dramaturgies, in Chapter 7 she returns to the work of the respected director Georges Lavaudant, and reads his practice through the philosophy of Gilles Deleuze. By focusing on both Deleuze's and Lavaudant's engagement with Italian theatre maker Carmelo Bene, she argues for an alternative approach to the politics of Lavaudant's directing, which stresses the importance of theatre's capacity to transform reality and to open up a space for potential becoming(s). This desire to tease out the political significance of contemporary theatre aesthetics via critical theory is reiterated in Chapter 8 by Bérénice Hamidi-Kim in her study of the company Théâtre du Grabuge. Through a detailed description of the on-going *Passarelles* project, which attempts to bring theatre to communities and places which have traditionally been deprived of it, Hamidi-Kim elaborates on Bradby's earlier point and shows how the republican tradition of *théâtre populaire* is currently being reconfigured to address the new exclusions and inequalities of life in a twenty-first-century France that is still struggling to deal with the consequences, both in the metropolitan centre and in its former colonies, of its imperialist past. The scholar and practitioner Chloé Déchery in Chapter 9 underlines, once again, the hybridized nature of experimental French theatre. In her essay, Déchery describes how two of France's most influential avant-garde theatre companies, Grand Magasin and Philippe Quesne's Vivarium Studio, expand the parameters of theatre by abandoning traditional notions of dramaturgy, character and *mise en scène* for ideas and practices borrowed from performance art, dance and cinema. In this way, she returns to Cantarella's definition of performance as a type of artistic practice that is more concerned with showing and sharing its processes, than with creating finished products. This allows Déchery to bring together the two central themes of this publication, and to suggest that the politics of Grand Magasin and Philippe Quesne reside in how they allow spectators to co-create the work with them and to question discourses of power and mastery.

The section on performance starts with Chapter 10, Elaine Aston's essay on the (in)famous body artist Orlan. Although Aston's contribution might initially appear to contradict the emphasis placed on new practices and lesser known works, her focus corresponds to the remit of the volume since it is the first time that Orlan has been discussed within a French feminist context. This allows Aston, one of the leading theatre scholars in the Anglophone world, to disclose the hidden theatricalism inherent in Orlan's performance practice and to argue that her politics recycle the past in order to point to a newly charged feminist future. Like Aston, Éric Vautrin is concerned in Chapter 11 to interrogate disciplinary boundaries, and his impressive and extensive survey of current examples of *poésie sonore* and action poetry highlights the astonishing extent to which French performance poetry has been able to borrow from the disciplines of theatre and performance to escape the restrictions of the page. Susan Haedicke's analysis in Chapter 12 of French street theatre continues the interdisciplinary theme. She argues that the work of Jeanne Simone, Illotopie and Le Phun is best defined in terms of 'performance' because of the way in which these companies produce the social space they inhabit. Haedicke is also reluctant to give up on the utopian politics involved in these 'performance installations', and she suggests in her provocative conclusion that 'taking back the streets [in France] just might lead to radical social change' (see p. 172 in this volume). In his analysis of the aesthetic politics inherent in the moving image installations of Dominique Gonzalez-Foerster and Philippe Parreno in Chapter 13, Carl Lavery refers to the same Situationist tradition as Haedicke. But, whereas Haedicke stresses the bodily co-presence of performer and spectator, Lavery places his emphasis on the performer's absence. By doing so, he claims that Gonzalez-Foerster and Parreno turn the virtuality of the image against itself and develop a politics of perception in which the spectator's experience of time and space is paramount. As with Haedicke, Lavery is interested in relating his observation to the wider social context in France, and he concludes by showing how these 'relational artists' are attempting, in their oblique and muted way, to heal a broken social bond.

The choreographer Bojana Cvejic's analysis of Xavier Le Roy, grounded in a long history of affiliation and collaboration with the artist, is the first in a series of essays to explore the performative and political aspects of contemporary French dance. Cvejic in Chapter 14 traces the evolution of Xavier Le Roy's work from a practice that initially sought to resist the logic of the 'signature' (what she regards as one of the dominant characteristic of modern dance in France and elsewhere), to an exploration of what Rancière in his key 1987 text *The Ignorant Schoolmaster: Five Lessons in Intellectual Emancipation* terms a politics of emancipation.

Nigel Stewart takes a very different approach in his study of the French-based choreographer Herman Diephuis's 2004 piece *D'après J.-C*. Unlike Cvejic, who draws on the ideas of Rancière, in Chapter 15 Stewart uses the theologically inspired phenomenology of Jean-Luc Marion to show how Diephuis's piece contests the opposition that Jacques Derrida sets up between a theological and non-theological stage. Stewart finishes his essay by touching on a transcendent form of ethics and politics that recalls the humanism of French Catholic thinkers and writers of the early to mid-twentieth century. In the final essay on dance perform-ance, the UK dance maker Augusto Corrieri in Chapter 16 explores how the influential French choreographer Jérôme Bel 'capsizes' assumptions about theatre and dance by fashioning a philosophy and practice of performance rooted in Roland Barthes' ideas of *bricolage* and the 'death of the author'. As Corrieri demonstrates through a close reading of *Nom donné par l'auteur* (1994) and *The Show Must Go On* (2001), Bel's huge impact on contemporary dance resides in how he weaves together a choreography of everyday surfaces, pop rhythms and quotidian bodies. According to Corrieri, Bel's willingness to embrace pop culture does not preclude a critical dimension, and in his contribution Corrieri shows how Bel's contemporary version of dance theatre offers a gentler, less oppositional articulation of Guy Debord's critique of spectacle and mass media communication.

The volume ends with an autobiographical essay by Geraldine Harris, one of the United Kingdom's foremost feminist theatre critics, in which she reflects on an all-too rare moment when French and Anglophone theatres were on the verge of a mutual dialogue and exchange. In Chapter 17, Harris shows how UK feminist theatre practitioners and scholars in the 1980s and early 1990s became interested in 'French Feminisms', and, in particular, in the writing of Hélène Cixous. Despite locating itself in the recent past, Harris's contribution is perversely the most contemporary of essays. By concentrating on a missed opportunity and unearthing a buried history, she inevitably discloses what is missing in the present and so fulfils the remit of the entire volume which, as we pointed out at the start of this Introduction, is to instigate new debates between French and Anglophone artists and scholars.

Notes

1. Some key examples of both tendencies are Judith Graves Miller (1977), Harold Hobson (1982), David Bradby (1991), David Bradby and Maria Delgado (2002), John Stokes (2005), Josette Féral and Donia Mounsef (2007).

2. The logic of this publication is to introduce new works to English-speaking readers. Although there is little academic writing on contemporary circus in the United Kingdom, companies such as Archaos and Cirque Plume are relatively well known and have a cult following. Likewise, the work of new circus practitioners – la Compagnie Chant de Balles and la Compagnie XY – often dominates the showcase events organized by the Cultural Services of the French Embassy, hence our decision not to focus on *le nouveau cirque* in this collection. See note 6 in this publication for more detail on this.

3. There have been numerous studies of Brook and Mnouchkine in English, and Koltès's plays have been translated and published by Methuen in two separate volumes. Koltès's final play, *Robert Zucco*, was staged at the Royal Shakespeare Company at The Other Place (1998). He is arguably the one relatively contemporary French playwright whom students in the United Kingdom and United States will have studied. For two excellent studies of Brook and Mnouchkine, see David Williams (1988 and 1999).

4. Christian Boltanski has pieces in the permanent collection at Tate Modern; Sophie Calle's recent retrospective *Talking to Strangers* was exhibited at the Whitechapel Art Gallery (October 2009 to January 2010); and Claude and Christo's staggered project *The Gates* (1979–2005) took place in Central Park in New York.

5. For an excellent discussion of French theatre's recent relationship with the State, see Robert Abirached (2005).

6. One exception that proves the rule is Oliver Py's 11-hour version of Paul Claudel's *Le Soulier de satin*, which was staged in its entirety (and with great success) at the Edinburgh Festival in 2004 (see Bradby, 2005). Another exception was the heavily subsidized *Paris Calling: A Season of Franco-British Performing Arts* that took place in London in the first half of 2008. However, this six-month festival increased the French theatre, dance and performance to which UK audiences were exposed in terms of quantity, rather than variety. The performances (apart from some of the dance work) programmed for the season tended mainly to represent French *nouveau cirque*, and to exclude many of the innovative performance practices taking place in France today. Despite its great success throughout continental Europe, for example, no UK theatre booked *La Mélancolie des dragons* by Philippe Quesne (see Déchery, Chapter 9 in this volume). Contemporary French theatre was only represented in the form of translated play-readings, and no full production took place. This lack of openness to unknown styles and practices was perhaps caused by the conservatism of UK programming policy, and its blatant phobia of foreign-language work.

7. One of the few critics to contextualize the work of French performance art is Kate Ince (2000 and 2005). Although Peter Collier and Victoria Best's collection *Powerful Bodies: Performance in French Cultural Studies* (1999) purports to look at performance, most of the essays deal with literature and film. In Timothy Murray's *Mimesis, Masochism and Mime: The Politics of Theatricality in Contemporary French Thought* (1997), there is very little mention of actual theatre and performance practices in France.

8. The relatively new discipline of Performance Studies has often been criticized as an Anglophone attempt to reduce the diverse theatre practices and traditions throughout the world to a single, hegemonic paradigm (see McKenzie, Roms

and Wee, 2010: 1–22). And, in this context, it is telling that no French scholar contributed to the 2010 volume *Contesting Performance: Global Sites of Research* which sought to offer a more internationalist perspective on Performance Studies. Similarly, as Jean-Marie Pradier points out in an excellent article on the troubled or (almost invisible) history of Performance Studies in France, 84 per cent of delegates at the 2001 international conference of Performance Studies (PSi) came from the United Kingdom. This figure has hardly changed in recent years, leading Pradier to pose the following question: 'For what set of reasons has the discipline of Performance Studies strongly influenced by Jerzy Grotowski's experiments in Poland had such difficulties in being accepted by researchers in Europe, and in particular in France?' (2008: 23; our translation). The only French and French-speaking scholars to contribute regularly to the influential journal *Performance Research* are Pradier, Pavis and Féral, although an article by Christian Biet has recently appeared (2010). However, irrespective of their absence (to date) from debates in the field of Performance Studies, it is evident that French theatre academics and artists are becoming increasingly interested in performance as an aesthetic practice. One thinks here of the international colloquium on the influence of the US avant-garde on European theatre and performance that took place at the Théâtre national de la Colline in Paris in January 2008, and which laid the foundation for the special edition(s) of *Théâtre/Public* that we cite in the main text. The conference was organized to mark the translation of Richard Schechner's *Performance Theory* (1988 [1977]) into French (*Performance, expérimentation et théorie du théâtre aux USA*, 2008).

9. See http://www.104.fr/fr/centquatre/4-missions (accessed 15 November 2009).
10. In the process of delivering the manuscript of this book to Palgrave Macmillan, we have learnt that Robert Cantarella, along with Frédéric Fisbach, have both resigned their posts as creative directors of le Centquatre. This does not, however, invalidate any of Cantarella's insights in his contribution to this volume (see Chapter 6 in this volume); and nor does it problematize one of the central claims in this volume, which is to highlight how French theatre and performance are engaging in ever more intimate dialogues.
11. For a debate on the definition of 'contemporary', see Jean-Pierre Han, Chapter 5 in this volume.
12. For the philosophers Gilles Deleuze and Félix Guattari, the artwork does not passively or simply express an artist's point of view; it provokes thought, what they call 'the sensation of the concept' (2003: 198). For a more detailed discussion of this, see Laura Cull, Chapter 7 in this volume.
13. For a comprehensive discussion of the French social and political phenomenon of assimilation, see Maxim Silverman (1992).
14. For further information on Serreau's controversial production of Kateb Yacine's play, see Jacqueline Arnaud (1982: 1017); Elisabeth Auclaire-Tamaroff and Barthélémy (1986: 114); and Saïd Tamba (1992: 18).
15. Whilst these publications, as well as the journal *frictions*, are invaluable companion pieces to essays in our book, unlike contributions by our authors, they do not provide analyses of particular artists or productions.
16. Both writers classify the work of theatre practitioners such as Robert Wilson, the Wooster Group and Forced Entertainment as performance.

17. See Josette Féral (2002) and Beth Hoffman (2009) for scholars who question rigid separations between theatre and performance.

18. In English, as Pavis points out, the word 'performance' refers, for instance, to a theatrical production, as well as to a transgressive form of art making.

19. This discourse of immediacy is of course already problematized by the role of the document in body and Actionist art.

20. For a further discussion of contemporary playwriting in France, see Clare Finburgh (2010).

21. France's international circuit is vast, and includes the Avignon Theatre Festival, the 'Festival d'automne' in Paris, and also a great number of smaller festivals including Bobigny MC93's 'Standard idéal' outside Paris, the 'Festival international des Francophones' in Limoges, and street theatre festivals in Aurillac and Chalon. The Théâtre national de la Colline under Stéphane Braunschweig has an increasingly internationalist remit, having invited numerous German productions in recent years, and the Théâtre national de l'Odéon was established in 1983 specifically to host European productions (see Bradby and Delgado (2002) for an account of the international influences that have impacted on the French stage). With respect to international playwrights, contemporary names are frequently staged, from the Austrian Elfriede Jelinek to the Serb Gianina Cărbunariu and the English Dennis Kelly.

22. For an extremely thorough and involved account of this militant tradition, see Graves Miller (1977); for further information on Mnouchkine's political involvement, see Neuschäfer (2002).

23. In spite of this evident emphasis on formal consideration in political theatre, many scholars, especially in the United Kingdom (for example, Whitton, 1987: vii), perpetuate a dichotomous opposition between theatre makers more preoccupied with stagecraft, and those who are politically *engagé*. Bettina Knapp, for example, categorizes Benedetto as a militant, and Georges Lavaudant as an aesthete (1995: 1).

24. See Olivier Neveux (2007) for a comprehensive account of French militant theatre.

25. This is exemplified by the art critic Hal Foster's foreword to RoseLee Goldberg's book *Performa: New Visual Art and Performance*. As opposed to artists of the 1970s who were obsessed with the 'immediacy' of the body, Foster argues that, for today's performance artists, 'the inextricability of body and media is taken as a given' (2007: 10).

26. See Charles Sowerwine (2009) for a good discussion of this point. He describes the great strike of October 1995 in France as 'the biggest strike wave since May '68' (2009: 403).

27. The interest that French artists have taken in politics has been mirrored by French art critics. As well as Nicolas Bourriaud, there have been key publications by Paul Ardenne (2000), Dominique Braqué (2004), Éric Troncy (2005) and Claire Moulène (2006).

28. Whereas Rancière would doubtless be willing to admit that Bourriaud's notion of relational aesthetics *might* reconfigure the world differently, he would query the prescriptive nature of Bourriaud's active model of participation where spectators are encouraged to make the work in the absence of the art object. Rancière is not interested in privileged models of the political, nor in the intentionality of the artist, but in contexts and capacities.

Writing about *The Deerhunter* (1978), Michael Cimino's film about the Vietnam War, Rancière notes, 'It can be said that the message is the derisory nature of the war. It can just as well be said that the message is the derisory nature of the struggle against the war. [...] There are no criteria. There are formulas that are equally available whose meaning is often in fact decided by a state of conflict that is exterior to them' (2006b: 61). See also, in this context, his essay *The Emancipated Spectator* (2009).

29. This desire to provoke in the spectator a renewed way of perceiving reality dates back in France to at least Jarry, who condemned the commercial theatre where people '[suffer] from a dearth of sensations, for their senses have remained so rudimentary that they can perceive nothing but immediate impressions' (1997: xxxiii).

30. During May 1968, a number of France's most prominent directors gathered at Roger Planchon's Théâtre de la cité in Villeurbanne to discuss the question of cultural democratization. They coined the term *non-public* to denote the silent majority of French citizens who had no access to public art and culture.

Works cited

Abirached, Robert (2005) *Le Théâtre et le Prince. Un système fatigué 1993–2004* (Arles: Actes du Sud).

Ardenne, Paul (2000) *L'Art dans son moment politique* (Paris: Flammarion).

Arnaud, Jacqeline (1982) *Recherches sur la littérature maghrébine de langue française: Le Cas de Kateb Yacine*, vol. II (Lille: Atelier national reproduction des thèses, Université de Lille III).

Auclaire-Tamaroff and Barthélémy, Elisabeth (1986) *Jean-Marie Serreau: Découvreur de théâtres* (Paris: L'Arbre verdoyant).

Biet, Christian (2010) 'Towards a Dramaturgy of Appearance: An Aesthetic and Political Understanding of the Theatrical Event as Session', *Performance Research*, 14: 3, 102–9.

Bourriaud, Nicolas (2002) *Relational Aesthetics* (Paris: Presses du réel).

Bradby, David (1991) *Modern French Drama 1940–1990*, 2nd rev. edn (Cambridge: Cambridge University Press).

—— (2005) 'Olivier Py: A Poet of the Stage: Analysis and Interview', *Contemporary Theatre Review*, 15: 2, 234–45.

—— (2007) (in collaboration with Annabelle Poincheval) *Le Théâtre en France de 1968 à 2000* (Paris: Honoré Champion).

Bradby, David and Maria Delgado (eds) (2002) *The Paris Jigsaw: Internationalism and the City's Stages* (Manchester: Manchester University Press).

Braqué, Dominique (2004) *Pour un nouvel art politique, de l'art contemporain au documentaire* (Paris: Flammarion).

Collier, Peter and Victoria Best (eds) (1999) *Powerful Bodies: Performance in French Cultural Studies* (Bern: Peter Lang).

Debord, Guy (1983) *Society of the Spectacle*, trans. Donald Nicholson-Smith (Detroit: Black&Red).

Defosse, Françoise (1971) 'La Nouvelle Compagnie d'Avignon', *Travail Théâtral*, 5 (October–December), 7–14.

Deleuze, Gilles and Félix Guattari (2003) *What is Philosophy?*, trans. Graham Burchell and Hugh Tomlinson (London: Verso).

Féral, Josette (2002) 'Theatricality: The Specificity of Theatrical Language', *Substance*, 31: 2/3, 94–108.

Féral, Josette and Donia Mousef (eds) (2007) 'The Transparency of the Text: Contemporary Writing for the Stage', *Yale French Studies*, 122.

Finburgh, Clare (2010) 'Introduction', *Paris Calling: Six Contemporary French Plays* (London: Oberon), pp. 7–18.

Foster, Hal (2007) 'Foreword', in RoseLee Goldberg, *Performa: New Visual Art Performance* (New York: Performa), pp. 10–11.

Fried, Michael (1980) 'Art and Objecthood', in Morris Philipson and Paul J. Gudel (eds), *Aesthetics Today*, rev. edn (New York: New American Library Edition), pp. 214–39.

Goldberg, RoseLee (2001) *Performance Art: From Futurism to the Present*, 2nd rev. edn (London: Thames & Hudson).

Grafton, Johnnie and Michael Sheringham (eds) (2005), *The Art of the Project: Projects and Experiments in Modern French Culture* (Oxford: Berghahn).

Guattari, Félix (2000) *The Three Ecologies*, trans. Ian Pindar and Paul Sutton (London: Athlone).

Hobson, Harold (1982) *French Theatre Since 1830* (London: Calder).

Hoffman, Beth (2009) 'Radicalism and Theatre Genealogies of Live Art', *Performance Research*, 14: 1, 95–105.

Ince, Kate (2000) *Orlan Millenial Female* (Oxford: Berg).

——— (2005) 'Games with the Gaze: Sophie Calle's Postmodern Phototextuality', in Johnnie Grafton and Michael Sheringham (eds), *The Art of the Project: Projects and Experiments in Modern French Culture* (Oxford: Berghahn), pp. 111–22.

Jarry, Alfred (1997) *Jarry: The Ubu Plays*, trans. Cyril Connolly and Simon Taylor Watson (London: Methuen).

Knapp, Bettina (1995) *French Theatre Since 1968* (New York: Twayne).

Labelle-Rejoux, Arnaud (2004) *L'Acte pour l'art: suivi de presque vingt ans après et de Let's Twist Again puis de quelques notules critiques* (Paris: Al Dante).

McKenzie, John, Heike Roms and C.J.W-L Wee (eds) (2010) *Contesting Performance: Global Sites of Research* (Basingstoke: Palgrave Macmillan).

Milin, Gildas (ed.) (2002) *L'Assemblée theatrale* (Paris: Éditions de l'Amandier).

——— (ed.) (2005) *L'Assemblée theatrale* (Paris: Éditions de l'Amandier).

Miller, Judith Graves (1977) *Theatre and Revolution in France Since 1968* (Lexington, AL: French Forum).

Minyana, Philippe (2008) 'L'Écrit', *Communications* special issue, 'Théâtres d'aujourd'hui', 83, 115–22.

Moulène, Claire (2006) *Art contemporain et lien social* (Paris: Cercles d'art).

Murray Timothy (ed.) (1997) *Mimesis, Masochism and Mime: The Politics of Theatricality in Contemporary French Thought* (Ann Arbor: University of Michigan).

Neuschäfer, Anne (2002) *De l'improvisation au rite: L'Épopée de notre temps. Le Théâtre du Soleil au carrefour des genres* (Frankfurt: Peter Lang).

Neveux, Olivier (2007) *Théâtres en lutte: Le théâtre militant en France des années 1960 à aujourd'hui* (Paris: La Découverte).

Pavis, Patrice (2002) *Dictionnaire du théâtre* (Paris: Armand Colin).

——— (2007) *La mise en scène contemporaine: origines, tendances, perspectives* (Paris: Armand Colin).

Pradier, Jean-Marie (2008) 'Regard anthropologique sur la Performance Theory', *Théâtre/Public*, 190, 22–3.

Rancière, Jacques (1991) *The Ignorant Schoolmaster: Five Lessons in Intellectual Emancipation*, trans. Kristin Ross (Stanford, CA: Stanford University Press).

—— (2006a) 'Problems and Transformations in Critical Art', in Claire Bishop (ed. and trans.), *Participation: Documents of Contemporary Art* (London: Whitechapel), pp. 88–93.

—— (2006b) *The Politics of Aesthetics*, trans. Gabriel Rockhill (London: Continuum).

—— (2009) *The Emancipated Spectator*, trans. Gregory Elliot (London: Verso).

Renaude, Noëlle (2004) 'Paroles d'auteurs', in Philippe Minyana, *Prologue, Entente cordiale et Anne-Marie* (Paris: Théâtre Ouvert), pp. 147–9.

Robertson, Roland (1995) 'Glocalization: Time-Space and Homogeneity-Heterogeneity', in Mike Featherstone et al., *Global Modernities* (London: Sage Publications), pp. 25–44.

Ross, Kristin (1995) *Fast Cars, Clean Bodies: Decolonization and the Reordering of French Culture* (Cambridge, Mass : MIT Press).

—— (2002) *May '68 and its afterlives* (Chicago, IL: University of Chicago Press).

Sarrazac, Jean-Pierre (1995) *Théâtres du moi, théâtres du monde* (Rouen: Éditions Médianes).

Schechner, Richard (1988) *Performance Theory* (London: Routledge).

Silverman, Maxim (1992) *Deconstructing the Nation: Immigration, Racism and Citizenship in Modern France* (London: Routledge).

Soulier, Emile (2007-8) 'Histoire(s) de la performance', *Art Press 2*, 7:4, 30–7.

Souriau, Étienne (1950) *Les Deux cent mille situations dramatiques* (Paris: Flammarion).

Sowerwine, Charles (2009) *France Since 1870: Culture, Society and the Making of the Republic*, 2nd edn (Basingstoke: Palgrave Macmillan).

Stokes, John (2005) *The French Actress and Her English Audience* (Cambridge: Cambridge University Press).

Tamba, Saïd (1992) *Kateb Yacine* (Paris: Seghers).

Thomas, Florence (ed.) (2007) *Produire la création* (Le Havre: Noÿs).

Troncy, Eric (2005) 'Manifeste du réalitisme, *Le Monde*, 13 October.

Ubersfeld, Anne (1996) *Lire le théâtre* (Paris: Belin).

Wallon, Emmanuel (2008) 'Expériences d'extraversion: les aléas de la performance dans l'espace public', *Théâtre/Public*, 191, 91–5.

Whitton, David (1987) *Stage Directors in Modern France* (Manchester: Manchester University Press).

Williams, David (ed.) (1988) *Peter Brook: A Theatrical Casebook* (London: Methuen).

—— (ed.) (1999) *Collaborative Theatre: The Théâtre du Soleil Sourcebook* (London: Routledge).

Part 1
Contemporary French Theatre

1

From *Mise en Scène* of *Texte* to Performance of 'Textual Material'

David Bradby

In 1985, the actor and director Antoine Vitez wrote that 'when they are over, we shall look back on these last 30 or 40 years as a golden age of theatre in France' (1991: 123; my translation).[1] By this he meant that theatre had finally liberated itself from being seen as dependent on literature, and that the art of *mise en scène* had come to be recognized in its own right. The energy behind this achievement came in large part from the expanding decentralization movement of the 1950s and 1960s, inspired by the ideal of *théâtre populaire*, or theatre for all. This had seen young theatre companies establish themselves all over France in regions previously deprived of live theatre. Following the lead of Jean Vilar, who founded the Avignon Festival in 1947, their aim was to bring productions of the classic and modern repertoires to a wide popular audience. In the late 1960s and 1970s, many of those working in the decentralized theatre had been dazzled by the visits to France of productions by, first, Jerzy Grotowski, then Robert Wilson, then Tadeusz Kantor. Inspired by these examples, many young directors saw their future in the exploration of all the corporeal and visual aspects of theatre production. Roger Planchon had developed a theory of *écriture scénique* (scenic writing) as the creative contribution of the director, to be put on a par with the *écriture dramatique* (dramatic writing), supplied by the playwright. These developments coincided with a period of steadily increasing state subsidies for theatre, and the result was a range of highly imaginative, visually rich productions, in which directors such as Planchon, or Patrice Chéreau, took on the role of cultural critics, presenting not just the familiar plays of the repertoire, but offering a critique of their historical period and (applying lessons learned from Brecht) emphasizing links with contemporary social and political reality.

In the course of the 1990s and the first decade of the new century, however, a strong backlash against this model of *mise en scène* was set in motion by a group of young independents, working outside the sub-sidized sector, who saw themselves as writers *and* actors *and* directors. The most vociferous of this group was Didier-Georges Gabily: in 1994, he condemned both the misuse of language and the abuse of directo-rial power that, following Planchon's lead, claimed to engage in *écriture scénique*: 'There is no such thing as the *écrivain scénique*. There are only (and *should* only be) artists, *passeurs* [guides] (to use Claude Régy's expression): actors and directors, who all serve the stage through study-ing and listening to texts that try to describe the world as it works (or doesn't)' (in Thibaudet, 1998: 58; Gabily's emphasis, my translation).

According to Gabily, Planchon's generation abandoned contempo-rary writing because they were afraid of it:

> That generation was rightfully suspicious of texts. The danger with texts (especially contemporary texts) is that they are irreducible to one primary meaning, and to the first image that the director-creator imposes on them. They have to be *inouï* [unheard of], in the literal sense, allowing space for things other than the obvious explanations of meaning through imagery.
>
> (ibid.: 57; Gabily's emphasis, my translation)

This accusation was based on two different qualities he identified in what he called 'text': its irreducibility and its resistance to interpretation through imagery. The art of *mise en scène*, in his view, was a veritable betrayal: terrified of the polysemic qualities of text, *mise en scène* tried to tame it by means of an image-based interpretation. According to Gabily, contemporary directing had a duty to find methods where the domi-nant form downplayed any mimetic realism, and where the language of the text itself became the site of action (see Chapter 4 in this volume by Clare Finburgh). With his company, T'chan'g (many of whose members had been students of Vitez), Gabily asserted his unwillingness to work towards a completed end result, opting instead for a sort of permanent rehearsal in which multiple forms could co-exist on stage. According to critic Bruno Tackels, this meant that Gabily's work was not forced to choose between the alternatives of emotion *or* intellect, entertainment *or* education:

> Gabily's direction – like his writing – is in mourning for the passing of collective knowledge. His theatre does not set out any truths, nor does it teach us anything. It shows us what happens when there is no knowledge, and truth falters under the weight of history. It gives

voice to the mind-numbing world that results from the attempt to understand a forbidden world that defies comprehension, a world of war, of memory, poetry and desire – *a world in conflict with the body*.

(1997: 43; Tackels' emphasis, my translation)

For all of these reasons, his productions were often difficult for an audience to watch, and even harder for a critic to describe. At every moment, they vehemently rejected any single stagnant image that could encapsulate the play. They refused the Pirandellian notion that defines itself as the theatrical lie that gives birth to the truth. These were productions that placed all their focus on the words and on the actors who spoke them. However, these words were often harrowing and violent, witness to an 'Artaudian' cruelty, linked neither to story nor to character.

His first production that registered with the critics was *Violences*, given at the Théâtre de la cité internationale in 1991. Those that wrote about this fragmented piece emphasized the difficulty faced in trying to describe it: 'It's like an artist's sketchpad; a free-flowing series of impressions, sketches and plans.'[2] Gabily's direction tried to give a material force to words: 'this unique and collective voice is passed from body to body like a relay baton. The performers never speak strictly as a chorus, but the words are often supported by an echoing murmur; a single melodious voice with pure intonations, soft and repetitive like a far-off lament.'[3] After *Violences*, Gabily directed *Enfonçures* (*Hollows*, 1992), then *Oratorio/Matériau* (*Oratorio/Material*; a title that shows the debt he owed to Heiner Müller) at the Avignon Festival in 1993, and a trilogy entitled *Gibiers du temps* (*Preys of Time*) that was performed in the course of the following three years. He died in August 1996, during rehearsals for a new show *Dom Juan/Chimère* (*Dom Juan/Chimera*).

Gabily's approach attracted support from a group of young writer/directors who shared his outrage at the dominance of elaborate reinterpretations of the classics by many directors at that time and who shared his rejection of theatre that could be reduced to issues. Another influential figure was Stanislas Nordey. Interviewed in 1997, Nordey proclaimed the end of the 'reign of the director':

One thing is certain: the reign of the all-powerful director is over. The future lies with the writer and the audience. They have been largely overlooked for the last ten years. Contemporary creativity has ignored and abandoned them. Not enough energy has gone into promoting new writing. [...] Theatre responds to moments of social fracture in new writing. It is one of the main challenges for the coming years, along with establishing a new relationship with the audience.

(1997: no pagination; my translation)

According to Nordey, the key failure that needed addressing was the abandonment of contemporary creativity by the major state-subsidized theatres. For him, it was up to theatre to 're-establish the ancestral relationship between text and audience' (ibid.). This is more easily said than done, but Nordey attempted it when, in January 1998, he was appointed as director of the Théâtre Gérard-Philipe, becoming (at 30 years old) the youngest director of a Centre dramatique national (CDN) in France. He immediately published a manifesto that confirmed his intention to shake up a theatrical institution that had long been resting on its laurels. The theatre would be open every day of the year, with a programme of 32 productions, and tickets were sold at a fixed rate of 50 francs (about £5) with a season ticket costing 200 francs (£20). The new programme was geared towards the people of Saint-Denis and many activities, performances, readings and participatory events were planned for the region's centres, schools and public spaces.

This radical approach had interesting consequences for the debate on the responsibility of the director. On the one hand, ticket sales for the first year were very positive, increasing from 25,000 to 46,000, which compensated for the price reduction and generated a substantial audience for the productions (many of which were co-productions with young, invited companies). However, looking at the larger budgetary implications, the theatre was near bankruptcy, with a deficit of 5.5 million francs (£600,000). This shortfall was due to the increase in productions: in the public sector, where relatively low ticket prices are needed to justify subsidy, income from ticket sales only covers part of the production costs, so the more productions there are, the more money is lost. For Nordey and his supporters, this absurd situation highlights the structural contradictions of the CDNs that result in them being unable to support new writers and develop that vital relationship between text and audience for which he was aiming. In fact, he argued, the structure and budgetary protocols of the CDNs only serve to maintain their role as museums of classical texts. After three years, and a cumulative deficit of 10 million francs (about £1 million), Nordey's contract was not renewed.

Another writer/actor/director who began working with an independent group of friends, and who is now a key figure in the subsidized sector is Olivier Py, appointed director of the Théâtre national de l'Odéon in 2007. In an interview given in 2004, Py stated that: 'I have always had a problem with issue-based theatre: when I'm asked what a play is about... well, it has to be about everything. Because if not, then it wouldn't interest me: desire, faith, the spirit, theatre, men, women, unhappiness, everything' (in Bradby, 2005: 242). This attitude led to a method that intentionally blurred the distinctions between writing and directing, creating a collective work where one form learnt from another, and the process was as important at the resulting show. As Py said in 2001: 'my vocation didn't particularly lie in playwriting, or performance or directing, but rather in the whole theatrical event' (in Perrier, 2001: 1; my translation).

On taking up his appointment at the Odéon in 2007, Py published a manifesto under the title *Discours du nouveau directeur de l'Odéon*, which consists of a monologue (spoken by him), broken up by a series of interruptions, each leading to a short passage of dialogue. The people who interrupt him are, successively, his cheese-seller, an art critic, a politician, his mother and death. This witty sketch demonstrates the ambition of his generation of writer/directors to distance themselves from the previous generation whose success was so often based on the image and depended on their collaboration with exceptional designers, such as Richard Peduzzi, who designed all of Chéreau's productions. Rejecting this model of *mise en scène*, he proclaims a new relationship between word and image: 'the theatre is the opposite of an image, it is presence. For the word is not opposed to the image, the word is image, it is the real presence which is both the origin and the other of the image' (Py, 2007: 16; my translation).

In common with his peers, Py sees the media as mind-numbingly dangerous, and positions theatre as utterly different: 'theatre is not the media because it has no message. It has no other message than itself' (ibid.: 17; my translation). It would be hard to find a more striking definition of art for art's sake, and Py's own plays are poetic, lyrical, dream-like (for a related position in French performance, see Chapter 13 by Carl Lavery in this volume). But, interestingly, Py also sees himself as part of the *théâtre populaire* movement. He argues that the individual who enjoys a really profound theatre experience discovers, *through* that experience, her/his symbiotic link to the wider community. He refuses the debate which starts from political definitions, preferring to start from the real presence of both actor and audience in real time and space, and arguing that any theatre performance which celebrates presence, and touches the individuals in its audience, achieves, through that, the elusive quality of the 'popular'.

Py's attempt to define a theatre that is both poetic and popular depends on the rather Brookian idea that the theatre is the place where we can recover a sense of the sacred. He sees the twenty-first century as being all about speed, instant e-mail communication, virtual reality, whereas theatre, for him, is summed up by three words 'attente, recon-contre, communion' ('expectancy, encounter, communion') (ibid.; my translation). Others of his generation are less inclined to the mystical, but arrive at a similar conclusion from secular sources stressing theatre's physicality. Pier Paolo Pasolini's *Manifesto for a New Theatre* (1968) was a shared point of inspiration for several of them. In it, Pasolini developed the idea of a theatre of words that was in opposition to what he called a 'chattering' theatre on the one hand, and a theatre of gesture on the other. Stanislav Nordey recalled how this manifesto had influenced the beginning of his career: 'I decided to believe Pasolini when he said that his theatre, which he also called poetic theatre, could do without the stage and be performed in any brightly lit space; what was important was the relationship of the actor and the audience, with the poet at the centre' (2005: 81; my translation). Nordey goes on to explain how his main concern is to make things heard rather than to make things seen, and that what should be seen is the actor swept up by the poet's words: 'I like the idea that theatre is created when an actor physically tackles words, that theatre is found in this mastication, this physical act' (ibid.; my translation).

Robert Cantarella also claimed to be influenced by Pasolini when, with the writer Philippe Minyana, he created his own theatre of words (see Chapter 3 by Céline Hersant in this volume for a discussion of Minyana). Cantarella stated that he was motivated by the need to find the future of theatre, and the terms that he chose to describe his directing are remarkably similar to Gabily's: 'What is there to say about the sudden appearance of a form of theatre that was not there before, and that manages, relatively easily, to make us aware of a previously unseen, or unheard of, consistency – bodies speaking in a space?' (2000: 91; my translation).

Cantarella proved to be very conscious of the need to find another form of theatrical art that allowed for an undecided or unspecified element, a quality important to the texts of both Minyana and Gabily. Working on *Pièces* (a homonym meaning both *Rooms*, *Pieces* and *Plays*) by Minyana, he set out to 'explore the text on stage in order to find various resolutions, using experimental techniques, repetitions, sketches and different textures' (ibid.: 92; my translation). In 2000, Cantarella was appointed as director of the CDN Dijon-Bourgogne, where he adopted techniques as rigorous as those used by the Théâtre du Soleil – long

rehearsal periods, the allocation of roles during the process, the sharing of discoveries with both the audience and the entire theatre staff.
For him, 'what is known as the rehearsal period is a place to build a
democratic environment where people can invent new ways of living
together' (2003: 31; my translation). Text-based theatre, when seen from
this point of view, cannot be solipsistic, but actually has the opposite
effect of confronting the modern world, he claimed.

One of the playwrights whose work Cantarella has directed is Michel
Vinaver and an account of tendencies in current French theatre would
be incomplete without a mention of this playwright whose work, most
unusually, spans the whole period from the 1950s to today and who is,
arguably, the greatest living playwright in France. As has been seen, an
underlying principle of *mise en scène* is that, where it does not choose
to dispense altogether with the playwright's text, it creates the expectation of a novel interpretation of that text. Thus the majority of directors
who are in charge of theatres in France today have established their
reputations through new productions of classic plays whose claim to
distinction lies in bringing inventive or challenging new interpretations
to well-known texts.

This privileging of directorial interpretation in any new production ran
precisely counter to the compositional method elaborated by Vinaver.
His was a dramaturgical method that sought to privilege multiplicity
of viewpoint rather than providing any one, dominant interpretation
of the events depicted on stage. In fact, Vinaver had begun his writing
career as a novelist, and moved to theatre precisely because he valued
the opportunity to compose without the necessity of an authorial viewpoint. As a young aspiring writer, Vinaver had been much influenced
by T. S. Eliot (he made a translation into French of *The Waste Land* in
1947). He borrowed from Eliot a juxtapositional method of composition
in which the most important thing is not the material itself but what
he called 'mises en relation' ('bringing into relationship or contact') at
the level of language: 'These are *material* in nature – that is to say that
they take place at the level of the linguistic material – rhythmic effects,
collisions of sounds, shifts of meaning from one sentence to another,
collisions setting off what one might call mini-phenomena of explosive
irony'(1998: 129; my translation).

Vinaver enjoys comparing his compositional methods to those of
painters or musicians. At the head of his play *Iphigénie Hôtel* (1960), he
set a quotation by Georges Braque, in which he emphasized that what he
painted was not so much the objects depicted on the canvas as the space
in between, and Vinaver stresses the importance of the 'in-between' for

his writing. From musical form, he adopted the method of superimposing different voices simultaneously. On stage it is not possible to have several people talking over one another, or all the audience hears is a babble; but Vinaver aims for a similar effect to that, say of the string quartet, in which four instruments play separate melodic lines, by juxtaposing and intermingling two or more conversations, so that different discourses overlap and the reader of his plays is frequently uncertain as to whom a given remark is addressed.

The result of this compositional method is a series of complex, fragmented dramatic structures which superimpose different voices, situations, stories, presenting the world in an unexpected light and opening up cracks in what is perceived as the established order. Microcosm is juxtaposed with macrocosm – for example, an intimate conversation between two individuals about their private lives is set in counterpoint to a discussion about investments between two business leaders, whose decisions may turn out to affect the private lives of the two individuals. Or a character finds that she is attempting to face up to a problem in her private life using the language and the mental structures learned in her workaday environment. In any given one of Vinaver's plays, several different stories and situations are juxtaposed with the result that it becomes impossible to identify a linear plot leading to a recognizable climax in the classical manner, or even to distinguish between main plot and sub-plots. Instead, one finds an interwoven texture of events, characters and situations. In order to identify his method, Vinaver establishes a distinction between *les pièces-machines* (machine-plays), in other words, those modelled on the rules of classical dramaturgy, and his own plays, which he terms *pièces-paysages* (landscape-plays), explaining that a *paysage* can be mapped in a wide variety of ways. It can be a place to be lost in, as well as a place in which one can discover oneself, but no one way of entering it can be said to be better than any other (ibid.: 99–100; my translation). Michel Corvin recently summed up the originality of Vinaver's method by saying that he short-circuits at one and the same time concepts of focus, of sequential chronology, of differential spatiality, in favour of a whole which can only be grasped by the reader's or audience's imagination (2006: 13; my translation). (See the translation of Corvin's essay in the following chapter for further discussion of this point.)

Vinaver's work has been enormously influential on a whole generation of theatre makers, writers, directors and actors, who have adopted the model of the *pièce paysage* and have sought out new ways of presenting on stage the material conflicts of speaking bodies in a form closer to concrete poetry than to traditional models of Tragedy or Comedy. Other key influences have been those of Heiner Müller and Edward Bond. Müller's densely textured speeches (often not attributed to *dramatis personae*), combined with his oppositional political stance, inspired many French playwrights, and enhanced their sense of the possibilities of 'textual material'.[4] Bond, now more frequently performed in France than in Britain, offered models for expressing the sense of violence latent in the apparently orderly structures of the late capitalist world.

Some French playwrights have gone much further down the road travelled by Gabily, producing texts that embody extreme violence. Valère Novarina, for example, batters his audience with repeated acts of verbal violence that recall the work of the surrealist poets and have been praised by some critics as sounding the alarm signal in the face of the banalities of mediatized language. Others, such as Noëlle Renaude, Gildas Bourdet, Michel Azama or Patrick Kermann have proved very inventive in exploring the poetic possibilities of language when presented on a stage liberated from naturalistic or traditional dramatic modes of expression. Often this results in work that consists of extended monologues, or lists, genealogies, and other methods of making the language itself the focus of the audience's fascination (see Éric Vautrin, Chapter 11 in this volume).[5]

No longer a separate genre, governed by rules that have become so elastic as to permit anything the writer's imagination can dream up, theatrical 'text' now aspires to a poetic status close to that of abstract art: it can be taken or left as *matériau* (raw material) and only fully exists in the interaction between real bodies and real voices present in a dedicated playing space. If any transcendence is to be found, it is in language itself and although this can lead to navel-gazing, it can also produce ambitious texts that aim to rival classical tragedy and to achieve a form of universality (for a very different relationship to language and text, see Bérénice Hamidi-Kim, Chapter 8 in this volume, pp. 111–21). Artaud, Genet and Adamov were among the great French masters often cited as inspirational sources by young writers. This is undoubtedly due to the poetic qualities of their writing. But writers did not so much seek to place themselves in a theatrical tradition as to write 'against the theatre', following the example set by Vinaver.[6] In their desire to create an autonomous world based on the power and process of art, they turned towards the great modernist novelists of the early twentieth century, especially James Joyce. The dense texture of Joyce's work seemed to a number of young writers to offer a model of a new theatrical dynamic. In his work they found a dazzling array of themes and characters, often expressed through monologues and streams of consciousness. They also appreciated his ability to approach everyday situations through the filter of classical antiquity. But most importantly, they discovered a structural freedom, a rejection of the laws that governed literary genres and an environment that became more defined as the text progressed – an environment that could be either an entire city or the thoughts and dreams of a single illiterate character.

The fact that Joyce (or at least the Joyce of *Ulysses* (1922) and of *Finnegans Wake* (1939)) had written prose, not drama, was no hindrance to their enthusiasm: they claimed the freedom to invent without reference to any fixed forms. The line that had separated dramatic form from epic form, seen in the opposition between Aristotle and Brecht and universally recognized before 1968, had been eliminated as a result of the challenge to all traditional models in the melting pot of 1968. The new texts that emerged in the 1990s laid claim to a poetic autonomy reminiscent of Rimbaud, Mallarmé and the symbolist poets.

As a result of this wave of experimentation, it became difficult at a certain point to differentiate between dramatic text and 'text' *per se*: the general characteristics that defined traditional dramaturgy (whether Aristotelian or Brechtian) lost their potency and, to use Patrice Pavis's expression (applied to Jean-Luc Lagarce), 'dramaturgy dissolved into textuality' (2002: 184; my translation). The structure of these texts rejected classical criteria (story, action, character), creating instead a 'textual material' that owed little to traditional and generic form. In these circumstances the question arose of whether it was still possible to define a theatrical specificity. One of the few people who attempted to do this was Michel Azama, in his anthology of Francophone writers from 1950 to 2000. In his research into this specificity, Azama (himself a playwright) found 'two fundamental features in theatrical texts. The first could be called its "respiration": its ability to enter the actor's body and create "play". This "verbal potential" is as essential to theatre as it is to poetry. [...] The other quality of theatrical writing is its "dramaturgy". If a text's respiration is represented in "verbal potential" then its dramaturgy is represented in "stage potential"' (2003: 20; my translation). The ambiguity of this definition shows how difficult it is to establish adequate criteria in the analysis of texts by many contemporary theatre writers. A sense of poetry is certainly an important criterion, but this does not help to differentiate the wide variety of plays ranging from the few written in verse, to the majority that are almost like prose poems. This definition of a verbal and scenic poetry can only really be assessed on stage: ultimately, there is no way of judging the quality of 'respiration' or 'stage potential' other than in and through performance.

Writing for the theatre in France since the start of the 1990s embodies a paradox reminiscent of the theatre of Antonin Artaud: on the one hand, it is constructed in successive verbal layers creating a dense and poetic texture, in which language is put to the test and the clichés of everyday speech are questioned or transformed; on the other hand, it aims to shatter language in order to touch life; that is to say, to achieve the reality of physical presence through its invention of hitherto undreamed of verbal structures. A large part of new French dramatic writing is concerned with this seemingly impossible fusion of text and body. The struggle of the performer's body with language, which might have been thought to have reached its last gasp in Beckett's minimalist late plays, is now finding a new flowering in the densely layered 'textual material' of today's French playwrights.[7]

The texts they produce no longer recognize the old dichotomy between performance and literature; like poetry, they incorporate both the word embodied in physical expression and the word as vehicle of reflection or thought. They are difficult, and do not allow for easy absorption into the visual framework of a *mise en scène*. However, the rejection of *mise en scène* did not mean the refusal of an essential physical dimension of their writing. Noëlle Renaude spoke for many writers of this generation when she claimed that: 'if there is one thing, one single thing, of which I'm sure, it is that theatrical writing – and theatrical writing alone – is a physical form' (1991: 93; my translation).

Notes

1. Antoine Vitez (1930–1990) was the artistic director of the Théâtre national de Chaillot (TNP) and later the Comédie-Française. See Chapter 4 by Clare Finburgh in this volume for a more detailed account of Vitez's work.
2. Review in *Le Monde*, quoted in *Le Guide des 129 metteurs en scène*, *Théâtre/Public*, hors série no. 7, 1993, p. 129.
3. Review in *Libération* quoted in ibid.
4. This is the title of one of Müller's most widely performed pieces, *Medeamaterial*.
5. An example of this can be seen in the opening scene of the first text by Renaude to be published in English translation, *Le Renard du nord* (*The Northern Fox*) (1998).
6. See Michel Vinaver (1998: 305).
7. For a more detailed account of the work of these writers, see David Bradby (2007) chs 13, 14 and 15.

Works cited

Azama, Michel (2003) 'Introduction', in *De Godot à Zucco 1* (Paris: Théâtrales), pp. 17–25.

Bradby, David (2005) 'Olivier Py: A Poet of the Stage: Analysis and Interview', *Contemporary Theatre Review*, 15:2, 234–45.

—— (2007) *Le Théâtre en France de 1968 à 2000* (Paris: Champion).

Cantarella, Robert (2000) 'Du Grain à écrire', in *Philippe Minyana ou la parole du visible* (Paris: Éditions Théâtrales), pp. 91–4.

—— (2003) 'Bilan du travail 1', *Spectres*, 1, 29–31.

Corvin, Michel (2006) 'Jusqu'où un auteur dramatique peut-il être intelligent?', *Europe*, 924, 7–14.

Nordey, Stanislas (1997) 'C'est la fin du règne des metteurs en scène', *Figaroscope*, 24 September.

—— (2005) 'La Cape d'invisibilité', *OutreScène* (*La Revue du Théâtre national de Strasbourg*), 6 May, 79–85.

Pavis, Patrice (2002) *Le Théâtre contemporain* (Paris: Nathan).

Perrier, Jean-Louis (2001) 'Le théâtre de combat d'Olivier Py', *Le Monde*.

Py, Olivier (2007) *Discours du nouveau directeur de l'Odéon* (Arles: Actes-Sud).

Renaude, Noëlle (1991) 'Un pari désespéré', *Théâtre/Public*, 100, 93–4.

Tackels, Bruno (1997) *A vues* (Paris: Bourgois).

Thibaudat, Jean-Pierre (1998) *Où va le théâtre?* (Paris: Hoebeke), pp. 49–60.

Vinaver, Michel (1998) *Écrits sur le théâtre 1* (Paris: L'Arche).

Vitez, Antoine (1991) 'L'Art du théâtre', reprinted in *Le Théâtre des idées* (Paris: Gallimard), pp. 123–6.

2
The Spirit of a Place: Place in Contemporary French Theatre

Michel Corvin

What will happen when the conventions of place and/or of the stage are exploded? With writing no longer structured or governed by strict spatial codes, the doors will be open to all attempts to create a fluid and changing style of writing that will spread in the mind and in the imagination, well beyond the boundaries of the stage, and which will broach anything that can be written in the fascinating but frightening absence of any reference points. A curious phenomenon occurred in France in the 1970s, when directors, whose job it is to translate a text into space, ascended to power and cared little for the spaces suggested by writers. They provided a scenography that was independent of the text's propositions, in order to assert their own interpretation. As a result, dramatic writing in France between 1970 and 1980 was consigned to the wilderness, until playwrights came up with the simple yet ingenious idea of writing a textual theatre; that is to say, a theatre that comes under the remit of writing alone, and is completely independent of the demands of the stage. From this point on, dramatic space became an entirely mental construction. It took shape with complete freedom in the minds of the writer and reader, with the result that, unlike in the years from 1950 to 1970, playwrights writing in France from roughly 1980 onwards – though this is only a provisional and partial affirmation – have cared little for dramatic and theatrical space, leaving that to directors. These playwrights implement a code of practice with stage practitioners, in the form of a hostile peace. Each has their own domain: the writer is simply dedicated to writing, whilst the director can create theatrical spaces with all the freedom that is granted by the disappearance of old oppositions inside/outside, interior/exterior. The latter is free to create a universe, her/his universe. It is also up to the writer to demonstrate the same creative independence.

Playwrights have embraced their newly acquired freedom: each one has created their own space, or non-space differently, and for themselves alone. This implies that the critic is required to produce a different detailed study for each style of writing. One approach might be to consider the use of stage directions in contemporary theatre. As we know, these have a status of exterritoriality: they belong to the writer, who manoeuvres at will whatever s/he wishes to turn into theatre, notably place and character. The writer can thereby set the location as a precondition to the dialogue which appears, according to the typographical layout of the first few pages, with the cast list, and details concerning set and settings within that place. This is the case in Philippe Minyana's *Drames brefs* (*Brief Dramas*, 1995 and 1997) and *Inventaires* (*Inventories*, 1993), Jean-Luc Lagarce's *Nous les héros* (*We, the Heroes*, 1993), and in Eugène Durif's *Tonkin-Alger* (*Tongking-Algiers*, 1988). Sometimes, additional information about place(s) is provided over the course of the play in order to set the scene, like in Durif's *L'Arbre de Jonas* (*Jonas's Tree*, 1991).

The stage directions might continue to be written in italics, which makes them instantly recognizable, such as in Didier-Georges Gabily's *Corps et tentations* (*Bodies and Temptations*, 1991). They still belong to the writer, but they 'novelize' what s/he says. The playwright stops directing what s/he writes exclusively towards what is said next. The playwright speaks either on her/his own behalf, or about the characters in a sort of descriptive gratuitousness, or else with analytical perceptiveness. The narrator is therefore implicated in the narration, which can only lead to a scrambling of places, times and events, and to a sort of *va-et-vient* between the story, and the writer's subjectivity.

An alternative strategy is necessitated, on the other hand, when the reader is faced with the total absence of stage directions, which warns of a new potential status of place: from the outset, one does not know where the voices are coming from. Durif's *Les Petites heures* (*The Small Hours*, 1992) is divided into 16 sequences separated by subtitles which give no information on place. However, it is not difficult to work them out using the dialogue. Everything takes place in an unspecified house with an inside and an outside, an upstairs and a downstairs, and where metaphorical values are clearly decipherable (aggression/proximity, threat/attraction, distance/fear). It is therefore not the materiality of the place that counts, but rather the undertones and connotations that characters attach to it. Place becomes metaphorical and symbolic when, for example, one considers Durif's *Meurtre hors champ* (*Murder Off Screen*, 1997), where it is clear that the places in which the characters Oreste and Pylade evolve are defined by an extreme violence which is intrinsic, even if it is not overtly shown.

These are merely general points, which do not enable us to understand the construction of place by a writer. In particular, how does one know that certain writers do not let themselves get carried away by some or other randomly chosen place, which will then become the driving force as much for the work's plot, as for its characters? This must occur more often than one might think, but few writers explain the spatial genesis of their plays. We know that Ionesco, whose dreams fuelled visions that became *The Chairs* (1952) and *Rhinoceros* (1959), does, but what about contemporary writers? Koltès does too, since he states clearly that he is interested in how the materiality of a place conditions behaviour and speech. Thus, with reference to *Quai Ouest* (1985), he says, 'The true meaning of the scene will be rendered if, above all, one takes care to show two people who are trying to walk on a slippery floor' (ibid.: 104), and, 'what is important about Charles, is the time that it takes him to get from one place to another, and the way he goes about it' (ibid.: 105). The osmosis is complete between place and play; one equals the other; one begets the other: 'I wanted to write a play in the same way that one constructs a hangar; in other words, by first building a structure from the foundations to the roof, before knowing precisely what would be stored in it; a large mobile space, a form solid enough to contain other forms within it' (1990: 111). Koltès sets himself a spatio-literary challenge, which he pushes to the limit. With this installed, the play then needs to be infused with its own driving force, which itself is spatial. The characters, so he says, have only one wish, to escape from the stage: 'I see the stage as a temporary place that the characters are always thinking of leaving. It's a place where these problems arise: this is not real life; how can we get out of here?' (1990: 119).

Koltès is a wanderer (his close resemblance to Genet, whom he admires, is no coincidence) and his characters are made in his image. A number of his contemporaries, notably Lagarce, Minyana and Durif are, on the other hand, sedentary, and write their plays about and within a house. This does not necessarily involve – far from it – metaphors of the protective cocoon, the mother's womb, or safety and tenderness; but rather, those of the coffin, entrapment and alienation (whether voluntary or not), or contrastingly, of liberating rebellion. The house is both a pole of attraction and repulsion. To say that a play is based on the theme of the house does not of course mean that the action takes place in the house. Rather, it means that the house, with all its materiality, its smells, its secret cupboards, its mould and cracks of light, with all the emotive charge that a house lived in for a long time leaves in the heart and mind of the person who may or may not have spent their childhood there, is the raw material of the work.

Two plays by Lagarce, *Juste la fin du monde* (*It's Only the End of the World*, 1990) and *J'étais dans ma maison et j'attendais que la pluie tombe* (*I Was in My House Waiting for the Rain to Fall*, 1994) are constructed in this way and counterbalance each other. They are like the obverse and reverse of a same place, with an inverted viewpoint. In *It's Only*, the house is the place towards which a dying man is walking: 'I decided to return [...] to announce [...] my impending and unavoidable death' (1990: 207–8). *I Was in My House* develops the point of view of the female occupants of the house, who are waiting for the return of the prodigal son. He has just arrived, and is going to pass away. The theme of returning home is a highly affective myth (we know that the word nostalgia derives from the Greek word *nostos*, meaning 'return'), but Ulysses, who embodies *par excellence* the successful homecoming, longs for happy reunions, and is always full of the joys of life. The main character in the two plays by Lagarce, on the contrary, is afflicted with a fatal illness and does not find the acknowledgement for which he hoped amongst those surrounding him. Either he leaves unrecognized (*It's Only*), or he remains, invisible, as a sort of *punctum caecum*, a blind spot around which the whole play – the whole house – revolves and evolves (*I Was in My House*). Lagarce builds his work on an elusive subject, on an absence, on the account of an absence.

Narrative is the place of the other, of the person we will not see. In *It's Only*, the five female wardens of the home, who represent the five ages of life and its principal stages, go back into the past, revisiting their non-life since the departure of the son, and, underlying this, the reasons for the rift between the father and son. They relive the anxiety of his departure rather than the joy of his return. The entire play draws on a past that is not just constructed, but reconstructed, as well as on a future that has already passed, and establishes the immobility of a house which no one will leave. The characters indulge in the workings of mourning before mourning, as does Lagarce himself, who modestly and lucidly anticipates his own death. The bias of the writing which shuns the *hic et nunc* of active speech to take refuge in fantasized comments, is usually the asset of novels, which are always free to follow the perambulations of dreamy subjectivity. Yet it is also the result of a poetic vision that tries, through words, images and extended metaphors, to weave a network of subtle sensations that, directly or indirectly, turn the house into the metaphor for something concrete, expressed in the guise of a journey that takes place within the space: 'Still in my dream, all the rooms in the house were a long way from each other, and I could never reach them' (Lagarce, 1990: 256). This is another way of signifying the need for and failure of dialogue. All in all, place in Lagarce's work is the story of a permanent misunderstanding.

Can it be anything else? Durif's *Eaux dormantes* (*Stagnant Waters*, 1992a) echoes Lagarce's voice, since the story of three women who hide in the cocoon-womb of a house to seek protection and safety has a familiar ring. The house is both described as real, and is charged with eu- and dysphoric metaphors: 'the house smells musty' (Durif, 1992a: 60). There is also hope that the house might be filled with something other than old memories: 'But who is still waiting for them at the house?' (1992: 62). The pronouns do not refer to the speakers, who talk about themselves in the third person – a sort of heightened novelizing – since this distancing ends up evacuating any notion of being-there, or rather, showing how being there is elusive and difficult to pin down. Marthe declares, 'We are here, everything has stood still. Some time has passed, nothing has changed, how can I describe this sensation? A hand movement to catch something and then nothing, and yet it was there. It seemed that it was easy to grasp, and then...' (1992a: 66). This is the theatre of feeling and of deferred feeling, which is the most subtle and evanescent kind. The three women leave at the end and Marthe concludes, 'What did we come to do in this house? The shadows, you can't cradle them. It's a real disaster as soon as you want to look back over your shoulder believing you can find them again and give them a tangible form' (1992: 68). Everything that refers to the house (its dilapidation, its quiet air) is equally appropriate and without any need of symbolic adaptation, since it all describes the feelings and mind-sets of the three women: fear, disgust, pleasure, boredom.

The paradox of place in Durif's work, just as in Lagarce's, lies in becoming attached to the nitty-gritty of the situation, while noticing that the horizon recedes the more one appears to approach it. The five women in *I Was in My House* revolve around an absence, as does the narrator of Durif's *Le Petit bois* (*The Little Wood*, 1992b). In his 'Présentation' to the play, Durif describes his character in the following terms: 'He loiters around the scene of a crime to which he cannot return.' (ibid.: 8). The crucial place – the place of the last meeting and of the murder – is so internalized that the distancing effects of narration could not be used, even if they were to narrate the impossibility of approaching the place. Yet there are stages in the motionless and invisible voyeur's approach, and he is aware of his failures: 'I wanted to approach her again [...] and

I lost my footing and fell [...]' (ibid.: 77). The account in the end reveals little, and the silky manoeuvres of the narrator towards and around the coveted, but absent goods that he desires are the best demonstration of the goods' mental and symbolic connotations, even though, at the heart of the forest, a crime has indeed been committed. The distinctive characteristic of Durif's protagonist is that he is a sort of village idiot who lives in direct contact with animals and nature. He adheres too closely to what he desires, and to what he sees, for any form of self-awareness to creep into his behaviour, other than the fact that he is a sort of basic upholder of the law, in the sense that he shares something of the nature of the elements that make up the earth. The question of place, consequently, no longer applies.

However, it still arises in terms of language, if one turns towards Vinaver or Novarina, albeit for very different reasons in each case. In order to discuss the writing of place in Vinaver, one has to take a considerable amount of time, since it goes to the very heart of his conception of dramatic art. He no longer wants anything to do with a form of linear or homogenous writing where characters follow each other on to the stage to elaborate their points of view or their conflicts, where stories quietly weave their different threads. He promotes a tabularization of perception that has commonalities with Marcel Proust's analysis of Vermeer's 'small section of yellow wall' in *À la recherche du temps perdu* (1913–27). In itself, the section does not represent anything, yet it is around this small block of yellow pigment that the colours and shapes of the painting are articulated. For Vinaver, a representative of an organic style of writing (whether musical or visual), the plurality of viewpoints on the world and its complexity require not so much fragmented tales, as interpenetrating stories in a sort of combinational analysis that brings into contact apparently unconnected particles and dialectizes opposites: the here and the elsewhere, the private and the public, the emotional and the political, the white woman and the black man, the bourgeois and the rebel, the young and the old, the lawful and the outlawed. Consequently, each element (by this I mean each of the characters' lines or emotions) reveals the full extent of its value when connected with the preceding and ensuing elements. Indeed, each of the 30 fragments of the play in *La Demande d'emploi* (*Situation Vacant*, 1973), for example, only makes sense when assembled with the other 29 in a cohesive totality, which has nothing, or very little, to do with their numerical succession. In short, Vinaver simultaneously bypasses the concepts of focus, homogenous and successive temporality and differentiated spatiality, in favour of a whole that is only perceptible in the imagination of the reader who is able to establish the 'situation' in the most localized meaning of the term: characters apparently (and visually) situated in the same space.

Reading habits make it tempting to establish links of contiguity between characters who are in fact each in their own bubble, and of causality between lines A and B, when in fact they simply follow on from one another, or are at best intertwined. With the near total absence of stage directions, readers are not able, unless they shut their eyes and simply stick to the content of the lines, to establish the sub-spaces that are essential in order to locate the different speakers and different situations of enunciation. This is all the more important since Vinaver makes things even more confusing by establishing tenuous links (based on polysemy and metaphor) between A and B, as if theme A rubbed off on theme B, with words re-forming connections which could be seen as poetic beyond the objective boundaries of conceptual relationships.

In fact, by creating these often humorous pile-ups, Vinaver, who has a very dry sense of humour, sends a veiled message to the reader. He breaks the parallelism of the lines of dialogue by building bridges of words and images from one sentence to another, to such an extent that meaning travels across discontinuous lines that are not spatially connected. In order to read Vinaver's works both efficiently and pleasurably, an education in perception is required, especially since a large number of characters talk simultaneously, for example in *L'Ordinaire* (*The Ordinary*, 1979a) or *Les Travaux et les jours* (*A Smile on the End of the Line*, 1979b). It is therefore of paramount importance to spatialize the reading, to create a concrete location where the words can take shape. The main question for the reader is no longer 'What are they talking about?', but rather, 'Who is talking to whom?' This means identifying one of the fundamentals of theatre: address. Since the concept of who addresses whom is no longer signposted by extra-diegetic information, notably the use of pronouns, and since the identity of the speakers and the listeners is not always clear, it is necessary when reading the text to imagine it spatially. This, of course, renders another form of spatialization, the stage performance of the text, almost redundant. In order to have a secret understanding with Vinaver, the reader becomes an audience member at a performance that does need to take place, and that does not require a place – hence his concept of 'over-staging', which has caused such as stir.[1] Here lies the paradox: constructing meaning does not entail drawing out ideas or uncovering a hidden message which, incidentally, Vinaver would never include, but finding, through logic and reason, one's own path through this solar system of planets, fixed stars and meteorites that Vinaver maps out differently in each of his plays.

Vinaver writes about non-place, since the connections between the different spaces of speech are made mentally, somewhere other than on the page, somewhere else – namely, in the reader's mind. Space is the place from which I am speaking, one of Vinaver's characters might say, and it is up to the reader to become the spatial vector of this 'I'. Equally, in Novarina's work, space is the place from which the speaker speaks, but as a result of criss-crossing the cosmos of his toponymic references, this speaker, who is subject to a process of perpetual transformation, is everywhere and nowhere: the speaker is the voice of space that takes on body and shape. A heavy body – 'space is heavy: heavy, heavy, heavy' says a character in *L'Opérette imaginaire* (*The Imaginary Operetta*, 1978: 15) – in the shape of death, since Novarina is heavily marked by the Bible and by the theme of death: 'Since I set foot on this earth, it's been the pits', declares the character named The Mortal in *L'Opérette imaginaire*. And a little further on, the Man-from-Beyond sings:

> In my little Peugeot that's no tin can,
> Yes really I crush the passers-by [...]
> But what I prefer, I openly say
> Is to stop at the cemetery, to leave behind
> The torments of all this parking
> So here I am in the dead zone, you might say.
> (Novarina,1978: 51)[2]

Novarina is no doubt being playful, but in one of his writings, the Prologue to *Je suis* (*I Am*, 1991), the concept of space with regard to Self is turned completely upside down. He seems to look at all the possible interplays between inside and outside, not for the pleasure of language, but in order to point out that there is no answer to the question that philosophers have long pondered: does the world have a status of exterritoriality, or is it simply a figment of my perception: *esse est percipi* (see Chloé Déchery in Chapter 9 in this volume). The last lines of the play, by steering the discussion back to the theatre, pose the question of place indirectly: 'Is there a world – this theatre in front of me and everything we see here – that is in itself, and that is not simply in front of me? These people, their eyes... why have we been given language?' The answer to this question is: 'Every being is spoken: even you. There is no being without speech, within us. I am within speech within you. Only what is spoken is alive' (Novarina, 1991: 214).

This sentence is filled with an amazing vitality if it is applied to a theatre of words where speech incessantly creates the world by speaking it. I am thinking here of Noëlle Renaude and her world-in-a-book *Ma Solange, comment t'écrire mon désastre, Alex Roux* (*My Solange, How Can I Write You My Disaster, Alex Roux*, 2004). We witness a logorrhoea of words, of all words, whether assembled into sentences or not, words of multiple dialects, half-heard, random mumblings, and all that this entails: the contraction of time, the uprooting of speakers, whose space is not stuck on to the soles of their shoes, but to their words (see related points made by Clare Finburgh, Céline Hersant and Éric Vautrin in this volume). Hence the multiplication of viewpoints, the fragmentation of sequences, all space having disappeared, whether it be space as an aid to, or constraint on creativity. This is space created out of, and by speech. There is no doubt a privileged speaker, Alex. He floats along, blown about, and curls himself up, turns in on himself, the space of his Self very much resembling a prison. We follow a whole part of his history. He is tempted by the great outdoors, but half-heartedly: 'Ah, how I wish I were elsewhere, ah how I wish I was no longer shut up, locked up within myself' (ibid.: 21).

If, when reading, one is able to get beyond the point of view of the speaker, whoever that may be, it becomes apparent – this is a major feature, whether covert or manifest, of novelistic, and of Renaudian writing – that the only real speaker is God the Father. He knows everything, sees everything, hands out speech to one or other of his creatures, whether they have a name or are no more than a pronoun. It is therefore pointless identifying the mass of anonymous grammatical elements that populate *Ma Solange*. They quite simply do not exist. The God Noëlle surveys her world, tours her world, visiting her beings, who are all made of speech. This omni-directional feature of Renaude's writing strikes me as the sign of her Luciferian ambition to build a parallel world, one composed of the memory of all the little things in all the little lives which, when forged together, make up Life. Balzac, it is said, was like a civil register. As for Renaude, she does not weave any fates. She is like the schoolboy Cleophas in Alain-René Lesage's 1707 novel *Le Diable boiteux* (*The Devil on Two Sticks*). She lifts the rooves off houses and quickly takes a peek at the rustling words that fly away like fragments of life; and off she flies, to reveal more indiscretions. She is ecumenical, in the sense that in her work, the world features, but not any old world. It is the world linked to the Greek etymology of the word ecumenical, in other words, the familiar world of the 'house'.[3] *My Solange* is the House-of-the-Earth.

Whatever the textual foundations used, it is clear that for this generation of writers in France, anchoring writing in a predetermined space
is no longer either necessary, or useful, since space has ceased to be
a prerequisite for theatrical perception. Since the writing is spatially
disorientated, it is consequently no longer either owned, or directed
at someone. Speakers speak within themselves rather than looking at
their interlocutors. It is a decentred theatre where the characters – if
they still exist – are blown about, pulled here and there, never finding
their centre of gravity. The demon of ubiquity is at work in the modern
world and, by extension, in the theatre. Writing, created from the word
of chance, wanders towards a distant world within.

Translated by Clare Finburgh and Dominic Glynn

Notes

1. Editors' note. See Vinaver's article 'La Mise en trop' (1998: 137–46), originally
   published in 1988, in which he criticizes directors who, in the 1980s, considered verbal text to be no more significant in their productions than lighting,
   scenography or the actor's movement. *Mise en scène*, according to Vinaver,
   had become *mise en trop* – a play on words in which *trop* indicates that production values had become 'too much'.
2. Avec ma p'tite Peugeot qu'est pas un cageot,
   Oui vraiment j'écrase les passants [...]
   Mais c'que j'préfère, j'le dis carrément
   C'est m'garer au cimetière : quitter les tour-
   ments, d'tous ces stationnements...
   Me v'là en zone morte, en quelque sorte... (Novarina, 1978: 51)
3. Editors' note. The word *ecumenical* derives from the Greek terms *oikoumenē*
   and *oikosm* meaning 'the inhabited work', or 'house'.

Works cited

Durif, Eugène (1988) *Tonkin-Alger* (Paris: Théâtre Ouvert).
—— (1991) *L'Arbre de Jonas* (Paris: Théâtre Ouvert).
—— (1992) *Les Petites Heures* (Paris: Théâtre Ouvert).
—— (1992a) *Eaux dormantes* (Paris: Théâtre Ouvert).
—— (1992b) *Le Petit bois* (Paris: Théâtre Ouvert).
—— (1997) *Meurtre hors champ* (Paris: Théâtre Ouvert).
Gabily, Didier-Georges (1991) *Corps et tentations* (Paris: Théâtre Ouvert).
Koltès, Bernard-Marie (1985) *Quai Ouest* (Paris: Éditions de minuit).
—— (1990) *Roberto Zucco* (Paris: Éditions de minuit).
Lagarce, Jean-Luc (1990) *Juste la fin du monde*, *Théâtre complet*, vol. 3 (Besançon:
les Solitaires intempestifs).
—— (1993) *Nous les héros*, *Théâtre complet*, vol. 4 (Besançon: les Solitaires
intempestifs).

—— (1994) *J'étais dans ma maison et j'attendais que la pluie vienne, Théâtre complet*, vol. 4 (Besançon: les Solitaires intempestifs).

Minyana, Philippe (1993) *Inventaires* (Paris: Éditions Théâtrales).

—— (1995) *Drames brefs 1* (Paris: Éditions Théâtrales).

—— (1997) *Drames brefs 2* (Paris: Éditions Théâtrales).

Novarina, Valère (1978) *L'Opérette imaginaire* (Paris: P.O.L.).

—— (1991) *Je suis* (Paris: P.O.L.).

Renaude, Noëlle (2004) *Ma Solange, comment t'écrire mon désastre, Alex Roux* (Paris: Éditions Théâtrales).

Vinaver, Michel (1973) *La Demande d'emploi, Théâtre complet*, vol. 1 (Paris: Actes Sud).

—— (1979a) *L'Ordinaire, Théâtre complet*, vol. 2 (Paris: Actes Sud).

—— (1979b) *Les Travaux et les jours, Théâtre complet*, vol. 2 (Paris: Actes Sud).

—— (1998) 'La Mise en trop', in *Écrits sur le théâtre*, vol. 2 (Paris: L'Arche).

3
The Landscaped Narratives of Phillipe Minyana and Noëlle Renaude

Céline Hersant

As soon as one touches on the subject of the hidden geographies of theatrical writing – I say 'hidden' because the map around this literary area is at first glance difficult to read – one also touches not only on dramaturgy, but also, and most of all, on the practicalities of writing and its capacity to construct a referent (see Chapter 2 by Michel Corvin and Chapter 4 by Clare Finburgh in this volume). Space can be described, or can appear in writing in many different ways, and it is worth, from the outset, making the following distinction of scale and perspective: *space* represents a continuous environment, the boundaries of which are relative; *place* is a specific, named setting; *context* is a set of referents that must be interpreted in relation to each other. In writing, these three dimensions can appear in various ways, bringing into play complex relationships between inside and outside, requiring inventories of real or invented place names, and using the referential power of deictics such as pronouns to create a temporal and spatial situation. In this chapter, I explore the construction and function of these spatial dimensions, these geographies of writing, in the dramatic texts of two of France's most experimental playwrights, Philippe Minyana and Noëlle Renaude.

External pressures on the personal: Phillipe Minyana

Deictics serve as shifters in speech. They enable the speaker to be located, and clarify the conditions of space and time in the enunciation. Since his very first texts, Minyana has always used them profusely. One only need consider the three monologues by Angèle, Barbara and Jacqueline in his 1987 play *Inventaires* (*Inventories*). In a television game show format, three contestants pour out their private lives in a public arena and take stock of their existence. What is striking when reading these accounts of their lives is the effort to which the three women go to situate their personal stories by means of great lists of dates and places. By listening to them, one embarks on a journey through history – of the war, or different family tragedies – and also through French geography – via places where the women lived or visited when on holiday. Recalling these times and places provides a foundation for the drama by framing the theatrical discourse and accounts of the three women. Given the precision of the information provided, it would be easy to trace the journey of each contestant before they ended up in the television studio.

This work on the private sphere is characteristic of almost all Minyana's plays. He is known for putting his speakers within a confined and intimate space often limited to a bedroom, sitting-room or corridor – in other words, inside a house (see, for example, *Chambres* (*Bedrooms*, 1993), *Drames brefs* (*Brief Dramas* (1995–97), *Prologue* (2004) and *Le Couloir* (*The Corridor*, 2004a)). But the safety and continuity of the house always seem to be under threat from an outside intrusion, such as in *La Maison des morts* (*House of the Dead*, 2006), *Pièces* (*Rooms*, 2001), *Habitations* (*Dwellings*, 2001), *Anne-Marie* (2004), *Entente cordiale* (2004) and *Histoire de Roberta* (*Roberta's Story*, 2006a). It is as if the exploration of the personal for Minyana could only take place in a small-scale or compartmentalized space. Most interesting of all, is the fact that the establishment of these micro-perimeters, along with the confinement of the speaker to a very clearly demarcated space, produce such conflicting results: effects of repression; the conflict between inside and outside; and the crossing of thresholds separating these two spaces. Tragedy resides partly in the impossibility of protecting oneself from the outside, this other threatening space, which might at any moment tamper with the safe space of the house. This is exactly what happens in *Histoire de Roberta*, where hands appear through a window to strangle Roberta. The play underlines the liminal function of doors and windows as fragile interfaces with, or fragile barriers against, the outside world.

An almost identical set-up is used in Minyana's *Anne-Marie* (2004), where 'watchers' scrutinize Anne-Marie's family problems through the window. Ever since his early work, Minyana has displayed a definite fascination with 'the space enclosed behind glass doors' (Nores, 1997: 5). And in this play, he creates a large house split in two, in which two generations are unable to cohabit, since there is the Old Lady's space, and the space occupied by the rest of the family. This *dispositif* (set-up) enables the division of various actions and fictions: on one hand,

two voyeurs, in the background, recount and comment on the action
at which they gaze (at certain points, one of the watchers, who cannot always see what is happening inside the house, has the situation
explained to him by his companion); on the other, the mute figure of
the Old Woman is watched as if she were part of a mime show.

SECOND WATCHER: The mother sighs can you hear her
she sighs and paces about
(oh deary me her old footsteps)
she's eyeing something out the window
I wonder
what there is to eye up
[...]
the mother listens
she sees us can she see us
the door is ajar
we whisper
she sees us whispering
you told me she was deaf is she really
Pause, they look at each other and perhaps nod in consent?

(Minyana, 2004: 72–3)[1]

Caught between the two spaces, Anne-Marie's status remains ambiguous: she is involved in both narratives, since she becomes either a
silhouette in the house, or a figure capable of interacting with the
watchers and calling out to them: 'Still spying on / the misfortunes
of others / and gossiping about them (*The woman says quietly*, "Clear
off")' (ibid.: 91). This utterance, to which are added the effects of direct
address to the audience or to other undefined speakers, changes the
outline of each fiction and gives each speaker a relatively unstable status. For example, the watcher can become the watched. This study of
voyeurism juxtaposes two viewpoints, one on the inside, the other on
the outside, and implies a specific way of writing about bodies in space
through the distances separating them or the looks they exchange.

Another important feature of Minyana's work is that houses, stones
and walls, as well as furniture and other domestic objects, contain all
the components of someone's life, becoming a sort of personal archive,
a tangible biography. This biographical material forms a space of memory. Minyana describes the house as an 'enclave' or a 'supplementary,
improved space' (*Entente cordiale*, 2004: 61); it is a fragment of space

clearly detached from its surrounding environment, and marked by the sedimentation of traces from the past. One of the characters in *Entente cordiale* says:

> Large cold house only the little sitting room was welcoming (bathed in sunlight) in the little sitting room time for reconciling intimacy (intimate traces diary knitting) time of the entente cordiale (of course there were truces).
>
> At that time it was almost the countryside and then the world changed (factory close by) the environment completely changed it was like our world had shrunk (despite the partition being brought down it was like our world had shrunk) our father went to the factory (before he worked in the shop next to where we lived).
>
> (2004: 64–5)[2]

Unfortunately, the house is a fragile 'enclave'; walls can come down at any moment. And the collapse of a partition can be experienced as marking the beginning of a family tragedy. The opening lines of *Entente Cordiale* are, 'it was then (when the partition came down) that it all kicked off' (ibid.: 65).

It can also happen that intruders interfere in or even upturn a character's personal life by removing or literally hollowing out the familiar, domestic space s/he has created for herself/himself. In *Pièces* – the play's title is eminently polysemous[3] – Tac's apartment is filled with so many piles of newspapers and leaflets that the floor tilts, and access is impossible. He is even forced to sleep on the doormat. However, one day, following a leak, the owner breaks down the door and sends the entire contents of the apartment to the skip. Here, violence stems not so much from Tac's expulsion by his landlord, as from the intrusion of an outsider who lays bare a private space, as well as from the drastic erasure of the character's memory. With no fixed abode, Tac returns to his native village, where some disappointing news awaits him. He is unable to stay with his sister, since her house has just been razed to the ground.

Themes of dwelling, eviction, or the lack of private space surface everywhere in Minyana's work. Characters are never housed in a safe environment. Rather, they seem constantly to be pushed to, or snatched by, the outside. This feature is all the more noticeable, since his use of narrative is often disjointed. The text, just like the homes it represents, is shattered – this feature is particularly apparent in *La Maison des morts*, where each fictional level is founded on a specific location. The houses follow on from each other, whilst the different stages in the life of the woman with the plaited hair are related in a stop-start fashion. The fractured narrative structure accentuates the character's lack of a stable abode in which to dwell.

Space in Minyana's work unravels like a phylactery.[4] In *Histoire de Roberta*, the text amasses spatial vignettes just as it accumulates fictional levels. Like in *La Maison des morts*, Minyana develops a succession of micro-environments around the different stages of Roberta's life. However, the spatial and temporal divisions provide little continuity. Indeed, the scenes alternate between views of the interior – of what happens at Renée's, Ingrid's mother's, Mme Fils's or Roberta's – and shots of the exterior – a street, meadow, bridge, deep forest or the countryside. The complexity of the spaces created by the text suggests that the 'play with space' and the 'space for play' have become the '"objective" intention' of the dramatic discourse, as Louis Marin writes in *Utopiques, jeux d'espace* (*Utopics: Space Games*, 1973: 88). What is particularly striking, especially when reading the text of *Histoire de Roberta*, is space's ability to dilate, as well as its relative permeability. Interiors are always hemmed in, for example, a window always looks out on to an exterior, whether this is in the town or countryside. The opening out of this private space, notably the episode where the country house is located on the edge of a deep forest, evokes Chekhov's dramaturgy. But there is the sense that an outside danger lurks within each of the perimeters provided by Minyana, and that this underlying threat renders any attempt to pin down the character of Roberta almost impossible. Outsiders invade her personal space, hands appear through the window to strangle her, and furniture proliferates to crowd her out. In the end, she becomes a figure moving in relatively unstable spaces. This effect is no doubt induced by the appearance of the play on the page, with its multiple subtitles and subheadings. In this respect it resembles *Madame Ka* (1999) by Noëlle Renaude. There is little separating Mrs Ka's story and Roberta's chronicle, and the two plays are also linked by the fact that the same actor, Florence Giorgetti, played in both.[5] These obvious indicators of intertextuality between the two authors reveal common concerns, but these concerns are resolved by the authors in different ways with respect to how they treat space, and how speakers evolve in their environment.

Taking it to the edge: Noëlle Renaude

In Minyana's work, as I have demonstrated, the spatial dynamics are founded essentially on the exploration of private space, on a centripetal force. This is diametrically opposed to the spatial forces driving Renaude's theatre, which tend to be centrifugal, and to explore landscape.

Scale is considerably different in Renaude's work, since she covers vast geographic and textual territories. In most of her texts, she plays – her writing is indeed very playful – with moving her speakers about like pawns, and elaborating complex itineraries made of meanderings, twists and turns and dead ends. This cartographic dimension is a common element in all her works, and her taste for labyrinthine journeys might almost be thought of as the underlying condition of her writing. This is confirmed by the Blois episode in *Ma Solange comment t'écrire mon désastre, Alex Roux* (*My Solange, How Can I Write You My Disaster, Alex Roux,* 2005);[6] the zigzaging narrative in her play *8* (2003); Bob's roamings in *Promenades* (2003); and the speakers' peregrinations in *Ceux qui partent à l'aventure* (*Those Who Go on an Adventure,* 2006). These texts are almost always structured in the same way, namely, by a set of stock features such as a train station, building, living room, veranda or garden, around which characters gravitate, or to which they often return. The landscape appears to be produced by walking and journeying, and the end result is often the same: simultaneous, contradictory journeys without any real point of convergence, and characters ending up in opposite locations to where they were heading.

To find one's way around Renaude's geographies, a real road map comes in very handy. The sites she describes often create fictional worlds in the form of treasure hunts, where the character, just like the reader, becomes disorientated or lost in the midst of a textual landscape. The importance attributed to place names is fundamental to Renaude's construction of movement in space. In fact, it seems that by naming places, she seeks to measure the referential potential of the topographical sign, which is capable of superimposing fictional spaces on reality. Landscape is therefore often associated with ideas of walking and duration, since to watch a landscape unfold in front of one is to signify and measure the passage of time.

Walking is itself an odd idea for a playwright to try to represent, since it is foreign to the narrow confines of theatre. It suggests that space extends beyond the physical limitations of the stage, though it is of course a common occurrence in cinema, where landscapes unfold via travelling shots or panoramas. Such strangeness is at the heart of *Par les routes* (*By the Way,* 2005a).[7] Here, Renaude includes a number of place names and actual chunks of the country such as Paris Île-de-France, Loir-et-Cher, Nievre, Aquitaine and Savoie. A multitude of geographical signs is accumulated as the text progresses, marking out the journey of the two speakers, who travel across France by car. Their trip is complicated by various hesitations, stops and detours. Indeed, it is built on a succession of fictional vignettes that produce movement, and landscape particular zones. With regard to the formalist aspect of *Par les routes*, Renaude attempts to describe a sense of landscape, speed and movement that all lead towards a limit, or 'edge'. The text's great strength resides in her meticulous cartography of all the signs that invade our visual environment. Our reality, according to Renaude's play, is a muddled heap of words (signs, billboards, arrows, markings). This quasi-anthropological viewpoint echoes Marc Augé's research in *Non-Places: Introduction to an Anthropology of Supermodernity* (1995) on the construction of landscape as a migratory space, the perception of which is only possible through movement in today's world.

The journey of the two travellers in *Par les routes* replicates the unravelling of the landscape, to the point that when the two speakers arrive at the Franco-Swiss border (and therefore at the edge of the map), they disappear in a cloud that covers the mountain, and are lost in the vastness of the landscape. *Par les routes* has all the features of a 'theatrical road movie' and can be read like a long travelling shot of the landscape that is interspersed with blackouts and road signs. The focus is no longer on character, but on the road, on time and space traversed. These elements make the text into a veritable landscape play, providing the reader with 'image-places' (Renaude, 2005b).

In *Ceux qui partent à l'aventure*, Renaude goes even further with this idea of spatial demarcation, by providing, in the first third of the text, a staggering list of places and times. When the virtual narrator decides to tell a group of ramblers 'the story of a guy who went bankrupt', he explains:

> Where does your little story take place Marinette?
> Well you see Ulysse it starts
>> quite simply along a corridor in a bank just before midday, then one evening after work in front of a window that opens on to another window, then on an office terrace during a beautiful mid-morning in autumn, later in a factory car park at 11 o'clock on a Thursday, just after that opposite two lift doors during a downpour, then in the middle of the entrance hall to a block of flats that's 20 stories high the eve of the day when it starts, then somewhere in the south under an inky sky, then at a table with four chairs several times in succession, then finally by a patch of garden adjoining a new house after a heavy storm [...].
>> (2006: 65–6)[8]

This monologue seems at first glance to be completely random and without context, but in fact it prepares and exposes the narrative that is embedded in the ramblers' conversation. Initially, it is impossible to understand to what all these places and times refer, since the actual event and diegetic content seem to have all but disappeared. However, this monologue actually establishes the structure of the whole text, even if the subject it seeks to pin down always seems fleeting. It summarizes and explains in full the setting and chronology of the 'guy who went bankrupt' even before the fictional sequences in the quoted monologue come into play. The displacing and condensing of these elements at the start of the play can only be understood retrospectively, meaning that the text gains from being read again and again. The virtual narrator's exposition, which, like a rough draft of a stage direction, needs to be reconnected with the times and places scattered throughout the play, presents *Ceux qui partent à l'aventure* as a sequence of itineraries and temporalities. Considerable patience is therefore required, to piece together the play's narrative with respect to this initial 'stage direction'. This involves redistributing the unities of place and time mentioned in it throughout the rest of the text.

As such, the great difficulty in transposing the play to the stage lies in the fact that in a single location (a black box studio), multiple spaces must be created. This style of writing requires a polysemous stage, which can, at the same time, represent inside and outside. Moreover, faced with the absolute nature of the linguistic sign, such a staging cannot accommodate a fixed set. Ultimately, the writing of space in Renaude's theatre is a 'gestural practice': the text makes provisions for movement in space, but more particularly, it implies and contains its own staging by anticipating the movement of actors as well as the choreography of bodies on stage (see Éric Vautrin in Chapter 11 of this volume).

This is not all, for the invention of textual territories in Renaude's work can also reside in her typographical strategies (her use of page layout or font, for example), which create in the play's narrative fabric different points of view from which to observe the story as it is being told. For example, the distance or proximity between characters or places might be shown literally on the page. As I have demonstrated, Renaude generates fictional landscapes via place names that she embeds in the narrative. She also creates these cartographic effects by exploiting the possibilities of word-processing and page design: just like reading a map, scrolling through the page on the screen indicates vertical and horizontal journeys through space – polarities – around which it becomes possible for a reader to imagine, mimetically, the

NOËLLE RENAUDE	CEUX QUI PARTENT À L'AVENTURE		PROFONDE?	
Où ça me chante Madame?	La piscine	C	C	
	On n'a plus de terrasse papa	E	E	Plus de terrasse
Oui? Je lisais. Des Élégies. Oui?				
On dit, on fait où on dit, si on ne dit où on doit, si on ne dit pas où, on	Le type au fait demande 30 % tout de suite	T	T	J'ai pas
Jeune homme apprenez à travailler à l'arraché				
À l'arraché / À l'arraché / À l'arraché / Je suis là j'ai mon engin et mon gars	Il revient finir le travail seulement si on lui donne ses 30 %	T	T	
				J'ai pas
Oui? Je lisais? Pardon. Des Élégies.		E	E	Cependant j'avais
Peux creuser là?	Quoi?			un plan
			F	Cependant j'avais
Oui? Allez.				dit
Sur la terrasse?		F		
Oui? C'est ensoleillé. Non?			O	la pelouse
Je peux?	Quoi?	O		cependant j'avais
Oui. Allez. / toujours seule? / oui	Quoi?	S	S	
en reconnaissance?				dit 10 mètres
passe sa vie désormais à ça renifler la viande froide			S	Comment fait-on pour sortir dans
Chérie le monde est un paradis et un enfer mais ce n'est que le monde	Comment fait-on pour sortir dans le jardin?	S	S	entrer dans la maison?
J'ai mal aux reins chéri				
Il faudrait ne connaître du monde que sa représentation chérie	Tu n'as pas salué ma petite sœur Elle s'installe Salut Chez nous un stage	E	E	Non
J'ai mal aux reins chéri				
Ho taxi				
On était là avant				Non
Deux heures qu'on attend				Non
Laisse tomber chéri				
C'EST QUOI?				

Figure 1 Extract from Noëlle Renaude (2006), *Ceux qui partent à l'aventure* (Paris: Théâtrales), p. 93

theatrical space. The border of the page might become, by analogy, the limit of the stage. This is clearly illustrated in the page lay-out for *Ceux qui partent à l'aventure*, where the text is located around three sides of an empty oblong, providing clear indications for staging: the speakers are gathered around a swimming pool (see Figure 1).

Typographical playfulness for Renaude erases the habitual syntax of the theatrical text, by refusing the well-worn framework of conventional stage directions. The positioning of the speakers on the page is enough to define the spatial limits of the performance. For example, as soon as a speaker's lines move to another part of the page, the actor knows that s/he must also move. The text is no longer to be considered as a self-evident continuity, but instead exists as a succession of typographical units.

Page layout in Renaude's works can be very visual, since it draws space by framing speech on the page. It demonstrates, moreover, her highly self-reflexive discourse, by commentating on the means and materials of writing today, which is conditioned by the use of computers. By opting for typographical stage directions capable of combining the staging, time and space of the play's production, Renaude inscribes the production's set design directly on to the page, and, at the same time, exposes, in a highly visual way, the problematic treatment of space in theatre. Reading can no longer be a cursory or passive activity, but is dynamic, and takes on the form of a number of choices to resolve, possible outcomes to explore and trajectories to demarcate.

So what do they tell us, these two types of writing, both of which question traditional theatrical techniques for creating dramatic space in the theatre, by staging in their texts conflicts between inside and outside, microcosm and macrocosm? In the end, both Minyana's and Noëlle Renaude's dramaturgies or fictions are anchored in reality, and the names of places, environments and objects work as triggers for the narrative. The incisiveness of their writing stems from the fact that, by describing space, they do not attempt to talk about the world, or about contemporary issues: they do not include a message. Instead, Minyana's intention is to question how we construct personal spaces and intimate territories, and Renaude's is to interrogate the possibility of creating landscapes and places that theatre habitually refrains from representing. In other words, these writers question, in the very fabric of their texts, the way in which a textual object can question or problematize the mechanisms of the stage.

For these writers, everything starts from the manipulation of stage conventions and the specific codes of theatre writing. Fiction is above all else a topographical environment in which, after the event, speakers evolve. As Michel Corvin notes, regarding contemporary playwrights, 'each one has created their space, or non-space differently, and for themselves alone', in order to produce 'form-meaning' (2006: 39). These writings of Minyana and Renaude are extremely self-reflexive, perhaps even formalistic. They provide linguistic systems, contexts and modes of enunciation that are strange and hybrid, half-way between theatre and the novel. Above all, they provide spatial systems that always overflow the physical limits of the stage, and that require of us, the reader who is always looking for landmarks, to rethink our practice and consumption of play-texts.

Translated by Clare Finburgh and Dominic Glynn

Notes

1. REGARDEUR 2:   La mère soupire tu l'entends
elle soupire elle fait les cent pas
(oh la la ses vieux pas)
et zieute par la fenêtre je me demande
ce qu'il y a à zieuter
[...]
La mère écoute
elle nous voit est-ce qu'elle nous voit
la porte est entrouverte
on chuchote
elle nous voit chuchoter
tu m'as dit qu'elle était sourde est-ce qu'elle l'est
   Pause: échanges de regards, de signes (d'assentiment?)

2. Maison grande qui est froide seul le petit salon était accueillant (il était ensoleillé) dans le petit salon temps de la réconciliation de l'intimité (traces intimes journal tricot) temps de l'entente cordiale (bien sûr il y a eu des trêves). [...]
   A l'époque c'était presque la campagne et puis le monde a changé (tout près l'usine) l'environnement était tout autre notre univers il avait comme rétréci (malgré la cloison abattue il avait comme rétréci) notre père est allé dans cette usine (avant il travaillait dans la boutique qui jouxtait notre habitation)

3. Editors' note: The French term *pièce* can denote at the same time 'room', 'piece', 'coin' and 'theatrical play'.

4. Editors' note. A phylactery, used in Jewish prayer rituals, is a small leather case comprising compartments which house prayers written on thin slips of paper. The phylactery is bound to the worshipper's arm with very long straps.

5. The actor Florence Giorgetti, to whom *L'Histoire de Roberta* is dedicated, commissioned Renaude to write *Madame Ka*.

6. Editors' note. In this section of the play, Alex, driven by his niece, his nose in a map, gets lost in Blois on his way to a wedding (Renaude, 2005: 286).

7. Editors' note. Renaude's play *Par les routes* is translated by Clare Finburgh as *By the Way* (see www.bushgreen.org).
8. Ça se passe où dis-nous ta petite histoire Marinette ?
   Eh bien vois-tu Ulysse ça commence
      banalement le long d'un couloir dans une banque juste avant midi, après ça un soir après le boulot devant une fenêtre ouvrant sur une autre fenêtre, puis sur la terrasse d'une entreprise au beau milieu d'une matinée d'automne, plus tard sur le parking d'une usine à onze heures un jeudi, juste après en face de deux portes d'ascenseur pendant une averse, et au milieu d'un hall d'un immeuble de vingt étages la veille du jour où ça commence, ensuite quelque part dans le sud sous un ciel d'encre, puis autour d'une table sur quatre chaises plusieurs fois de suite, puis alors devant un bout de jardin avec une maison neuve tout au fond après un gros orage [...].

Works cited

Augé, Marc (1995) *Non-Places: An Introduction to an Anthropology of Supermodernity* (London: Verso).
Corvin, Michel (2006) 'L'Esprit du lieu', *Théâtre/ Public*, 183, 2006, 36–44.
Marin, Louis (1973) *Utopiques, jeux d'espaces* (Paris: Éditions de Minuit).
Minyana, Philippe (1993) *Chambres* (Paris: Éditions Théâtrales).
—— (1995) *Drames brefs 1*(Paris: Éditions Théâtrales).
—— (1997) *Drames brefs 2* (Paris: Éditions Théâtrales).
—— (2001) *Habitations*, followed by *Pièces* (Paris: Éditions Théâtrales).
—— (2004) *Prologue*, followed by *Entente cordiale* and *Anne-Marie* (Paris: Éditions Théâtrales).
—— (2004a) *Le Couloir* (Paris: Éditions Théâtrales).
—— (2006) *La Maison des morts*, version scénique (Paris: Éditions Théâtrales).
—— (2006a) *Histoire de Roberta* (Paris: Éditions Théâtrales).
Nores, Dominique (1997) 'Préface', in Philippe Minyana, *Fin d'été à Baccarat* (Paris: Théâtrales), pp. 5–6.
Renaude, Noëlle (1999) *Madame Ka* (Paris: Éditions Théâtrales).
—— (2003) *Promenades* (Paris: Éditions Théâtrales).
—— (2003) *8* (Paris: Éditions Théâtrales).
—— (2005) *Ma Solange, comment t'écrire mon désastre, Alex Roux* (Paris: Éditions Théâtrales).
—— (2005a) *Par les routes* (Paris: Théâtre Ouvert).
—— (2005b) Email correspondence with the author, 6 November.
—— (2006) *Ceux qui partent à l'aventure* (Paris: Éditions Théâtrales).

4
The Politics of Dramaturgy in France*

Clare Finburgh

What do 'dramaturgy' and 'dramaturg' mean in a contemporary French context? To explore these questions, I interviewed French theatre makers who practise dramaturgy today. Bruno Tackels has worked as dramaturg with two highly experimental French contemporary playwright-directors, Didier Georges Gabily and François Tanguy.[1] Whilst Tackels has worked essentially with and on contemporary artists, Anne-Françoise Benhamou serves as dramaturg, primarily on classic texts, for director Stéphane Braunschweig.[2] Joseph Danan, practising dramaturg and academic at the University of Paris III, offers a definition of dramaturgy with respect to contemporary French playwriting. I therefore also invite a contemporary French playwright to respond. Noëlle Renaude thus completes my panel.

Owing to the vast array of artistic and intellectual pursuits to which my interviewees dedicate themselves, it was impossible to bring them all together. Instead of including each of their interviews intact, I permit myself to juxtapose, or 'dramaturgically stage' their varied responses to my questions. In this way, I enable tendencies and consistencies on the one hand, and conflicts and contradictions on the other, to emerge, this tension reflecting the diverse and unresolved definitions of dramaturgy present in French theatre.

I enquire as to whether dramaturgy in France bore, or still bears the same ideological intentionality and social function as the German Brechtian dramaturgy from which it originates. The strong association between dramaturgy and ideology leads Bruno Tackels to describe the first encounters between France and German dramaturgy as a 'failure'. Interviewees explore this notion of failure and the fact that the term dramaturg is taboo in France today. Concurrently, participants demonstrate that whilst the professional role of the dramaturg carries problematic connotations in France, the actual function of dramaturgy is present in all aspects of theatrical production. From here have emerged concepts of *mise en scène* and *écriture de plateau*, where a particular production offers an original interpretation of, a point of view on, a classic play.[3]

This 'round table' explores French dramaturgy in relation to contemporary readings of both classic texts, and new writing. In more recent decades, the failure of Communism as a utopian ideal has rendered the idea of unequivocally upholding ideologies on stage less convincing or viable. French playwrights and directors have subsequently appeared to retreat from overt political *engagement*. I therefore ask what role dramaturgy plays with regard to these contemporary experimental texts. I identify a shift from an external dramaturgy, which is mapped on to a text in order that that text might echo in our contemporary society, to an internal dramaturgy, where the stylistic, aesthetic, formal features of the text determine and direct analysis. I conclude by asking in what ways this emphasis on form might be obliquely, rather than overtly political.

Clare Finburgh: To understand what the concept of dramaturgy means in France, it's useful briefly to examine its origins and evolution.

Anne-Françoise Benhamou: For me, the notion of French dramaturgy derives from the desire to bring critical theory to the theatre. The emergence of dramaturgy in France coincides with the staging of the Berliner Ensemble's *Mutter Courage und ihre Kinder* at Paris's Théâtre des Nations in June 1954. Directors, notably Roger Planchon, had been attempting to read, or re-read classic texts via critical theory, for example psychoanalysis, sociology, Marxism and sociocriticism.[4] Moreover, critical theories such as structuralism had started to have their impact on artistic production in France. Added to this, Roland Barthes and Bernard Dort, mainly responsible for introducing Brecht's theories to France, had already been sensitized by Jean-Paul Sartre's concepts of the *théâtre de situations* and political commitment, to the idea of combining the arts with other disciplines such as politics (see Barthes, 2002: 162–5 and Dort, 1960).[5] Brecht was therefore particularly welcome, since theatre makers had already been searching for ways to integrate politics and sociology into the theatre. Planchon didn't always work with an actual dramaturg, but he and his creative team brought a specific dramaturgical reading to their plays.

Brecht, via Planchon and the Théâtre national populaire (TNP) in Villeurbanne, had made a great impact on what we understand by dramaturgy in France today. Brecht and critical theory continued to be dominant forces in the theatres of successive generations of French directors such as Antoine Vitez and Patrice Chéreau, who had trained with Planchon.[6] Then, Braunschweig, for whom I'm dramaturg, worked with Vitez, and he continues the tradition of incorporating critical theory into *mise en scène* today. So this interrogation of the text's meaning derived from Brecht, and then passed through Planchon, Vitez, Chéreau, and up to the present day with Braunschweig and other directors like Alain Françon or Bernard Sobel, both of whom prioritize social concerns in their work.[7] For all these directors, interpretation, meaning, point of view, in other words, dramaturgy, are central to their projects.

C. F: Bruno Tackels, for you, the German model of the dramaturg can carry more insidious connotations.

Bruno Tackels: From the start, the relationship between French theatre and the dramaturg was never simple and was, to my mind, marked by what I'd call 'failure'. The problem was that the French imported what they *thought* to be the Brechtian conception of dramaturgy. The first dramaturgs – for example, Michel Bataillon working with Planchon at the TNP in the late 1960s; and the second wave, Jean-Marie Vincent's team working at the Théâtre national de Strasbourg (TNS) from the 1970s[8] – turned Brecht's theories into a doctrine, into what in France we call 'Brechtism' – a term that's now an insult. In other words, they based their practice on fixed ideas they had on how to be faithful to Brecht's theories. In France at this time, his theories were too closely associated with the far-left ideologies of the French Communist Party, which was blind to the atrocious historical events taking place in the Eastern bloc. Dramaturgs seemed to be employed with the remit of conceiving and imposing a specific political line. They consequently had the potential to become aggressively controlling and authoritarian. It's no surprise that at the time, Antoine Vitez called dramaturgs *les flics du sens* (the meaning police), a kind of dramaturgical politburo (1981: 168).

Today, there are relatively few dramaturgs who advertize themselves as such in France. Very few are employed permanently by theatres. Instead, they go by the name of literary adviser, collaborator, assistant director, even translator. Therefore, I'm not saying dramaturgy doesn't exist in France; on the contrary, many people perform the function of dramaturg, but the term itself has become taboo, for reasons I've explained.

C. F: Here, we're speaking about the role of the dramaturg. What about the practice of dramaturgy? Are practice and role inextricably associated?

A.-F. B: We need to distinguish between the terms dramaturgy and dramaturg. A production can be 'dramaturgical' without someone explicitly performing the role of 'dramaturg'. In the 1970s, Vitez insisted that he didn't want to work with dramaturgs. And yet, a 'dramaturgical' approach was patently evident in Vitez's productions.

Dramaturgy, according to Brecht's theories, has nothing to do with ideology, because Brechtian dramaturgy involves precisely the opposite, namely, dismantling dominant ideologies in order to renew our outlook on the world. It's true that Brechtian theories were co-opted for didactic purposes. But crucially, Brechtian theories met the need in France for a renewed approach to classic texts, and propelled the emergence of the art of *mise en scène*. This wasn't necessarily politically ideological at all.

C. F: You explain elsewhere that, in order for you to function effectively as a dramaturg, each and every member of the creative team must search for a 'point of view', a dramaturgical interpretation: the director, the actors and designers (Benhamou, 2008: 46). Scenographer Marcel Freydefont would agree, since he, too, considers himself a dramaturg (2008: 103). Playwright and theorist Jean-Marie Piemme, influenced by Roland Barthes's semiology, extends dramaturgy beyond the sphere not only of the dramaturg, but also of the stage, speaking of the dramaturgy of a theatre's architecture, and of geographical location (1984).

Bruno Tackels describes this fusion of analysis and practice: 'German dramaturgy invents an unprecedented posture in the history of the arts: for the first time, the critical dimension of an art becomes an integral part of that art, and does not come after, or outside that art. Here, thinking about art, and making it, participate in the same movement' (2001: 103).

German playwright Heiner Müller declared in the early 1980s, 'there has never been as much dramaturgy and at the same time as little playwriting as today' (in Dort, 2008). He was alluding to the fact that dramaturgy in the 1960s and 1970s was principally enlisted for the re-reading of classic texts. Since the late 1980s, France has witnessed a proliferation of playwriting, much of which has dismantled cohesive plot, recognizable character, time, space and logical dialogue. In what ways has dramaturgy been obliged to evolve in response to this new writing?

A.-F. B: People are often inclined to think that all contemporary
French theatre is post-dramatic. However, we can't generalize about
authors as diverse as Fabrice Melquiot, Valère Novarina, Philippe
Minyana and Jean-Luc Lagarce. There are many contemporary
French plays, for example those of Bernard-Marie Koltès, that
are constructed with great narrative coherence, and that contain
what we might recognize as characters, even if they're not exactly
naturalistic.[9]

C. F: I'm thinking more of playwrights like Novarina, Renaude, Minyana
or Michel Vinaver.[10] Part of their artistic project is to reinvent a theatre
freed from the dramaturgical practices, techniques or rules set out, for
example, in Aristotle's *Poetics* or Pierre Corneille's three discourses in
Trois discours sur le poème dramatique (*Three Discourses on the Dramatic
Poem*, 1660), both of which stipulate the main tenets of drama.

Joseph Danan: The answer to this question will vary depending on
each individual author or play. In the formal experimentation that
characterizes the evolution of contemporary dramatic writing both
in France and elsewhere, one must distinguish between at least two
directions. I say at least two, because there are many others between
these poles. At one pole, one finds plays (I still call them *plays*)
that, as audacious as they might be with regard to their writing,
nonetheless include a fundamental internal dramaturgy which
one must take account of when staging these plays. This is the
case, for example, with Vinaver, with the exception of one or two
of his works. The plays at this pole contain a certain organization
at the level of narrative, action, time, space, relationships between
characters that inherently constitutes the dramaturgy of the play
according to the original meaning of the word. Here, the work of the
dramaturg or director-dramaturg is no different if we stage Vinaver,
Corneille, Marivaux or Chekhov. Therefore, contemporary plays
by authors like Vinaver don't require us to redefine the notion of
dramaturgy.

Contrastingly, other works appear to elude this dramaturgical
model in more or less radical ways. The most extreme example is
Noëlle Renaude's *Ma Solange, comment t'écrire mon désastre, Alex
Roux* (*My Solange, How Can I Write You My Disaster, Alex Roux*).
It eludes classical dramaturgical models to such an extent that
I would describe it as *texte-matériau* (textual matter), albeit written
for the theatre, and not a play (see David Bradby (Chapter 1),
Michel Corvin (Chapter 2) and Jean-Pierre Han (Chapter 5) in this
volume). Textual matter, in my opinion, abandons the internal

organization we understand as dramaturgy according to its original meaning, leaving the invention and elaboration of a dramaturgy, in other words, representation, to the dramaturg or director. Most of Novarina's texts also fall into this category. In addition, we can include Vinaver's *King* and *11 septembre 2001*, originally presented by him as an oratorio, the organization of which is perhaps musical, rather than dramaturgical.

C. F: Noëlle Renaude, you're a contemporary author. Would you agree with Joseph Danan, that your texts constitute 'matter', the dramaturgy of which the dramaturg or director must define?

Noëlle Renaude: I agree with his hypothesis in certain respects, but not in all. For him, there are theatre plays on the one hand, and texts intended for the theatre on the other, the former being characteristically dramatic, the latter potentially theatrical; and my texts belong to the latter. Up to this point I agree, like I agree with Vinaver's distinction between 'machine-plays' and 'landscape-plays'.

C. F: For Vinaver, plays can be divided into those that run like a machine, where the cogs are set in motion and turn in a predetermined direction along a single classical dramaturgical continuum; and those with the constitution of a landscape, where valleys and peaks are crossed using a range of different routes. In the first instance the journey is predictable; in the second, it's up to author, actor, director, dramaturg, reader or spectator to map the route (see Chapter 1 by David Bradby in this volume).

N. R: I also agree with Danan's definition of textual matter that abandons the internal organization we understand as dramaturgy, leaving the elaboration of a dramaturgy up to the dramaturg or director. This category could include the montage, collage and assemblage texts of Heiner Müller, which don't anticipate staging at all. But I don't agree that my play *Ma Solange* (1996–8) belongs in this category. My texts *are* dramaturgically organized – extremely precisely – even if this internal organization doesn't obey classical doxa, be they Aristotelian or Corneillian. Moreover, my plays don't leave the invention of a dramaturgy up to the director or dramaturg. On the contrary, they impose a specific set of questions, shifts, modes of reading... that bring with them on the stage a parallel set of questions, shifts, modes of acting. The dramaturgy of my plays isn't open to reinvention on the stage. It's present, inscribed, fused into the writing itself.

Each of my texts is organized according to a single dramaturgical question: time, space, fictional situation, character. I select a rule, analyse it, explore it, experiment with it, whether this be in a visible, or a covert way. Each text thus reinvents its own dramatic position. And it's this new position that the dramaturg must learn to read and analyse. It's admittedly a deconstructed, dissonant, eviscerated dramaturgy, but it's nonetheless a dramaturgy; a way of accessing meaning, making meaning appear.

In the case of my writing, the word *organization* might be more suitable than dramaturgy. But then, what text isn't organized? With the example of *Ma Solange*, organization corresponds to the chronology of when it was written. At first glance, it's true that *Ma Solange* might appear to be what Danan terms 'textual matter'. However, a crucial element governs the text: time; or rather, temporality. Not time in terms of dramatic duration, but the time at which each fragment or segment appears in the text. Each fragment is like a closed unit. The units are in no way linked to each other via narrative, character or situation. And yet, each fragment is intimately bound to the preceding and proceeding ones, thereby constituting hour by hour, page by page, an account of the task of writing, of the different modes I used in order to advance through, to progress with the actual act of writing.

C. F: Just one example amongst many from your plays: a character, who recounts travel plans to Morvan, Lozère and Pisa, says that a bloke he met has room for him in his trunk bound for Greece. Whilst this scene makes little sense in logical terms, it's linguistically coherent, since Greece (Grèce) rhymes with trunk (caisse). This acousticity serves to structure the next fragment in the text: '*À propos de caisses. Si je peux me permesse. À propos de caisses*' ('Speaking of trunks. If I may. Speaking of trunks'). Here, trunks are mentioned again. Moreover, in a moment of overblown formality, the new character invents a subjunctive (permesse), which prolongs the rhyme (Renaude, 2004: 21). As you say, the *mode* of writing creates an internal organization, or dramaturgy.

N. R: This accumulation of proliferating fictions, this new dramaturgy, must be uncovered by the reader, actor, dramaturg or director. Language for me is an essential dramaturgical tool. The director and dramaturg are obliged, when confronted with my texts, to change their habitual ways of seeing. A hiatus between two words, or a sentence with unsteady syntax, provide crucial information on how the text can be staged. Were one not to stop at one of these points, not to question these elements, one would no doubt overlook the text's meaning.

Dramaturgs often refer to themselves as 'the guardians of meaning'. When form itself carries meaning, when form is structure, or vice versa, both dramaturg and director must revise their conventional ways of understanding and find the dramatic value, the direction, in other words, the meaning of the form itself.

I agree that one can't force texts that have been crafted and conceived according to rules radically different from those of Aristotle or Corneille, to try and comply with those rules. On the other hand, it's wrong to think that texts like mine are devoid of all dramaturgical rules.

C. F: It seems that, according to Noëlle Renaude, when presented with experimental French theatrical texts, dramaturgs must learn to discover their internal dramaturgies, rather than imposing pre-existing external dramaturgies.

Would you agree, Bruno Tackels, that much contemporary French playwriting requires a different dramaturgical approach?

B. T: It requires us to observe how it behaves from the point of view of the stage, rather than the page. Contemporary French texts, most notably the post-Aristotelian works of Novarina, often need first and foremost to be expressed via the actor's voice and body. The text needs to be heard and felt in order to be understood. This is because these texts rarely provide simple and easily identifiable entry points, like a particular theme or idea. On paper, they can appear indecipherable, opaque, hermetic. For this reason, I try to push, in the reading committees on which I sit, for work to be read aloud before being judged. I think this is the only way we can understand much new French writing dramaturgically.

C. F: So it seems that dramaturgy in France in the 1960s and 1970s involved enabling theatrical texts – mainly classic texts – to resonate with a world contemporary to their staging; whereas today, much contemporary French theatre, notably that of authors like Novarina or Renaude, who foreground form, style and structure, withdraws from the world, and into the text. So does this highly aestheticized theatre exclude a politically engaged dramaturgy?

J. D: From the 1970s in France, we began to be wary of ideology, notably of communist ideology. The problem is, we didn't know what to replace it with, other than a retreat into aesthetics. In order to feel worthy – renouncing all sense of political conscience is hardly acceptable for a dramaturg – we tried to theorize the idea that political commitment could be communicated via an experimentation with form, which would precipitate a transformation of the spectator's mental reception of representations. I'm drastically oversimplifying because, from the 1970s to today, there have been many overtly political productions – far more than France is given credit for – where the political standpoint can't be reduced to questions of aesthetics and representation.

Getting back to the supposed politics of aesthetics, as a dramaturg I think it's all very well wishing to transform form in order to counter dominant ideologies, but the question is, for whom? For which audience? This is a dramaturgically crucial question. The dramaturg must construct the answer by working on the ground, taking into account each artist, each creative team, above all, each audience. If theatre only addresses its stock audience, the transformation of form might be laudable, but it has no real ideological effect.

C. F: So where does this leave the role of the dramaturg, or director-dramaturg in the original sense, namely, an agent who brings socio-political meaning to the theatrical text?

A.-F. B: Texts like Novarina's, that manifest explicitly the impossibility of making meaning through language, aren't something Braunschweig and I would choose. In writing like Novarina's or Renaude's, language becomes an end in itself. We must, in my opinion, sense an urgency in theatre, an urgency in relation to the world we live in. In our world, meaning itself is deconstructed. It's not that I wish to bring meaning to a meaningless world. That would be pretentious. However, my aim as dramaturg is to ensure that a work provides a point of view on the world. So myself as dramaturg and Stéphane as director try to stage plays not because they're beautiful or because we're attracted to them, but because they appeal to our sense of necessity with respect to the world.

C. F: I'll summarize the main arguments to have emerged from this discussion.

Whilst the leftist ideologies of the first French dramaturgs, notably those of the TNS, have all but disappeared from French dramaturgy today, the quest to utilize the theatre for the purposes of understanding and articulating the world – an enterprise close to the hearts of the first director-dramaturgs like Planchon or Vitez – still prevails in the work of many theatre makers, notably Braunschweig (see Chapter 8 by Bérénice Hamidi-Kim in this volume). Plays should resonate in the social context in which they're staged, rather than archeologically evoke the past in which they were written. In contrast, numerous contemporary French plays, as Noëlle Renaude explains, contain their own unique dramaturgies, woven into the actual fabric of the theatrical text. More than formulating and representing the world around them, they present their own materiality – their own syntactical, semantic and rhythmical effects. I wonder, however, if these two currents are really opposed and unrelated (see Chapter 7 by Laura Cull in this volume). Do some contemporary French texts entrench themselves in formalist aestheticism precisely so as *not* to be co-opted by dramaturgs for socio-political comment?

Moreover, perhaps these contemporary texts bear an intrinsic political dimension with respect to today's society. For Danan, French theatre after the 1970s 'retreat[ed] into aesthetics'; and Benhamou states that she and Braunschweig would not stage a text by Novarina or Renaude, since they do not provide 'a point of view on the world'. In numerous conversations I have had with Noëlle Renaude, she insists that she is not a politically committed author. However, when she states that each of her texts poses a central question concerning time, space, voice, body and character, she demonstrates how she interrogates the very foundations of representation, and thereby is entreating the dramaturgs, directors, actors and spectators who encounter her texts to 'change their habitual ways of seeing'. Danan rightly maintains that politicizing aesthetics *per se* can be an exercise in conscience-absolving. But entreating humans to question, revise and recreate the ways in which they see themselves and their surroundings is surely of social significance. The seminal contemporary French director Claude Régy sums this up: 'the only thing that matters when we create an image, write a text, or rewrite a text, is that what we see or hear refers us back to the uncreated, makes us aware of it' (1999: 64).

Notes

*All translations are mine.

1. The plays and productions of Gabily (1955–1996), who worked in collaboration with his group T'chan'G', dramaturgically wove together encounters between mythical figures, for example, Theseus, Phaedra, Hermes, and the Amazons. Tanguy (1955–), who has worked with the Théâtre du Radeau since the 1980s, employs dramaturgical analysis to adapt classic texts, for example, by Molière or Shakespeare, or mythical figures like Faust, into spectacles with great visual, aural and sensory appeal.
2. Braunschweig, a philosophy scholar, mainly stages the classics – Molière, Ibsen – to which he brings acute analytical rigour and dramaturgically charged scenography.
3. *Écriture de plateau*, as understood by Tackels, is a way of approaching theatrical production that prioritizes a range of different media, rather than simply the text (see Tackels, 2001).

4. Brechtian dramaturgy enabled Planchon (1931–2009) to demonstrate how history is determined by the social relationships between the privileged and poor.
5. Theatre scholar Dort (1929–1994) was one of Brecht's main advocates in France. Throughout his career he promoted an understanding of theatre's social and political role.
6. An advocate of what he termed an 'elite theatre for everybody', Vitez (1930–1990) applied his hallmark style of montage, poetic stylization and free association to the classics, creating productions that were at once aesthetically arresting, and accessible. Whilst Chéreau (1944–), like many important French directors, is highly influenced by Brecht, this influence is aesthetic rather than political, since he defends theatre primarily as art.
7. Françon (1945–) is reputed for his austere minimalism, which he combines with a Brechtian preoccupation with social concerns; Sobel (1936–) has a direct association with Brecht, since he worked at the Berliner Ensemble in the late 1950s.
8. Vincent (1942–) is one of France's foremost politically committed directors, and one of its main exponents of Brechtian theory. His productions focus mainly on the classics, employing dramaturgical analysis in order perpetually to interrogate the relationship between theatre, history and society.
9. Melquiot (1972–) often treats contemporary themes, which he distorts to create a grotesque atmosphere of humour and anxiety; Novarina (1942–), conversely, is a playwright for whom the treatment of language supersedes thematic consideration. His is a dramaturgy of destruction – of theatre as one recognizes it – and celebration – of the human voice and its rhythms, tones and textures; the language of Minyana (1946–) also foregrounds sonority, but his theatre is anchored more in realism, exploring relationships between humans and their material surroundings; Lagarce (1957–1995) is renowned for his use of complex rhetorical syntax, that renders meaning elusive, and language incantatory; Koltès (1948–1989), announces a return in French theatre to narrative and linear coherence, after Beckett's deconstruction of story and Brecht's emphasis on fragmentation. These playwrights vary widely in the themes they treat and the styles they adopt (for detailed readings of these playwrights see Céline Hersant and Michel Corvin in this volume).
10. Whilst these authors are eclectic in the subject matter they treat – Novarina explores the French language; Renaude explores the potential of theatrical space, time and language; Vinaver treats social and political themes, from the Algerian War of Independence to unemployment; and Minyana examines individuals and their relationships with objects – many members of this generation of authors concern themselves with theatrical form (see Chapter 1 by David Bradby, Chapter 2 by Michel Corvin and Chapter 3 by Celine Hérsant in this volume).

Works cited

Barthes, Roland (2002) *Écrits sur le théâtre* (Paris: Seuil).
Benhamou, Anne-Françoise (2008) 'Bref aperçu de dramaturgie expérimentale', in Philippe Coutant (ed.), *Du dramaturge* (Nantes: Joca Seria), pp. 45–50.

Dort, Bernard (1960) *Lecture de Brecht* (Paris: Seuil).

—— (2008) 'Dramaturgie', in Michel Corvin (ed.), *Dictionnaire encyclopédique du théâtre* (Paris: Larousse).

Freydefont, Marcel (2008) 'Panurge le dramaturg et Panique la dramatique', in Philippe Coutant (ed.), *Du dramaturge* (Nantes: Joca Seria), 101–12.

Piemme, Jean-Marie (December 1984) *Le Souffleur inquiet*, special issue of *Alternatives Théâtrales*, 21–2.

Régy, Claude (1999) *L'Ordre des morts* (Besançon: Les Solitaires Intempestifs).

Renaude, Noëlle (2004) *Ma Solange, comment t'écrire mon désastre Alex Roux* (Paris: Théâtrales).

Tackels, Bruno (2001) *Fragments d'un théâtre amoureux* (Besançon: Les Solitaires Intempestifs).

Vitez, Antoine (1981) *De Chaillot à Chaillot* (Paris: Hachette).

5
An Unlikely Scene: French Theatre in the New Liberal Economy

Jean-Pierre Han

Theatre commentators and even practitioners are frequently asked to provide a survey of theatre today; to press pause on what seems to be developing or unfolding a little too quickly in the eyes of those who prefer to reflect on the matter. Legitimate though such requests may be, particularly when they come from people far-removed from or unfamiliar with our practices, and who simply wish to be better informed, they are nevertheless somewhat vain. It is as if the ephemeral nature of live performance were so unbearable, that it was necessary to fight against it by altering its very essence. 'Surveying' is a game that we have all played more or less felicitously. It would consequently even be possible to chart, if not a sort of history, at least a plot of our various assessments or depictions of the state of play. Indeed, this is natural since, to state the obvious, the situations described necessarily evolve with the passage of time. But as observers, we also change with time, and therefore our approach, our critical standpoint and analytical tools change, too.

The brief

I wish to confine myself to the most recent requests I have received to paint a picture of the situation of theatre in France. Alongside teaching on various different university Masters programmes, I have also been trying for a number of years to provide future administrators and managers of artistic organizations with a basic understanding of the aesthetics of today's theatre. From one year to the next, it becomes apparent that what I said the previous year has become obsolete. It is impossible to repeat oneself in these conditions, and it is simply not enough to change the names of some of the productions and artists. Rather, the very structure or framework of the classes I give needs to be revised each time.

On closer inspection, even the titles of the briefs are subject to variations. These slight shifts in the suggested topics for reflection are very revealing. Thus, the overview that the journal *Théâtre aujourd'hui* asked me to provide in 2005 focused specifically on the 'state of directing today' and not on theatre in general. A critical angle is always imposed from the outset. A little later on, I was asked once again to reflect on the issue of new writing for *Théâtre/Public* (2007), and not long after, I was given yet another angle to consider, stage design this time, by *Scènes d'architectures* (*Stages of Architectures*, 2007). I appreciate that it no doubt pertains to me to stitch back together the scattered pieces of the 'tapestry', but I do not believe that this is the most appropriate way of broaching the subject of contemporary theatre (in France). Furthermore, the pieces of this tapestry are also ensnared by temporality, and cannot be adjusted.

Nevertheless, of the many reservations voiced in my written or spoken commentaries on the matter – some of which put forward the idea of an 'impossible panorama', to quote the title of an article by Jean-Loup Rivière (2003) – I wish to concentrate on the following issue: which corpus must one choose to work on in order to provide a considered opinion? The exponential increase in the number of shows on offer, in spite of the fact that subsidies awarded to theatre companies have decreased steadily up until 2008, when, under Prime Minister Fillon's government, the cuts have been drastic – a tendency which is due to pick up speed, as is already forecast in the 2010 budget for the performing arts – means it is impossible to have a satisfactory overall view of theatre production. For instance, the students of one Masters programme are 'sponsored' by the Théâtre de la Ville. They are regularly and generously invited to attend a number of shows at the theatre. They therefore see this theatre's productions first and foremost, to the detriment of others on offer elsewhere. Needless to say that the overview they are asked to provide at the end of their course is heavily influenced by the artistic programming of the theatre, now under the leadership of the young director Emmanuel Demarcy-Mota, which is heavily biased in favour of contemporary works, and which cheerfully mixes dance and theatre. It is therefore important to know where one is positioned, from which perspective one is coming. As a theatre analyst, even if one is granted a great freedom of choice, one will nevertheless choose the shows one goes to see in accordance with the editorial line of the publication for which one is working.

The nature of the chosen (or imposed) corpus therefore always influences one's reading of the situation. How – today more than ever – might the outlines of this corpus be defined? After all, in this post-dramatic era, which Hans-Thies Lehmann (2002) has discussed at length, the following question arises: what can be classified using the terminology of theatre? Indeed, theatre has expanded its horizons by borrowing from (as well as feeding into) the visual arts, dance, music, circus and several other disciplines. There are shows nowadays that are hard to define and describe. In short, it is the very definition of theatre that needs to be reformulated.

The roots of the problem

Two questions arise as a result of providing overview after overview of the theatre at various points in time: why choose to consider such or such a particular moment (unless there is no objective reason, and even then, the answer lies with those who place the order), and which history should one provide? Indeed, it is the very thread of history that needs to be unravelled each time. But where does one start? More specifically with regard to French theatre, should the starting point be (as it often is in my work) the end of the Second World War? This almost seems the obvious choice. Not so long ago, it provided a round figure: '50 years of decentralized theatre'. On a more serious note, it corresponded and still corresponds to a symbolic or perhaps mythical time in the country's reconstruction. As theatre critic Renée Saurel, who edited the journal *Les Temps modernes* with Jean-Paul Sartre, noted pertinently in 1967, 'In 1946, when France was liberated, all dreams seemed possible, even when it came to the theatre' (2008: 49).

However, Diane Scott has criticized this way of proceeding in an article that has recently been published in the journal I edit, *frictions*. In her words, 'To provide an assessment means postulating a starting point and, in this case, the appraisal of "50 years of cultural decentralization" functions in tandem with the Liberation as a mythical time of new beginnings, which is a very expedient way of negating all the trade union and working-class roots from which popular education derived prior to the Second World War' (2008: 41). What, therefore, should be the starting point for providing a picture of theatre today, without having to go too far back in time? Two other equally emblematic dates might be put forward: May 1968 (the 40-year anniversary of this aborted 'revolution' was recently celebrated with great pomp and show), because the very infrastructure of our theatre was almost overturned. The illusion was short-lived, and the return to the old habits of the bourgeois theatre strikingly fast (it occurred with the start of the 1968 winter season). Nevertheless, retrospectively, this date marks a break, if only in the mentality of audiences and artists. Another pertinent starting point, which the young scholar Bérénice Hamidi-Kim has taken in her invaluable thesis *Cités du 'théâtre politique' en France de 1989 à 2007* (*Cities of Political Theatre in France Between 1989 and 2007*), is 1989, the year of the fall of the Berlin Wall. What stands out from all of these introductory considerations is that it is almost impossible to provide an accurate description of the current situation.

Initial points to consider

The requests to assess the situation, as I have said, are on the increase. No doubt this increase indicates our inability to grasp how things really are. But this powerlessness is in itself revealing and, in a way, contributes to the sketching, if not the composition, of the desired description of the scene. There are many reasons for this helplessness. Theatrical life in France, as elsewhere, has been almost completely transformed. It has changed according to societal developments and upheavals, in a society where the place given to culture in general, and to theatre in particular, are just melting away. The theatre is no longer an integral part of society and is considered superfluous, a sort of luxury. This is highlighted by the lack of exposure it is granted in the general-interest press. The press in fact no longer dares to use the heading 'culture' but prefers substitutes such as 'leisure', 'going out', 'ideas for tonight?', so as not to frighten its readership. In advanced liberal economies, of which France is now well and truly one – notably following Sarkozy's rise to power – it is clearly affirmed that 'all cultural products, whether an object, a book, a painting or a programme, are *necessarily* subject to market forces, their ups and downs and pernicious effects' (Slama, 2008; my emphasis). As one guru of current thinking trumpeted recently on the radio station France-Culture, theatre is nothing more than a dispensable item of leisure, which can be done without. It is easy to see why a number of artists, practitioners and theorists institute Greek society in the fifth century BC, with its great tragedians, as a mythical model. It is also clear why there is a sudden flood of questions (and publications) with evocative titles such as: *What Use is the Theatre?* Or, *Is Theatre Necessary?* With the following agonizing corollary, *Where is Theatre Heading?* (Guenoun, 1997; Dupuis, 1998; Cormann, 2003; Siméon, 2007).[1] The time is long gone in France when theatre was a societal concern and when certain questions relating to it, notably those with political implications, were evoked in Parliament during heated debates. One looks back nostalgically to the post-war period (notably with Jean Vilar and the TNP (Théâtre national populaire)) or indeed to the first French production of Jean Genet's *The Screens* in 1966.[2] Time has accelerated, as has the history of theatre, which Jean Jourdheuil believes stopped in France in the 1970s.

Have theatre productions become everyday consumable products subject to market forces? An entire infrastructure, an operating system, has been put in place. It is what Jean Jourdheuil has pertinently characterized in a number of articles as 'la dérive spectaculaire' ('the spectacular drift'). He makes the distinction between theatre as the 'concern of the city and its citizens' and spectacle which is 'business', whether consumer, electoral or other. This subtle distinction still applies. It is now necessary to operate under the banner of the spectacular and hope to get noticed, and to sell oneself, 'for shows are always presented to audiences as goods on supermarket shelves in what Martin Heidegger termed "uniformity without distance", driven on solely by advertizing campaigns' (Jourdheuil, 1994: 15). In this configuration, festivals have the heavy burden of acting like supermarkets, or at least their shop windows. One only need take a look at their programmes, which alternate between the chic, and the shocking (loss leader), and a great number of other things on offer which are enticing to greater or lesser degrees. And since artistic programming throughout the year is becoming more 'festivalized', even in the theatres, Jourdheuil has remarked that 'more generally, the end of theatre coincides with the growing appeal to programmers of questions of commemoration, festival tourism, and the prospective sociology of new technologies' (ibid.). This analysis was provided in 1994, approximately 15 years ago, and it seems ever more true today.

In addition, as I mentioned, since the number of shows has increased (Jack Lang's appointment as Minister of Culture in 1981 under the presidency of François Mitterrand further accelerated this movement, since for two years at least, the cultural policy was governed by the pronouncement that 'everyone is an artist'), different theatrical classes have emerged. I use the term in the same way as if to describe social class. Different production and circulation circuits, quite separate from each other and sometimes bearing no relation on either economic or aesthetic fronts, have been put in place. No common denominator exists between the productions of a 'young' theatre company, and those belonging to the newly created category of 'artistic excellence', which refers to the 'highest' echelon. Perhaps it is necessary to paint a distinct picture of each class (see Han, 2008).

Concerning artistic excellence – the label that is stuck on a product – there is a clear link with the new and thrilling touring of shows from

Russia, the United States, Poland, Hungary, Spain and so on. One cannot help but be delighted by such a movement. However, there is a flipside to this opening-up, namely, that the productions need to be 'excellent'. Again, this is a source of delight. But such travelling 'excellence' has its own set of requirements. The barriers of language having been more or less overcome (sur-titling techniques are improving). Moreover, it is preferable if the play and the imagery are easily identifiable. Any risks taken, if at all, must be minimal. The bias of these productions is always towards the conventional (identifiable), the accessible. Pushed to the extreme, this brings us to a form of (supranational) official art. These filtering mechanisms, moreover, play the role of policemen, since they always expect the 'image' of the producing country. Or else, a production must emphasize its disparity with the 'image', so that the production can be classed in an esoteric-folkloric category. Jourdheuil, again, notes, 'I am not convinced that this open-mindedness, this type of (superficial) integration of different identities does not abolish these identities under a cloud of generalized relativism, and that the productions in question do not simply produce routine exoticism' (1994: 15). I do not mean to deny the quality or value of certain productions. Nevertheless, for the most part, what is proposed, or conveyed, is nothing less than recycled aesthetics (these days, for example, the aesthetics of the 1970s are frequently borrowed) or else manufactured products, 'polished' by a few zealous assistants, trained for this purpose.

So much for the high end of the market, which can nevertheless procure a certain amount of excitement, even though the real aesthetic, and therefore political, concerns of our era no longer have any place there. As a result, the audience finds itself in a 'museographical' position. What is much more troubling is the exemplary effect that these luxurious productions have had (it would be interesting to talk figures in this time of economic crisis) on the younger generations, who do not rest until they have imitated their glorious elders. To thus see young thirty-something directors (or a little older) churn out products, which are well-oiled, manufactured and well-made, too well-made – nothing could ever jam the successful workings of the production (we should sing the praises of imperfection and impurity!) – is just frightening.

This artistic excellence in theatrical matters has produced a very closed caste (to which very few are admitted) which gives impetus to and imposes a dominant aesthetic with multiple facets. Conscious of the danger, the playwright and dramaturg Jean-Marie Piemme, in 1991, was already calling for 'as many minority aesthetics as possible'; he noted that 'today the theatre is no longer at the heart of collective life. It has become a minority art form', hence theatre's wish to counter the situation by embracing consumerism. Piemme added that if 'such internationalization (and what this implies in terms of the erasure of identity) and espousal of the media were to become the driving forces behind European theatre, it would be better to call it a day' (1991: 58). Twenty years later, here we are, but there is no intention of giving up. 'Something is giving way and its replacement has not yet appeared', Jourdheuil dubitatively notes (1994: 15). For the moment, this renewal has not yet appeared, but artistic excellence still serves as an alibi.

This concept of artistic excellence is interesting in that it manages to dispose of all critical perspective of, and discourse on, the products that are lucky enough to come under its banner. The 'creators' of these products even become untouchable. It is inconceivable that an ordinary pen-pusher or second-rate artist might say anything unpleasant about Patrice Chéreau and company. Artistic excellence has the good taste to close off any form of debate. Why should there be a need for debate? The products are complete, set in their own perfection, once and for all. This represents the opposite extreme to any notion of 'open work', and is poles apart from any form of experimentation, which alone might allow the theatre to reconnect with its history again, by going back to History.

An international aesthetic, which is the product of our liberal economies, has been put in place. To this are added the effects of fashion, which give us the illusion – that is their purpose – that we are completely... free. Contemporary theatre feeds, and even gorges itself on topics ranging from the supposedly provocative to the falsely scandalous. 'Artists' such as Jan Fabre, Jan Lauwers or Rodrigo García, who are very popular in France, have mastered the vocabulary of this type of timely production: they are but the voluntary products of our society of mass consumption. Their choice is a free one. And it is certainly not these people who have, or will have any problems with any form of censorship. Quite the opposite: performative filth and the staunchly pornographic are highly prized by the authorities; so they are exhibited, and sell well. Thus, the same productions can move indifferently from one international festival to another, from Seoul to London, Berlin or Paris. These productions are thus conceived with this in mind. Certain companies from the former Eastern bloc, for instance, have understood what types of conventional discourse and aesthetic are required in order to be admitted to the system. On the other hand, censorship (that dares not speak its name) keeps everything that might diverge from the norm out of the official discourse. A recent example (December 2008) is the 'impossibility' of taking on tour – a tour that had been agreed with the national funding body Cultures France – the production of Jean-Luc Raharimanana's *47* directed by Thierry Bedard. The production treated the theme of the largest massacre perpetrated by the French in their colonial Empire, in Madagascar in 1947 (between 80,000 and 100,000 people were killed).

Other points to consider

There are other points I should evoke quickly, which contribute towards making the depiction of theatre in France today difficult. French theatre resembles a ship at sea, which has literally lost its bearings. It no longer has any landmarks; the great artists who could have filled this role have either moved away from theatre (Patrice Chéreau), or no longer have the same creative energy (Peter Brook), or work according to the same (fixed?) modes of production, but the reception of their work is no longer the same (Ariane Mnouchkine). In any case, most have severed contact, which leads one young director, Frédéric Maragnani, to say that he belongs to an orphaned generation.

In terms of a tradition, there has been a real break between the generation that began to emerge in the 1970s, and which ended up managing the large institutions (Jean-Pierre Vincent, Jacques Lassalle, André Engel, Daniel Mesguich), and the following generations. The fact that in France, unlike in neighbouring countries, there is no training for directors (this question has only started to be considered in the last 15 years and at present, things are far from being clear, since the process has hardly started) only widened the gap; the generation of Éric Vigner, Robert Cantarella, Dominique Pitoiset, Christian Schiaretti and Stéphane Braunschweig was trained elsewhere, often in the fine arts, which explains the importance of the visual arts in the work of these directors. This no doubt also led to the emergence and increasing importance of stage design, now considered as an art form in itself. Some designers consider that they can only work on the condition that they can also direct actors (Gilone Brun), and others (Daniel Jeanneteau) have even become directors outright; a redefinition of each role seems necessary, but in any case, the way these categories are thought out has evolved considerably. As Jean-Loup Rivière has noted: 'what is unimaginable in our times is in fact to question heritage' (2003: 61). It is clear to see why the field is so fragmented when the governing logic is that each is out for their own. Nevertheless, a tension still exists between what might be defined as a desire for continuity and an attempt at rupture.

A changing landscape: between continuity and rupture

The defining characteristic of French theatre is that it remains marked by its affiliation to literature. The events of May 1968 did nothing to change this: the sacrosanct text remains at the heart of all theatrical activity. A number of young companies continue to operate according to the old, classical methodology. They do it well, with a degree of intelligence, thereby perpetuating a real tradition, even within a 'modern' aesthetic. This traditional theatre still occupies a considerable space in the landscape. Yet, even if the text is central to all theatrical projects, the former has in itself changed considerably. There has been a marked shift from the literature of the past. The notion of what constitutes a play has evolved, if not exploded, and today one speaks rather of a text, of writing, of dramatic material. Authors write in direct relation to the stage, sometimes directing their own plays. Michel Vinaver or Philippe Minyana, for instance, have invented a new type of writing, as has Noëlle Renaude whose *Ma Solange, comment t'écrire mon désastre, Alex Roux* (*My Solange, How Can I Write You My Disaster, Alex Roux*) was written for – with? – the actor Christophe Brault. Others team up with a director (Georges Lavaudant–Jean-Christophe Bailly, Patrice Chéreau–Bernard-Marie Koltès, Robert Cantarella–Philippe Minyana, David Bobée–Ronan Chéneau), or explore new ways of approaching theatre. There are also those who hold several positions concurrently, as stage and company directors. Here, it is worth mentioning Didier-Georges Gabily, who died in 1996 at the tender age of 40, but whose influence is still felt today by young companies. A new mode of operating based on the group (not to mention the collective) has surfaced. These groups intend sometimes to mark a complete break with traditional theatre. Using writings not intended for the stage, they create productions that include elements taken from other art forms, such as circus, puppets, and of course dance, since the body is an integral part of their experimentation. Or, if they do indeed work on recognized texts, they do not hesitate to interrogate them by deconstructing them if need be. The influence of Heiner Müller in this domain is palpable. Furthermore, new technologies also need to be mastered. This only occurs rarely with any pertinence, but the works of directors and video artists such as Cyril Teste or Véronique Caye (and a few others) are already promising.

What unites this small world is the deliberate and sometimes erroneous desire to speak about and account for the world of today through the prism of personal experience. Connecting the personal with the universal: this is, after all, the mission that has always been assigned to the theatre. 'The world has been created as many times as an original artist has appeared', wrote Marcel Proust. What defines artists is surely their singularity. How might one then force them into categories? France can count amongst its talented a number of unconventional artists whose strength and originality make them important: François Tanguy and the Théâtre du Radeau, Alexis Forestier and his Endimanchés, and a number of others. They do not fit into any portrait, any synthesis. This can only be a source of delight.

Translated by Dominic Glynn

Notes

1. Editors' note: See Works Cited for the French titles of these publications.
2. Editors' note: Roger Blin's production of Genet's *Les Paravents* in 1966 sparked violent demonstrations outside the Théâtre national de l'Odéon by a number of former soldiers who had defended French colonial interests in Indochina and Algeria, and who assumed that the play insulted the army. Certain members of Parliament were outraged that public subsidies were being spent on a play that criticized the State, but the serving Minister for Culture, André Malraux, successfully defended the production. This affair is credited with being one of the most politically charged in French theatre history.

Works cited

Cormann, Enzo (2003) *A quoi sert le théâtre?* (Besançon: Les solitaires intempestifs).

Dupuis, Sylviane (1998) *A quoi sert le théâtre ?* (Geneva: Zoé).

Guenoun Denis (1997) *Le théâtre est-il nécessaire ?* (Belval: Circé).

Han, Jean-Pierre (2008) *Derniers feux (essais de critiques)* (Morlanwelz: Lansman).

Jourdheuil, Jean (1994) 'La Dérive spectaculaire', *Libération*, 16–17 July, p. 15.

Lehmann, Hans-Thies (2002) *Le Théâtre postdramatique*, trans. Philippe-Henri Ledru (Paris: L'Arche).

Naugrette, Catherine (2005) *Théâtre Aujourd'hui 10: L'Ère de la mise en scène* (Paris: Théâtrales).

Piemme, Jean-Maire (1991) 'Le plus d'esthétiques minoritaires possibles', *Cahiers de la Comédie-Française*, 1 (Autumn), 58–62.

Rivière, Jean-Loup (2003) 'L'Impossible panorama', *Le Monde de l'éducation*, July–August, 316, 59–61.

Saurel, Renéé (2007) *Scènes d'architectures: Nouvelles architectures françaises pour le spectacle* (Paris: Les Éditions du patrimoine).

—— (2008) *Le Théâtre face au pouvoir: les temps modernes, 1965 –1984* (Paris: L'Harmattan).

Scott, Diane (2008) 'Crise mais encore', *frictions, théâtres-écritures*, 13, 41–7.

Siméon, Jean-Pierre (2007) *Quel théâtre pour aujourd'hui?* (Besançon: Les solitaires intempestifs).

Slama, Gérard-Alain (2008) 6 June (Paris: France-Culture).

Théâtre/Public: Théâtre contemporain, écriture textuelle, écriture scénique (2007), 184.

6
The Construction and Production of Performance

Robert Cantarella

The term *création* (new production) has been used for some time now in various contexts, in situations which, most of the time, allude to the fact that to create a new production is the hallmark of originality, of a unique position, of risks taken by those participating in the theatrical process.[1] Theatre directing is usually associated with staging these events. When, thanks to the organizational ability of the director, theatrical signs are prepared and arranged, a new production comes into being.

If I begin in this way, it is because in my essay I attempt to trace the thought processes that led me – after having practised in France from the 1990s onwards pretty much every method for assembling and constructing work into a new production – to think about the possibility of building a different theatrical venue, the Centquatre, provoked by these very reflections. I shall try to understand the reasons for the fact that the new production, in theatrical circles, is seen as the dominant element in the whole chain of transformations that leads from an idea, to its realization. I shall then define how the Centquatre might escape the logic of the new production, and in doing so respond to the new requirements of the contemporary art scene in France.[2]

The Centquatre is the logical conclusion to the fact that the term 'new production' has been overvalued, first and foremost in the field of theatre, but also in the other arts, as I have come to discover. The excessive importance attached to the new work has determined ways of functioning and, most of all, the hierarchy or, as some might say, the regulation and organization of artists' and audiences' desires. Indeed, by dealing with new productions, by financing them, by establishing criteria that deem whether or not a project will be staged, 'regulators' – whether cultural officials or publicly funded producers chosen to select an artistic season – determine which aspects of French theatrical creativity gain exposure, and which do not. My intention is not to denounce a perverse machine that is cruel to the destitute and the forgotten. Rather, I seek to highlight the consequences of an ingrained and fiercely defended insistence on new theatrical productions. As a result of focusing the entire evaluation apparatus on the visible part of the creative process – the new production – theatre auditoria have justifiably developed in such a way as to accentuate the division between what falls within the remit of preparation, and what is presented to the public. Which means to say, that everything is conceived and built around the premise that the theatrical work is concocted behind closed doors and that its ensuing presentation must occur via a magical process which can only take place according to this secretive format. All the focus is on building conventional theatres; very little, if any, is on creating alternatives that would also enable the public to see work spaces, rehearsal rooms, places of exchange that do not usually fall within the framework of showing new productions. New productions are the very *raison d'être* of these buildings. New productions represent the raw material both of consumer exchange and artistic exchange in the field of modern-day theatre. This dominant ideology presupposes that contact with the new production will provoke or change something in the audience's consciousness.

A new production ('une création'), as its French linguistic origin indicates, is a genesis which leaves its mark on history; becomes legendary. Since it is the work of God above all else, it is not easily shared by those who have been produced ('créés'). How can you produce anything original or truly new when you yourself are the product of divine creation? ('Comment créer en étant soi-même une création?').[3] It would be flagrant blasphemy. But the shifts in meaning and different usages of the term mean that it has become diminished and secularized, such that it can nowadays signify a theatre premiere, for example. However, the word premiere also has a nebulous, or rather vast meaning. Indeed, a premiere implies the idea of starting something new, this notion becoming both its reason for being, and its very constitution. But premiere for whom? The opening night is of course a premiere. So premiere is the term adopted by those who play in front of, and for, the audience for the first time. It is they, the audience, who create the new work. What happens afterwards is something else (everyone has their own ideas about what happens on the second night). The premiere is invested with considerable value. It represents a transitory or liminal moment when members of the cast give each other presents, say 'break a leg', and where various pre-performance rituals ease the transition from rehearsal to production. The audience acts as the missing ingredient that either brings everything together, causes illusions to tumble down, or perhaps adds nothing new, but nevertheless the presence of spectators in the theatre space transforms the show into a new production. A new production takes place when contact is established with those for whom the work was prepared. The audience gives meaning to something that, until its arrival, had only been a projection, a promise, an event put on hold but not yet delivered. The audience must be involved in the production. The audience 'produces' the play. When it comes into contact with the new work for the first time, the audience creates memories, interpretations, questions and experiences pleasure, boredom, frustration, and so on. Contact is made with the audience and the production takes place, as does the premiere, and already people are talking about the next production. In this respect, the premiere is inherently paradoxical, since whether in the auditorium or on the stage, everybody thinks they are 'producing' something that is always, to an extent, already produced and never in the place it should be: a premiere is something intangible, it inhabits the ephemeral time and space separating and joining actors and spectators.

If I go through this complex process in some detail, it is because implicitly underpinning this model is the idea that theatrical creation constitutes part of, and is dependent on, the outside world, which must be anticipated as a condition of that new production. The community of human beings assembled at the moment of a new production supposedly receives a certain creative energy, and these spectators thereby supposedly become agents for the event produced for them: they will supposedly be the 'producers' of new theatrical creativity.

The supposition that the work will activate a passive audience, or at least one on standby or on pause, is the fundamental reason for the fact that new productions are overvalued in the chain of events leading to the construction of a piece of theatre both today, and in the past few years. Let us consider the vast amounts spent on the construction of sumptuous sets, magnificent stage machinery and immaculate finish, at the expense of the amount spent on welcoming the audience. I draw on my own personal experience in order to explain my views more clearly. When I used to go to the theatre religiously, I was (and still am) surprised, on the one hand, by the care and attention given to organizing theatrical signs on the stage, an effort carried out by a number of intelligent people who have been granted the human and financial resources to accomplish this task; and on the other, by the negligible amount of thought invested in the relationship between signs around the stage: lights, café, staircases, entrance hall, access to the venue, starting times of shows and the like. The logic behind this situation was (and still is) determined by a preconceived idea that the important moment takes place in the auditorium, when one is seated before the stage, face-to-face with the action, before the production. According to this set-up, ideas supposedly become fewer and poorer, the further one moves away from the stage. Which leads me to question why so much energy and creativity are now invested in this idea of the new production? Because, even when I am not physically present as an actual audience member, I still receive a host of signs, which I invariably experience and link together. When I walk into the auditorium, which is in fact a kind of theatre or stage in itself, my emotions merge with what I am. Why is this fact forgotten or denied? Primarily, in my view, to persuade us that what is important lies elsewhere, namely, in the performance itself. I saw (and still see) the intention to make the production appear in all its intimidating splendour and sacredness. I was (and still remain) terrified, just as when faced with those live bodies that are at work and seek to educate our consciousnesses. Bodies that think through our consciousnesses by implementing traps in order to lure energies into the auditorium with the aim of changing us either by supposedly educating us or by giving us a pleasurable experience. Whatever the intention, I feel others are thinking on my behalf.

The over-investment in new productions has a number of practical repercussions. There are, for instance, multiple intermediaries between the artists responsible for the work and the audience, since the exposure of the production needs to be orchestrated, as I mentioned at the beginning of this essay. Exposure involves publicity for the production, and also fixing the calendar of events and new releases. Knowing how to market a field of creativity has become a profession in itself, as is knowing how to manufacture interest in it. A whole legion of staff and a whole programme of events have been created around this job. Invariably, new productions promise to give us 'a good time'. To do this, they must emphasize their own appeal, meaning that details that will attract special interest are underlined, starting with who will play what part, and what part is the most important. A certain set of values must therefore be maintained in order to feed expectations and promises. In theatre, a new production usually starts with the casting of parts, which of course anticipates the moment of creating and producing something collectively. This is another way of predicting the future reception of the work and its intentions, in other words the coming into being of an aesthetic and sensory communal experience. Once again, all this is supposedly intended for the 'common good', and different means are used depending on the events and artists involved.

There is one particularly striking example of this denial of the development process, in favour of the completed form. When I say completed, I mean a finished artefact or product that is waiting for an audience to activate it. Even if, as many directors claim, a production changes every night according to the performance, it still remains a relatively stable entity, recognizable via certain hallmark features that characterize the particular production [for a related point, see Chapter 14 by Bojana Cvejic in this volume]. The example to which I refer involves the plays of Jean-Luc Lagarce. In the recent history of what in France we call 'living' or 'contemporary authors' the gap has never been so great between the difficulty in having plays performed during an author's lifetime, and the subsequent proliferation of performances after that author's death. During his life, Lagarce was forced to rely on his own tactics and *savoir faire* by staging tried and tested plays – Molière, Ionesco – in order to raise the financial means to perform his own writing and his own productions. One critic for *Libération* admitted that the only good author is a dead author, since one can 'capture' a dead author's work. Indeed, since Lagarce's death, analysts have been able to set to work on his texts; directors have been able to stage them; and audiences have been able to appreciate them.

What relationship does this bear with my definition of the term new production? It is easier to provide an expert assessment, or perform an autopsy, on a motionless corpse than on a living body, since the latter is unpredictable. I am saying nothing new here. What the middleman between artist and audience foresees is the reception of the new production. Predicting the effects of a new production is what makes such intermediaries act and react. Their mission is to control exposure to the production, its appearance, and its inherent worth. They themselves might be artists, but in their capacity of deciding what exposure a production might enjoy, their most important task is to predict what effect that production might have on others. As a result of this, when Lagarce was still alive, he constantly shifted direction and varied his work. Usually, when a new play is being staged for the first time, it is, by definition, an unknown quantity, because it depends on external factors such as which venue hosts it, what the audience's reaction will be, what the critics will think – in other words, on parameters that are often difficult to anticipate. However, since Lagarce's plays have now, after his death, become relatively well known and part of the canon, they guarantee large audiences, and considerable exposure. This is relatively commonplace. Over time, what had appeared as experimental and complex has attracted critical and popular attention, and won people over. So several criteria or indicators that characterize Lagarce's case give me food for thought when I discuss the subject of new productions. First, the speed of the turnaround – only a few weeks after Lagarce's death, a seminar was held on his complete works; and second, the difficulties and obscurities of his plays were suddenly forgotten; it was as if a writer who had always been accepted and understood was suddenly born out of nowhere.

A new production is the main reason why financing bodies mobilize themselves to find necessary resources. I am still speaking here about the field of theatre. If one wanted to produce a play that had not already been staged, one would have to think about where, and especially how to do it. The habitual path followed by directors who have not yet been granted the financial means afforded to someone running a national institution, or someone who is subsidized sufficiently in order to make further funding applications, starts with them speaking about their plans for future theatre productions. They must describe their projects, make a pitch. In this regard, the production proposal marks the first step. A proposal is necessary in order to sell the production; to find money. Most of the time, the proposal is a dossier of documents that clarify the project – it defines how the project will be produced; its context; the director's artistic vision; the author's vision (if s/he is not the director); images; and the CVs of those taking part. These elements compose an embryonic whole or virtuality, which is then subsequently developed through the 'mysterious' processes of artistic construction. The proposal can be more or less original and represent the director's signature ideas. Indeed, there are times when the proposal is in itself almost a kind of production. In order to sell the first production I staged in a warehouse in Paris while I was studying the art of 'shattering theatrical illusions' under Antoine Vitez, I compiled a dossier so huge that I could hardly carry it, and theatres certainly could not stage what was in it. It came complete with a recording, a pop-up of the venue, and a story-board of the production. It was pretentious and a little ridiculous, but started from a simple idea: since my proposal needed both to sell and to elucidate my project on Bertolt Brecht's play *Baal*, I needed to make it into a work of art in its own right. This would prove that I knew what I wanted, or else that I had good ideas, or that I was not a joker, or that I was committed. In short, I really acted the part. In French, the expression for alluding to the proposal for a new production works well: 'en mettre plein la vue pour prévoir'('to show off about the future show'). Interestingly, during the 1980s it was always the most idiosyncratic proposals that succeeded; it was as if creative energy was being channelled more and more towards attempting to guarantee wide exposure, and less and less towards genuine theatre research.

By talking regularly about how to construct theatre productions, and then about how to circulate ideas, I have gradually been able to identify the reasons for my sadness, both as an artist and audience member, when faced with the necessity of having to produce a new show. 'What's your next production?', we often used to ask each other after having just seen the first night of a new production. The other hackneyed expression was, 'I'm going to such and such's new production. Are you?' I pondered whether my constitution was not weakening, faced with the pressure exerted by this need to produce. In all seriousness, I was starting to wonder if I had lost faith in this work regime, this tripartite schema of, first, preparing a proposal, finding money and participants, getting them on board; second, rehearsing and organizing theatrical signs into a public performance (the date of which had already been communicated via public relations mechanisms); and, third, staging the production, holding a premiere and keeping the performances going. Perhaps, I was no longer cut out for this business.

Frequenting the company of other theatre practitioners who felt a similar pressure, as well as conversing with artists from different fields who were obliged to participate in a similar process, persuaded me when conceiving the Centquatre that, since we lacked the necessary tools, we needed to *use* the existing forms and structures rather than simply submit to them. We had to try to change the means of exchange between artists, in order to enable other modes of behaviour. Those listening to us often called us 'dreamers'. When all is said and done, their response was not so stupid after all: the tools of production exist, but we have to transform them in relation to the projects about which we dream. The story is well known: 'get yourself in there and subvert it internally'; as is the punch line: 'the system has some good sides to it, after all'.

On the other hand, the demand for theatre was booming. Writers wanted to read or stage their works in the theatre; people working in the visual arts desired the immediacy of performing in front of live audiences; other artists, too, solicited the stage (musicians, landscape artists, photographers) in an attempt to experience the human contact and sense of communion inherent in the theatre (see, in this volume, Chapter 13 by Carl Lavery and Chapter 11 by Éric Vautrin). But a stage conceived for theatre performances proved unsuitable for other art forms, since it was unable to be sufficiently modified to account for more collaborative and dispersed practices of art making. Equally, the pace of a conventional theatre rehearsal and production schedule did not suit the creative rhythms and processes of alternative modes of artistic creation.

Little by little, the term 'performance' slipped in between the terms 'new production' and 'artistic construction'. Performance has now become a buzzword for artists seeking exposure. The hybridization of disparate practices and techniques has contributed to the appearance of this term, which encompasses many ideas and fields. The aim of the Centquatre is to assemble in the same time and space the almost infinite variety of arts, and to nurture relationships between them. At its most basic, performance involves a moment of sharing between a group of people who attend, and one or several people who perform an action, or actions. One could say that, if the actions were spoken and if they were spread out over a considerable length of time, they would become a theatrical play. But performance differs from theatre in that its processes of construction are more disjointed, lighter, freer, more unconventional. Many artists who request a space at the Centquatre want to make a performance, that is, they seek to create something immediate and transient, something that will only be performed once. Even if the performance were to be re-enacted again, its eventness, that is to say, its unique articulation in space and time, is not reproducible. To reproduce it again would mean that everything would have to be exactly as it was at the original moment of creation. This is impossible, since the very fact that the artist has decided to recreate it again causes the disruptive play of difference to appear. In this respect, performance is the quintessential 'new production', in the extent to which it resists the very possibility of reproduction. Its spirit of freedom and atypical nature transform it into a spontaneous memory, a unique experience. 'You had to be there', and consequently the temporal and spatial paradox of theatre that I have already mentioned is either resolved or eluded, since both parts, the artist and the audience, produce the moment of performance together. There are significant demands from artists and audiences for performative events (these terms, too, have come to mean anything and everything). Since performance is not preconceived, one can actually see the conditions of its production; in other words, the new production is constructed in front of live witnesses. With performance, the construction of the act and the new production overlap. I, as a spectator, am witness to the construction of a new production before my eyes. In the theatre, this construction phase is put out of mind, effaced, superseded by the idea of reproduction, or reconstruction.

Performance is therefore above all predicated upon the interplay and possible resolution of two temporalities. It is a moment of pleasure and excitement, not to mention the fact that it advocates the shattering of dramatic illusion, which it does by revealing its own processes of construction. It can be a kind of X-ray of the theatrical act, its spectre, its residue, its detritus, its shadow, its transmission in the mechanical sense which, like the axle or a central structure in between the motor and the wheels, ensures movement (see the Introduction to this volume for a detailed definition of Performance).

The building that I imagined was a place where ideas would circulate constantly, a place where the building did not separate construction from production and performance. And in order to achieve this, this building had to avoid privileging one notion over another, one temporality over another. The Centquatre is the physical incarnation of this idea.

Translated by Clare Finburgh and Dominic Glynn

Notes

1. Editors' note: The term *création* in French bears several significations: it means the fabrication of something, both in an artistic and a religious sense (for instance, God's Creation as described in the Book of Genesis); it signifies the product of that fabrication, namely, the work or concept; and it denotes a theatrical production that is performed for the very first time. Cantarella mainly employs the latter meaning, though he also exploits the word's multiple connotations.
2. Editors' note: The Centquatre, a vast cultural complex, was opened in October 2008. As its two directors, Robert Cantarella and Frédéric Fisbach, state in their 'manifesto', *L'Anti-musée*, they did not want the establishment to become yet another museum that would showcase France's cultural heritage (2009). Instead, it would be a kind of laboratory, with three main missions: first, to enable the general public to watch artists in the process of creating work; second, to forge pluridisciplinary relationships between various arts; and, third, to involve the local community – it is located in the nineteenth *arrondissement*, one of Paris's more deprived areas. Whilst the Centquatre has attracted a wealth of artists from architects, to interior designers, playwrights, visual artists and musicians, from places as far afield as Cameroon and Peru, it has lacked exposure and audiences. Cantarella and Fisbach stood down in March 2010, and the future direction that the Centquatre will take is uncertain.
3. Editors' note: To grasp the full meaning of Cantarella's point, we have quoted the original French alongside the English translation.

Works cited

Cantarella, Robert and Frédéric Fisbach (2009) *L'Anti-musée* (Paris: Nouveaux Débats publics).

7
Performing Presence, Affirming Difference: Deleuze and the Minor Theatres of Georges Lavaudant and Carmelo Bene

Laura Cull

In this chapter, I want to explore the relationship between one of contemporary France's most prominent theatrical figures, Georges Lavaudant, and one of its most important recent philosophers, Gilles Deleuze. While Deleuze only came to the attention of British and North American scholars during the last ten years of his life (that is, from the mid-1980s), his ideas were unsurprisingly taken up earlier and more widely in his native France. For instance, *What is Philosophy?*, his last collaborative work with Félix Guattari published in 1991, became a French bestseller. Likewise, it could be suggested that the title given to a recent *Le Monde* interview with Lavaudant – 'Mettre un peu de mineur dans le majeur' – indicates the extent to which a Deleuzian vocabulary of the 'major and minor' has permeated French popular culture (Lavaudant, Darge and Salino, 2006: 4). However, it also adduces Lavaudant's specifically Deleuzian, as well as broadly philosophical, sympathies. As far back as 1977, Lavaudant had argued that the French theatre of his time was not 'philosophical enough' and supported Antoine Vitez's desire to 'begin the circulation of thought' in and *as* theatre (Lavaudant in Champagne, 1984: 87). Equally, in a 1994 interview, Lavaudant proposes a concept of theatre as a kind of live, communal event of philosophizing by describing it as 'one of the few spaces where we can still think in the presence of, and alongside, others' (ibid.: 43). But beyond this affirmation of a philosophical theatre *per se*, Lavaudant's theatrical project is directly characterized by explictly Deleuzian values, as Nicole Fayard suggests when she argues that Lavaudant 'radically transformed' existing French theatre traditions 'by inventing a theatre based on an impatience with all limits' (Fayard, 2003: 37). For Lavaudant, 'the theatre is about the enjoyment of having no rules to follow' (Lavaudant in Fayard, 2006: 205); correlatively, Deleuze's philosophy of immanence is premised upon the primacy of becoming over being and the resistance of any transcendent law that would place pre-emptive restrictions on the production of the new.

Given this connection between Deleuzian philosophy and Lavaudant's directorial practice, this chapter will suggest that we can employ Deleuze's thought to relate to Lavaudant's theatre anew: less as one that comes forward pointing to the mask of its status as representation and more as a theatre that 'surge[s] forward as something represent-ing nothing but what presents and creates a minority consciousness as a universal-becoming' (Deleuze, 1997: 256). In particular, I will look at Lavaudant's *La Rose et la hache* (*The Rose and the Axe*), a creative response to Carmelo Bene's *Riccardo III* that was first produced in 1979 and re-staged in 2004.[1] As such, the latter might be described as a revival or homage to Bene's own creative adaptation of Shakespeare. Too many steps away from a so-called 'original' for some, one French critic referred to Lavaudant's production as Shakespeare's '*Richard III* cleansed of its historic complexity' (Delord, 2006: 78). But as Deleuze remarks of Bene's *Riccardo III*, this is not a theatre concerned with the representation of (an official) History, but with extracting 'becomings against History, lives against culture, thoughts against doctrine, graces or disgraces against dogma' (Deleuze, 1997: 243). Finally, whilst focus-ing on Lavaudant and Deleuze, this chapter also obliquely demonstrates the close relationship that can exist in France between political philoso-phy, and theatre.[2]

Lavaudant's Deleuzism

Lavaudant refuses to assign theatre any fixed identity, arguing that 'all that is not theatre is theatre' and characterizing the theatre as a cease-lessly changing hybrid (Lavaudant, in Fayard 2006: 205). In this sense, Lavaudant's theatre is what Deleuze would call an 'assemblage' (*agence-ment*), a dynamic composition that gathers together different elements, beyond any subject/object relation. It is a kind of unity, but one that is given its specificity by its connections. For instance, in the opening of *A Thousand Plateaus*, Deleuze and Guattari describe the book as an assemblage, arguing that it can neither be attributed to a subject, nor be said to have an object which it represents (Deleuze and Guattari, 1988: 3–4). As an assemblage, the book is produced in the mutually transformative connection of the writer and world; indeed, it *is* that connection, rather than being reducible to either of the things con-nected. The assemblage is not a totality, but a collection of differential parts, like the diverse components of an ecosystem. Likewise, Lavaudant sets up a theatre that can enter into new assemblages with other art forms, including literature and painting, but also, more specifically, 'detective novels, poetry, history, the cinema, music hall... fashion, [and] advertising' (Fayard, 2003: 38). Lavaudant's entire theatre project is an assemblage, but there are also different assemblages within individual productions, particularly in 'collage' works such as *L'Education sentimentale* (*Sentimental Education*, 1975), which gathers together texts by Lavaudant with those by Flaubert and de Sade, plugging one literary style into another to create something new. When looking for texts, Lavaudant says he is attracted to 'a certain quickness of writing [...] that remains mobile, that I can demolish, remake' (Lavaudant in Champagne, 1984: 93).

Lavaudant's perspective also echoes Deleuze's in so far as he defines theatre in terms of its speeds and against any informational relation to its audiences. For instance, we might note his interest in unexpected tempos as explored via the slow motion movements of figures in works such as his 1976 production *Palazzo Mentale* or the slow motion battle scene in *Richard III*. Lavaudant argues that, 'theatre can take everything in. It must absorb everything. Theatre with its fragility and slower rhythm holds its own against the omnipresence of rapidly moving images. And I stand with it against all the "great communicators" who try to mystify us' (Lavaudant in Fayard, 2003: 37). In this way, Lavaudant's work of the 1970s and early 1980s disturbed existing concepts of theatrical meaning. As Fayard has implied, Lavaudant's assemblages were not concerned 'to make any sense' (ibid.: 41) but to *affect* the audience; not to produce performance as a recognizable object but to force the audience to think (genuinely) by creating what Deleuze calls a 'fundamental encounter' that eludes representation (1994: 139).

This is not to reinstate some kind of false dichotomy between feeling and thinking, or body and mind, but to suggest a different conception of the impact of performance beyond the notion of meaning received by the representational consciousness of a subject. For example, when Deleuze argues that the 'essential aims of the arts should be the subordination of form [...] to the variation of speed, and the subordination of the subject [...] to the intense variation of affects' (1997: 249), this is by no means a call to embrace a theatre of emotion over a theatre of the mind, to give ourselves over to the pleasures of the 'merely' formal properties of an artwork instead of wrestling with its conceptual dimensions. Rather, Deleuze's 'onto-aesthetics' posits the corporeal transformations of (human and inhuman) bodies in connection with one another *as* a kind of thinking (Zepke, 2005: 4) – specifically a kind of nonrepresentational, unconscious thinking conceived as affect or sensation. Understood in terms of their power to be affected, Deleuze suggests that bodies can think in ways which consciousness would do well to learn; he argues that difference in itself is that which 'can only be sensed', since consciousness works with identities (1994: 139).[3] For Deleuze, incomprehensibility is precisely where genuine thought begins; not being able 'to make any sense' is what makes us *really* think as audience members, rather than getting locked into thinking with a fixed set of ideas. As encounter, thought is involved in bringing something new into being, rather than simply reaffirming what has already been thought; it is creation rather than representation.

Lavaudant, Deleuze and Bene

More of these matters, and indeed of how they might allow us to reconsider the politics of Lavaudant's theatre, in due course. For now, though, there is one further connection between Lavaudant and Deleuze that I want to address: namely, their shared fascination with the work of the irreverent Italian actor, director and general 'enfant terrible' of Italian theatre: Carmelo Bene. Whereas Bene initially attracted attention for his work in 1959 with his staging of, and performance in, Albert Camus' play *Caligula* (1944), Lavaudant first came to prominence post-1968 as a member of the Théâtre Partisan group based in Grenoble, before going on to become the co-director of Grenoble's Centre dramatique national des Alpes (CDNA) in 1976. Lavaudant accepted the post of co-director of the Théâtre national populaire (TNP) in Villeurbanne in 1986 and later that of director of the Théâtre national de l'Odéon in Paris in 1996 (Fayard, 2004: 325). As director of the Odéon, one of the first invitations that Lavaudant issued was to Bene, who performed his *Macbeth Horror Suite* there in the year of Lavaudant's appointment. This was not, however, Bene's first presentation to a French audience; he and Deleuze had already met when the Carmelo Bene Company was in residence in Paris in 1977, 'staging performances of Bene's *Romeo and Juliet* and *S.A.D.E.* at the Opéra-Comique for the annual Festival d'automne' (Bogue, 2003: 116). Bene reports meeting with Deleuze after one of these Paris performances and discussing with him his ideas for staging *Richard III* (ibid.). It was here that the collaboration that produced the book *Superpositions* began.

First published in Italian in 1978, *Superpositions* incorporates an essay by Deleuze called 'One Less Manifesto' or 'One Manifesto Less' (depending on whose translation of the title you prefer) and Bene's script for a production entitled, *Richard III: or, The Horrible Night of a Man of War*. This essay is Deleuze's only sustained commentary on theatre and, as such, a vital text for anyone concerned with the relation between Deleuze and performance. But it is also of central importance for our purposes in so far as it provides an elaboration of the conceptual dyad of 'major' and 'minor' art that Deleuze and Guattari had already introduced in *Kafka: Toward a Minor Literature* (1986).

Riccardo III and *La Rose et la hache*

In 'One Less Manifesto' Deleuze defines a minor theatre as one that places all the different elements of theatre – its language, gestures, costumes and props – in perpetual variation, through a process of 'subtraction' or 'amputation' (Deleuze, 1997: 239). Whereas, in much dramatic theatre, the tendency is to submit the speeds and slownesses of performance to the organizational forms of plot and dialogue and to emphasize characters over transformative becomings that sweep them away, a minor theatre seeks to affirm the primacy of perpetual variation over the fixed representation of subjects, objects and a coherent fictional world.

For Deleuze, there is no fundamental separation between art and life, or aesthetics and ontology. Lived experience is not more real than aesthetic experience, nor is theatre a mere illustration of the force of difference to which Deleuze accords ontological priority; rather, it *is* that differential force (Zepke, 2005: 3–4). Indeed, we might even suggest that, for Deleuze, art can be *more* real than life, or at least bring us closer to the reality of difference. Differently from in everyday consciousness, where we tend to experience affect as mediated through the subject/object relation, art can provide transformative, material encounters in which audiences are carried away from themselves as subjects in order to enter into composition with the pure affects of a painterly, musical, literary or theatrical 'body'. The work of art makes perceptible 'the imperceptible forces that populate the world, affect us, and make us become' (Deleuze and Guattari, 1994: 182).

As such, 'One Less Manifesto' merits being read in the light of Deleuze's wider philosophical project, and the notion of the perpetual variations of minor theatre alongside the idea of life as constituted by becomings rather than beings, process rather than substance. However, given his onto-aesthetic position, it is also important to note that there are no *essentially* major or minor theatres for Deleuze, but rather different *usages* of theatre and its elements that we can call major and minor. In the first instance, Deleuze argues that Carmelo Bene's practice constitutes a minor usage of theatre because he employs a tri-partite, subtractive method that removes the 'elements of power' from theatre – eliminating both representations *of* power and representation *as* power in order to set free the movement of difference. This process involves: '(1) deducting the stable elements, (2) placing everything in continuous variation, (3) then transposing everything in minor (this is the role of the company in responding to the notion of the "smallest" interval)' (Deleuze, 1997: 246). This subtraction (or amputation) consti-tutes what Deleuze calls a process of 'minoration' – the undoing of the major in order to release the minor, which he defines as a revolutionary practice (ibid.: 243).

Lavaudant, like Bene, chose to perform this subtractive operation on a number of plays by 'the great Will' (Leonardini in Bradby, 2008: 110). As I have noted, Lavaudant started practising theatre in and around 1968 when the wider concern of many was to liberate theatre from institutionalized conventions. In common with other French groups at the time, such as the Théâtre du Soleil, Le Folidrome and Théâtre du Radeau, Lavaudant and the Théâtre Partisan experimented with the process of collective creation; however, much like Carmelo Bene, Lavaudant first came to notoriety on account of his productions of existing works from a more classical repetoire: Musset's *Lorenzaccio* in 1973 and Shakespeare's *King Lear* in 1975 (Fayard, 2003: 39). But there is no contradiction here. Indeed, David Bradby proposes that 'far from being dethroned in the aftermath of 1968, Shakespeare was produced by both the young Turks and the older revolutionaries', including those like Lavaudant 'who, in [the French critic] Leonardini's words "tear the great Will to pieces: unpick him, skin him, slice him, split him, crush him, pulverize him and rip him to shreds"' (Bradby, 2008: 110–11; my translation).

In this way, it is not so much that there are fixed major and minor authors; rather that Bene and Lavaudant subject Shakespeare to what Deleuze calls a 'minor author treatment' (1997: 242). But this minor treatment is by no means against a theatre of language, and neither is it concerned with simply amputating large parts of Shakespeare's scripts. On the contrary, 'with the exception of two passages taken from *Henry VI, Part III*, virtually all of the lines spoken by the actors [in Bene's *Riccardo III*] are translations of lines from Shakespeare's *Richard III*' (Bogue, 2003: 127). Yet at the same time, more than half of Bene's script is composed of elaborate stage directions which articulate a series of actions and events that bear no connection to Shakespeare's tragic plot, but instead transplant his words into a new imagistic *mise en scène*. Likewise, *La Rose et la hache* undoes the hierarchy between text and performance. Or, to transpose Deleuze's words on Bene to Lavaudant, it makes Shakespeare's words but one part of a totality that includes deformed movements and gestures, the a-natural blue light that glows at differing strengths from various surfaces and screens, a table so full of glasses that it has ceased to function as a table, and sculptural costumes 'limiting movement instead of aiding it' (Deleuze, 1997: 248). Indeed, in turn, each theatrical element matters less 'in itself' than in its function as the 'material for variation' (ibid.: 246).

The minor treatment also concerns *how* Shakespeare's words are performed. The major Shakespeare, Deleuze claims, speaks '"the king's English": homogenized and invariant' (in Fortier, 1996: 5), whereas a minor theatre maker must 'amputate the text because the text is like the domination of language over speech and still attests to invariance or homogeneity' (Deleuze, 1997: 245). In contrast, Deleuze argues that minor usages of language allow us to apprehend 'language's most inherent, creative property': a fundamental variability (ibid.). Whereas the structuralist distinction between *langue* and *parole* suggests that there is an underlying set of rules or constants, in relation to which specific enunciations are understood to be deviations from a norm, Deleuze's position implies that any given language ought to be understood as 'a multiplicity of semantic worlds' in which all possible differences of meaning are virtually present (Bogue, 1989: 147). Deleuze suggests that there are minor usages, which perform this difference within language in Bene's *Richard*, such as Lady Anne's differential repetition of the phrase 'You disgust me!'. There is no fixed meaning to this enunciation, Deleuze argues:

> It is hardly the same [enunciation] when uttered by a woman at war, a child facing a toad, or a young girl feeling a pity that is already consenting and loving [...] Lady Anne will have to move through all these variables. She will have to stand erect like a woman warrior, regress to a childlike state, and return as a young girl – as quickly as possible on a line of [... perpetual] variation.
>
> (1997: 246)

In this way, the actress playing Lady Anne transmits an enunciation through 'all the variables that could affect it in the shortest amount of time' (ibid.: 245), allowing the phrase to actualize its immanent difference. Likewise, at one point in *La Rose et la hache* there is a differential repetition of lines, as Ariel Garcia Valdes's Richard whirls into an energetic frenzy: 'When I was last in Holborn, I saw good strawberries: I do beseech you, send for some of them... because... when I was last in Holborn, I saw good strawberries: I do beseech you, send for some of them... because *etc*....(Lavaudant in Delord, 2006: 80). The theatre scholar Delord goes on to argue that this sentence, 'repeated endlessly in every possible way, is eventually emptied of all meaning, in a delirious re-writing of the scene that ends with Hastings' condemnation' (Delord, 2006: 80).

As Deleuze says of Bene, the power of language to differ perpetually is also exposed by a musical treatment of language, in which changes in tonality and speed take priority over the emphases that might derive from a communicational approach. With both Bene's and Valdes' Richard (s), this takes the form of rapid mumblings that deform words into what Bene called the 'articulations of a troglodyte' (Bene in Deleuze, 1997: 250), and which, in *La Rose et la hache* are also punctuated by coughs and splutters. Equally, in Lavaudant's *Hamlet* the actors deliver their lines in what Fayard (after Yann Ciret) calls '"chanté-parlé" (speech patterns which are a cross between chanting and speaking)' (Fayard, 2006: 222). This produces an effect akin to the kind of *Sprechgesang* (literally spoken-song) that Deleuze admires in Bene's poetic performance in the piece *Manfred*. This musical approach to language is also exemplified by Lavaudant and Bene's rejection of conventional dialogue in favour of the construction of an assemblage of overlapping recorded and live voices in a complex score. In this way, the voice is not a representation of a stable presence that comes before it (it does not, for instance, secure the identity of the speaker). As a consequence, in *La Rose et la hache*, the audience is disorientated as it watches characters lip-synching to songs; hears the heavy accents of actors being made to perform sections of the play in languages that are evidently not 'their own'; and is subjected to outbursts of disembodied and deranged laughter.

Finally, and again like Bene's piece, *La Rose et la hache* involves itself primarily with the creation of Richard on stage, as the actor performs a process of self-fashioning, not with prostheses but with bandages recalling the protagonist of Bene's film *Our Lady of the Turks* (1968). With his face in full theatrical make-up, Richard performs the act of bandaging a body (unclothed and unmade-up but for the single black glove on his 'bad hand') that does not seem to belong to itself. And in another scene, we see Richard being fed soup by Buckingham – becoming-invalid or child – rather than arriving at the molar identity of being a powerful 'King' despite his desperate, repetitive assertion in the strobe-lighting scene: 'I am King! I am King'. As Deleuze observes of Bene's Richard, 'one would not conclude that these characters have an "Ego"' (Deleuze, 1997: 241), since they are constantly differing from themselves, a refusal of linear development enhanced by the cinematic fades and cuts of Lavaudant's production which toss the audience from one scene to another.

And yet, as with 'One Less Manifesto', *La Rose* is no mere representation of Bene's *Riccardo III*; on the contrary, it performs the virtuality within Bene's Richard, creating a new work that puts role, as well as language, in perpetual variation. For instance, the actor who begins the performance playing Edward, later reappears, interchangeably as both Buckingham and then Hastings, sometimes leaving the stage as one character and re-entering it as the other, emphasizing what Deleuze calls 'the continuity of variation' rather than any continuity of identity or plot (1997: 249).

Becoming-minor

One productive result of conjoining Deleuze and Lavaudant (via Bene) in this way is the potential recuperation of the latter from the persistent equation of his work with a particular brand of postmodernism and certain strategies such as parody, irony and pastiche. For example, in his 1984 version of *Richard III*, Lavaudant's leading actor 'shifts from love to cunning and betrayal, callousness to fear, ugliness to charisma, boisterous youth to old age' (Fayard, 2006: 212). But whereas Fayard reads these actorly transitions as an indicator of Lavaudant's decision to adopt 'a strategy of conspicuous theatricality' that 'advertized the production as representation', Deleuze's text suggests ways in which we might read this perpetual variation as a presentation of difference as the 'really real'. That is, whereas Fayard sees Lavaudant's use of the actor as a self-reflexive effort to emphasize the 'power of illusion', 'One Less Manifesto' proposes, by contrast, a way to conceive Lavaudant's production as putting the actor in variation in order to create a minor theatre as non-representative force (ibid.: 212–13). Rather than categorizing Lavaudant's work as 'puzzling' or 'enigmatic' (ibid.: 222) – terms that betray a residual attempt to determine what it all *means* as representation – Deleuze's emphasis on variation in Bene, invites us to think performance more in terms of what it *does vis-à-vis* its production of 'differential presence'.

Fayard characterizes Lavaudant's work in terms of two distinct phases: a first phase of 'irreverent, iconoclastic productions' during the 1970s and 1980s and a second phase beginning in the 1990s that she describes as a 'magical theatre of images' (Fayard, 2006: 206). But arguably, this periodization operates at the level of content, rather than at the more abstract level of process. Lavaudant's Deleuzian concerns – with anti-representation, variation, assemblage – are largely consistent throughout his œuvre. While he does drop the method of performing surgical operations on Shakespeare's canonical texts in his productions of the 1990s, the refusal to treat performance as representation remains. In a 1994 interview, for instance, Lavaudant singled out *Hamlet* as a favoured work precisely because it 'lends itself the least well to interpretation. It frustrates any attempt to interpret or counter-interpret and to give an account of its dramatic structure from beginning to end' (Lavaudant in ibid.: 219).

This 'theatre of images' was also, of course, Bonnie Marranca's (1977) term for the work of, amongst others, Robert Wilson. As Champagne notes, a good deal of the so-called 'new' French theatre that emerged in the 1970s 'owes a debt to the staging of Robert Wilson, who has had an enormous influence on France since his *Deafman Glance* was staged at Nancy in 1971' (1984: 93). Whether they are addressing Wilson, Bene or Lavaudant, there is a tendency for secondary commentaries, including those of Marranca herself in later writings, to characterize these 'theatres of images' as other-worldly (Marranca, 1984: 121–2), or as that which excludes the 'real world' (whatever that means) in favour of constructing 'a sensual theatre of the mind in which imagination and theory are the ruling agents' (Champagne, 1984: 94). As such, a recurring question (and often it is a question that is asked in an accusatory tone) is: 'Is this political theatre?' (ibid.). For many, this aesthetic and unashamedly philosophical theatre appears to have abandoned the 'questions of the spectator or of social conditions' that had been of such pressing concern to the activist theatres of the generation before. But as Champagne goes on to point out, Lavaudant (at least) is far from a-political and forces us to rethink what we mean by 'political theatre'. Like Deleuze, Lavaudant rejects the Brechtian, dialectical model in favour of a politics of creativity. 'My first field of intervention', Lavaudant states, 'is creation. I ask what is the theatrical machine (a very Deleuzian phrase), and how to make it function [as a] zone of illusion, fascination, mystification. If the question: "How is your theatre political?" means only "What does it serve?," I prefer not to respond' (Lavaudant in ibid.: 95).

Likewise, in 'One Less Manifesto', Deleuze asks himself the question of the use of minor theatre 'for the outside world, since it is still a matter of theatre and nothing but theatre?' (Deleuze, 1997: 252). In response, Deleuze argues that Bene's minor theatre deviates from what he calls *majority rule*: a state in which groups such as 'women, children, the South, the third world, etc.' are, despite their numbers, constituted as subordinate minorities in relation to a standard measure: the supposedly universal model of Man, who in fact represents the specifically 'white, Christian, average-male-adult-inhabitant of contemporary American or European cities' (ibid.: 255, 253). A political theatre, for Deleuze, would not be one that aims to *represent* these minorities, or to represent *conflicts* between men and women, or the first and third worlds. Rather, a revolutionary theatre reveals the perpetual variation underlying these representational oppositions. Conflicts, Deleuze states, 'are already normalized, codified, institutionalized. They are "products". They are already a representation that can be represented so much better on the stage' (ibid.: 252). 'As a substitute for the *representation* of conflicts,' Deleuze argues, 'Bene proposes the *presence* of variation' (ibid.; my emphasis): an example of how theatre can help us to enlist in the revolutionary process Deleuze calls becoming-minor.

From a Deleuzian perspective, Lavaudant's practice is revolutionary because, like Bene's, it allows theatre 'to construct in some way, a figure of the minority consciousness as each one's potential. To render a potentiality present and actual' (ibid.: 254). For Deleuze, the suppression of difference or the failure to affirm presence as *perpetual variation* is a political as well as an aesthetic problem. The affirmation of difference is his overarching value – be it in philosophy, literature, science, politics or theatre. By entering into a becoming in the event of theatre, we are expressing a solidarity with those who are constituted as 'the minority' under majority rule. Like Lavaudant's minorations of language and role, their becomings and our own are not 'deviations from a norm' but affirmations of the difference in life.

Notes

1. I would like to express my gratitude to Juliette Caron from the archives at the Théâtre national de l'Odéon in Paris for providing me with the video documentation of the 2004 performance of *La Rose et la hache*.
2. Examples include theatre maker Jean Jourdheuil, whose productions since the 1960s have been greatly influenced by Marxist philosophy. In addition, he has created a production based around texts by Michel Foucault, *Michel Foucault: Choses dites choses vues* (*Michel Foucault: Things Said Things Seen*, 2004). Alain Badiou is another example: he is both a world renowned philosopher, and a prolific playwright. For a long meditation on the subject, see Denis Guenoun (2009).
3. Deleuze uses the term 'difference in itself' to invoke a concept of difference that does not derive from the comparison of identities. For Deleuze, there is not a world of permanent presences underpinning the differences between

substances or physical systems; what there is is difference as a kind of chaos or 'virtually existent pure duration' that generates the appearance of permanence and presence (May, 2003: 147). Difference is the immanent force that produces the difference between things. Alternatively, one might describe Deleuze's philosophy of difference as an ontology of perpetual variation, in which ceaseless change or the production of novelty is accorded ontological priority as well as aesthetic and political value.

Works cited

Bogue, Ronald (1989) *Deleuze and Guattari* (London: Routledge).

Bradby, David (2008) 'Book Review: *The Performance of Shakespeare in France since the Second World War*. By Nicole Fayard', *French Studies*, 62:1, 110–11.

Champagne, Leonora (1984) *French Theatre Experiment Since 1968* (Ann Arbor: University of Michigan Press).

Deleuze, Gilles (1994) *Difference and Repetition,* trans. Paul Patton (London: Athlone Press).

—— (1997) 'One Less Manifesto', in Timothy Murray (ed.), *Mimesis, Masochism and Mime: The Politics of theatricality in Contemporary French Thought*, trans. Timothy Murray and E. dal Molin (Michigan: University of Michigan Press), pp. 239–58.

Deleuze, Gilles and Félix Guattari (1986) *Kafka: Towards a Minor Literature*, trans. Terry Cochran (Minneapolis: University of Minnesota Press).

—— (1988) *A Thousand Plateaus: Capitalism and Schizophrenia*, trans. Brian Massumi (London: Athlone).

—— (1994) *What is Philosophy?*, trans. Graham Burchell and Janis Tomlinson (London: Verso).

Delord, Frédéric (2006) '*La Rose et la hache* [*The Rose and the Axe*], directed by Georges Lavaudant, production Odéon-Théâtre de l'Europe, Théâtre des Treize Vents, Montpellier, 12 November 2005', *Cahiers Elisabethains*, 69, 77–80.

Fayard, Nicole (2003) 'The Last Bastion of Resistance: Georges Lavaudant's *Theatrum Mundi*', *Contemporary Theatre Review*, 13:3, 37–46.

—— (2004) 'A Hybrid Shakespeare: The Shifting Frontiers of Georges Lavaudant's Theatre', in Yvette Rocheron and Christopher Rolfe (eds), *Shifting Frontiers of France and Francophony* (Bern: Peter Lang), pp. 325–36.

—— (2006) *The Performance of Shakespeare in France since the Second World War* (Lewiston, Queenston and Lampeter: Edwin Mellen Press).

Fortier, Mark (1996) 'Shakespeare as "Minor Theatre": Deleuze and Guattari and the Aims of Adaptation', *Mosaic*, 29:1, 1–18.

Genoun, Denis (2009) *Livraison et délivrance : théâtre, politique et philosophie* (Paris: Belin).

Lavaudant, Georges, F. Darge and B. Salino (2006) 'Mettre un peu de mineur dans le major', *Le Monde*, special supplement on the Odéon, 26 April, p. 4.

Marranca, Bonnie (1977) *The Theatre of Images* (New York: PAJ).

—— (1984) *Theatrewritings* (New York: PAJ).

May, Todd (2003) 'When is a Deleuzian Becoming?', *Continental Philosophy Review*, 36:2, 139–53.

Zepke, Stephen (2005) *Art as Abstract Machine: Ontology and Aesthetics in Deleuze and Guattari* (London: Routledge).

8
Théâtre du Grabuge: Ethics, Politics and Community[1]

Bérénice Hamidi-Kim

Since the term *théâtre populaire* entered the cultural lexicon towards the end of the nineteenth century, French theatre has been publicly charged to act as an agent of and for greater democracy. However, what democracy actually means in this context has been repeatedly questioned, with all parties concerned (government ministers, artistic directors and theatre makers) arguing fiercely over the best way to define it and to proceed. Whereas artists such as Romain Rolland and Armand Gatti advocated a form of people's theatre that would lead to a political revolution, others such as Firmin Gémier, Jean Vilar and, more recently, Ariane Mnouchkine have pursued a different objective: namely, to bring together and reunite all the sections of French society in or around a common stage. At a time when the economic gap between rich and poor in France is widening, and a vociferous and aggressive debate over what constitutes French national identity is on the governmental agenda, a number of artists persist in their attempts to realize the utopian aims of *théâtre populaire* with refreshed methods (see David Bradby, Chapter 1 in this volume). This chapter, based on the study of the *Passerelles* by Théâtre du Grabuge, purports to analyse one such attempt.

Two citations

Théâtre du Grabuge's on-going and extended theatre project, the *Passerelles* (*Bridges*), frequently begins with a citation from *The Inoperative Community* by the philosopher Jean-Luc Nancy, and ends with another from the essay 'Political Loss' by the writer Marguerite Duras:

> We know the scene: there is a gathering, and someone is telling a story. We do not yet know whether the people gathered together

111

form an assembly, if they are a horde or a tribe. But we call them brothers and sisters because they are gathered together and because they are listening to the same story. [...] They were not assembled like this before the story; the recitation has gathered them together. Before, they were dispersed, [...] shoulder-to-shoulder, working with and confronting one another without recognizing one another. But one day, one of them stood still, or perhaps he turned up, as though returning from a long absence or a mysterious exile. He stopped at a particular place, to the side of but in view of the others, on a hillock or by a tree that had been struck by lightning, and he started the narrative that brought together the others.

(Nancy, 1991: 43)

For a lot of people, an apolitical attitude mostly means a loss, or ideological void. To me, political loss is first and foremost a loss of self, a loss of one's anger as well as one's sweetness, of one's ability to hate as much as one's ability to love; a loss of one's recklessness as much as one's moderation, a loss of excess as well as restraint, the loss of folly, naïvety, courage and cowardice; the loss of one's dread of the world as well as one's trust in it, the loss of tears and joy alike.

(Duras, 1980: 15–16; my translation)

The two citations reveal much about the aesthetic aims and political goals of Théâtre du Grabuge. Whereas Nancy's comments suggest that public acts of story-telling – that is to say, theatre events – have the capacity to transform scattered individuals into a united community, Duras's statement implies that an 'apolitical attitude' is akin to existential depression. In the texts from which these quotations derive, Nancy and Duras both take as their starting point the disappearance of community and the erosion of political hope that the 'death' of communism has brought in its wake. This is the socio-political context in which Géraldine Bénichou, the artistic director and founding member of Théâtre du Grabuge, chooses to situate her work. She does so, as I proceed to argue, in the hope that theatre may constitute a tentative response to a need that traditional politics is unable to meet, in terms of ideology and established political party networks. According to Bénichou, theatre has the capacity to keep certain radical elements of the supposedly defunct Marxist project from vanishing altogether, such as, for instance, promoting a sense of radical equality, and investing in a necessarily internationalist vision of revolutionary change. However, despite these utopian ideals, Bénichou also realizes that in France a preliminary pre-political step is required before more inclusive forms of democracy can emerge. For Théâtre du Grabuge, this is focused, above all else, on disclosing an *a priori* sense of social solidarity between different social classes, marginalized ethnic and religious groups and disenfranchised individuals. As Nancy remarks, the very notion of politics presupposes that one is 'already engaged in the community, that is to say, undergoing in whatever manner, the experience of community as communication' (1991: 41).

The *Passerelles*: towards a 'theatre without walls'

Théâtre du Grabuge, which in English translates roughly as 'Theatre of Havoc', was founded in 1996, and since then has been under the artistic directorship of Bénichou. The company's name as well as its motto, 'pour un théâtre sans murs' ('for a theatre without walls'), are significant. They imply that theatre is not a self-contained entity divorced from life, but, on the contrary, part of a larger socio-political process whose exclusions and inequalities it should seek to question and redress. Bénichou's life and career evidence the same logic: she studied directing at the Conservatoire national supérieur d'art dramatique in Paris (CNSAD), and her shows have been performed in such prestigious venues as the Théâtre de la Croix-Rousse in Lyon (where the company is based) and the renowned Théâtre national populaire (TNP) in Villeurbanne. However, from 1998 onwards, she has concentrated her energies on creating full-fledged versions of the *Passerelles*, long-term projects, developed over several months with dispossessed sections of the population who seldom, if ever, go to the theatre and/or appear on stage – immigrant workers, abused women, the homeless. Crucially, Grabuge make no distinction between conventional theatre spaces and everyday sites, and much of their work is located in shelters, hostels and asylum centres (see Chapter 12 by Susan Haedicke in this volume). This desire to open theatre up to its outside is reflected in the mission statement displayed on the company's website:

> At the crossroads between the classics and contemporary voices, in pursuit of a discourse that would be both intimate and political, the shows created by the Théâtre du Grabuge are put to the test and developed in stages and via detours, through what we now refer to as *Passerelles* [...]. The *Passerelles* are works in progress, which represent moments when our artistic desires and our creative material are being shared and put to the test. We do this outside of theatres, so

as to experience on a daily basis the necessity to steep our discourse and imagination in the everyday lives of ordinary people, taking the risk of being constantly diverted from our original intentions, of having our commitment and our words constantly questioned and our imaginative world disrupted by social realities, all the while keeping our ears open to what we may learn from this dialogue about ourselves and about others. We also do this inside theatres, attempting to discover anew the necessary role of such places, where an indispensable questioning and dialogue can be conducted between imagination and reality, between art and the city.[2]

(my translation)

This statement draws attention to the fact that the *Passerelles*, as their name suggests, seek to connect – to form a bridge – between places, people and activities that are normally kept apart: art *and* the city, artists *and* non-artists, literature *and* everyday language, social *and* artistic venues.

A common theatrical narrative

The process of making the *Passerelles* is divided into two parts, which Bénichou brings together under one heading, but which I treat separately here. I refer to the first part as 'the workshop' and to the second as 'the presentation', by which I mean a theatrical event constituting the final outcome of the work, carried out in a specific place, with specific people and in front of a specific audience. In the workshop, Bénichou 'invite[s] some people not only to listen to a story that is part of a common heritage, but also to read that story out aloud' (Bénichou in Hamidi, 2006: my translation). She always takes this story from classical literature or the Scriptures of the three main monotheistic religions. Bénichou explains the logic behind her aesthetic choices: 'Take the *Odyssey*, or Antigone's or even Abraham's story. They all sound familiar but actually are not familiar at all; they are "commonplace" in the strongest sense of the word but they are also completely forgotten' (ibid.). In so far as these narratives, as Bénichou suggests, form part of a common, but submerged, folklore or mythical substrata, familiar even to those who have never read them as works of literature, they serve to bridge the gap between theatre artists and the non-professional participants with whom she works. In 2005, an important change manifested itself in Bénichou's aesthetics. From that date onwards, participants are no longer simply instructed to read out a section from the founding narrative (the pre-existing classic or biblical text); they are now invited to write their own stories as well. These self-authored tales are designed to resonate with the initial textual inspiration for the piece and grapple with similar themes of departure and exile. In this way, all the texts included in the *Passerelles* contribute to the creation of one common overarching narrative, in which actors and participants meld voices and swap stories.

Since 2005, the aim of the *Passerelles* has been to maintain a dialogue between classical narratives and contemporary life stories. The ambition is to blend past and present, and to endow anonymous lives with a potentially epic dimension and mythical destiny. The texts produced in the course of the writing workshops are aided by professional company members who edit and help to rewrite the participants' stories. The interweaving process is a complex one, since, in addition to the writing stage conducted during the workshops, the final presentation turns the participants into narrator/actors alongside the company members. Roles are not interchangeable, however. Each *Passerelle* is managed by the company members, who differentiate between those participants who walk up to the lectern and read part of the classical story, and those, by contrast, who perform one of the autobiographical texts. Theatrical labour in the *Passerelles* is thus both divided and shared: workshop participants perform classical texts; read out their life stories; and/or narrate those of other participants.

Founding a common place/creating common experience

Besides those involved in the workshop, the spectators attending the presentations comprise friends and relatives of the cast and company, and participants from former *Passerelles*. Importantly, these audience members are not, as in conventional theatre, simply permitted to watch the performance; they are asked to participate actively in creating a new one. For example, a spectator who has arrived to watch the latest presentation, but who took part in a previous workshop, may well find her/himself reading out her/his own text, although s/he did not take part in the preparatory workshop for the current presentation. A practice like this takes the interweaving of voices one step further, and Bénichou often integrates tales from former workshops into the latest presentation. By keeping the narratives circulating from voice to voice and presentation to presentation, Bénichou ensures the creation of a truly common narrative and of a common good, especially as the audience of the *Passerelles* is a deliberately heterogeneous group without a common culture, collective memory or shared sense of identity.

When I invited Bénichou to contribute to a practice workshop for third-year students on a Theatre Studies degree at the Université de Lyon 2 in 2005, she accepted, on the condition that the workshop would constitute both an introduction to the *Passerelles*, and a contribution to a new *Passerelle*.[3] In keeping with the usual practice of the *Passerelles*, the writing workshop took the theme of departure as its starting point. This gave rise to tales of geographical journeying, as some of my students shared their (more) privileged experiences of travel with other participants who were immigrants or refugees. As well as literal accounts of journeys taken in the past, other texts produced in the workshops at Lyon 2 were more personal and metaphorical, and recounted what happened to participants during (and not before) their experiences in the *Passerelles*.

One of the students, Amélie X, happened to read a text written by Rokia Y, a young Malian woman who had sought refuge in France to escape a forced marriage. Her path had crossed that of the Grabuge during the long making process for the *Passerelle* entitled *Dis-moi pourquoi dans le secret tu soupires et tu pleures?* (*Tell Me Why You Secretly Sigh and Cry*, inspired by Homer's *Odyssey*), which was finally staged in Eragny-sur-Oise, a north-western suburb of Paris in spring 2006. Rokia had to overcome two major obstacles. First, her aunt, with whom she was staying – and who seemed to regard her more as a maid than as a niece – was reluctant to let her take part in an activity that Rokia had chosen to do for herself. Second, Rokia was pensive because she feared the hostile reactions that her life-story might prompt in the workshop process itself. Other participants in the *Passarelle*, for instance, regarded pre-arranged marriages as perfectly acceptable. In order to calm her anxiety, company members did everything they could to put her at ease; and from the start of the process, she was seated next to an old Chilean political refugee, who took her under his wing and stood by her side while she read out her narrative:

Sunday in Bamako, the day set for the wedding / That Sunday in Bamako, on the day set for... / Me / I left on the Saturday to escape that Sunday / Me / I do not want to talk about what took place before / I do not want to utter the word ...: At home, they are saying that I brought shame on the family name / And maybe I do feel slightly ashamed today / But NO! / One cannot waste one's life like that / Even if they call me a witch now / That is why I came here / I do not look at anyone / I never laugh / Before, I used to fear that they would send for me / Now, I wish I could talk to my mother / Just one word / I wish she could begin to agree with me / Give me some advice / Inquire after me / Say: I think of you / Ask : Are you all right? / Some day, my mother is going to talk to me again / Some day, I will be able to return to Mali to see her / That old gentleman who wanted to [...] me / I wish I could see him and shout at him until I had no strength left in me.

(My translation)[4]

This is the very text that Amélie X read out, and which upset her so much that it disrupted her attempts to narrate her own story:

Whenever I read out Rokia's text, I start crying / I've tried and tried again / I still cry / When I lend my voice to her words, I truly become her / I become her suffering / I get separated from my own mother / It's a new situation / I do not want to say this / To experience this / It is the word / mother / which triggers / the first jolt / Something is the matter with my throat / I do not want / To cry yet another time / I start struggling / My mother is dead / For a moment, my mother is dead / A lump in my stomach, spasms / I try to utter the words / About her mother, about my mother / in vain / Little by little / I actually undertake her own journey / I give way to her / And by so doing, it is a part of myself I leave behind / Her voice, her life.

(My translation)[5]

Amélie X cried, not because Rokia's predicament reminded her of any situation she had personally experienced, but because, for a short while at least, she put herself in the Malian's shoes. A life experience was shared through the mediation of words; and a further link was forged when Amélie read her response aloud during the presentation of the *Passerelle*. Amélie's text, suffused with the strong affect pervading Rokia's tale, struck an emotional chord in the spectators and allowed them to open themselves to the experiences of others (see Chapter 15 by Nigel Stewart in this volume).

The efficiency – the performance efficacy – of the *Passerelles* lies precisely in their intense emotional power, in their capacity, that is, for provoking empathy. It is quite common for those who attend the workshops or the presentations to cry, which might suggest a comparison with art therapy. The comparison holds in so far as each participant is affected emotionally. However, the stakes are ultimately very different. First because theatre is not considered by the Grabuge as a therapeutic tool *per se*; and second, because the emotion released in each individual exposes that individual to the collective, thus making all those present part of a potentially political community rooted in affect rather than in identity. For Théâtre du Grabuge, to experience the affective ties that bind us to the other in such a sensory manner permits people to grasp, intellectually and emotionally, the necessity for (re)building the lost fraternity to which both Nancy and Duras allude in their respective critiques of the current *status quo*. To use Nancy's terms, theatre provides a new foundation for what one might call a (pre)political community, that is to say, a community based on *a priori* emotional bonds permitting what he calls 'an originary or ontological sociality' to emerge (1991: 28).

A theatrical assembley

Grabuge's determination to allow different groups and individuals to come together in what Nancy would call an 'impossible community' is diametrically opposed to the French republican model of integration. Unlike its multiculturalist counterpart, the United Kingdom, France has always striven to make ethnic and religious minorities renounce their differences and so impose a monolithic and abstract identity on all French citizens (for a similar critique, see Chapter 10 by Elaine Aston in this volume). In recent years, the republican model has broken down, and French society is now increasingly characterized by grave tensions between groups entrenched in their own jealously guarded notions of identity. In response to the increasing spectre of social and ethnic fragmentation, Grabuge uses the stage as a space to create an alternative assembly of people. This assembly is one that gives tangible shape to the endless gathering, substitution and circulation of words and places without ignoring the differences between individuals. The participants stand in front of lecterns in a semi-circle, facing an audience seated in an identical fashion. The construction of this circular space facilitates the alternation of places and roles. Every person is potentially an 'active participant' and can assume the position of either performer or spectator. The spatial exchange between participants and audience members embodies, in the most concrete way possible, the democratic quality of the *Passerelle*. Music, too, contributes to the production of 'equality in difference'. Whereas the texts are mostly written in French and then interspersed with words belonging to the multiple languages of the participants, the interludes between the episodes are sung in Arabic by the singer and musician, Salah Gaoua. The 'global language' produced conveys differences, while at the same time arousing feelings of fraternity and togetherness.

This linguistic interweaving is evident, for example, in *Sarah, Agar et les autres* (*Sarah, Agar and the Others*) which took place in Fourvière, a suburb in the west of Lyon in 2005. The text in this *Passerelle* was created from extracts of the Bible, the Torah and the Koran, and focused, specifically, on the story of Sarah, and Abraham, 'father to a multitude of nations'. Explaining the origin of this *Passerelle*, Bénichou states:

> It originated from the fact that I started rereading the Bible. Like everyone else, I find that religious issues are becoming a real nuisance; one can't even talk about them. Duras was right when she observed that political ideologies were being superseded by religious ones. [...] Take the Bible, the Torah and the Koran. All the stories in these books are being used essentially as propaganda, as weapons of war, so I feel it is a good thing to reread these texts and re-establish an intimate relationship with them, to find out what light they can throw on today's issues.
>
> (in Hamidi-Kim, 2006; my translation)

The decision to concentrate on the story of Sarah and Abraham is highly significant, since it belongs to that part of the Book of Genesis which is common to both Christianity and Judaism. That is to say, to the time before the seeds of religious division were planted, which subsequently led to the establishment of what Bénichou refers to as 'today's murderous frontiers' (ibid.). Bénichou is fully aware of the ecumenical activism which characterizes the *Passerelles*, and which can be accounted for by the social background of the participants, as well as by the venues which host them. Her objective is to produce a community that transcends 'ethnicity', a term that Bénichou uses, but not without reservations:

> Personally, I have few dealings with ethnic communities; this is more a phrase used on television. As for me, I deal with people. What lies at the bottom of my work is my interest in these dwelling-places, these shelters housing people who have nothing in common apart from their homelessness, who are thrown together but come from very different walks of life, and have very different interests. [...] The whole point is to constitute a chorus of residents who would be willing to take part in the show. To me, a chorus is by nature a reminder of Greek tragedy: representatives of the city going on stage. This is something I have been working on for a very long time.
>
> (in Hamidi-Kim, 2006; my translation)

For Bénichou, the chorus is the theatrical fulfilment of a social ideal, since it produces an assembly from people who have 'nothing in common' (Lingis, 1994). By constituting a chorus, her aim is allow the participants, many of whom are alienated from other people, to become united by virtue of their participation in a collective project, capable of both respecting and transcending potentially disruptive differences. As a result of the relatively long-term workshop process, each *Passarelle* is both an artistic and political event. Through a succession of shared experiences (the hours spent together in the workshops, the stage-fright experienced before the presentation, the hand-shaking that takes place at the end of the performance, and so on) the participants become a tangible federation of individuals.

The *Passerelle* which has arguably had the greatest impact, because it was spread over the longest period of time, was *Dis-moi pourquoi dans le secret tu soupires et tu pleures?* Its presentation ended with a dialogue that borrowed its language and format from a celebrated passage in *The Odyssey*. Bénichou read out the following question, 'Foreigner, tell us by what name your parents used to address you at home / Tell us what your land, your city, your people are.' In response, the participants, along with the company members and local residents, proclaimed their names as Ulysses does in Homer's text 'I am... I was born in... I am a noble citizen of...' (my translation). Each person was free to mention only her/his forename or surname and to state what meant most to her/him in terms of belonging, proclaiming themselves 'noble citizen of France' or 'noble citizen of Éragny'. In this suburb, with a large immigrant population, few people felt they belonged locally, even less nationally. When it was Rokia Y's turn to proclaim herself as 'noble citizen', her words took on a special significance, since at the time, she had not yet become a fully legalized French citizen. The sense of belonging created by the *Passerelle* not only anticipated her actual French citizenship, indeed it may have made it possible. She received her identity papers a few weeks after the presentation, and immediately telephoned the Grabuge to express her gratitude, both for the letter the company had written to the town hall on her behalf, and for the opportunity they had given her to take part in a collective project. This *Passerelle* also had a strong impact on the other participants who, in its wake, decided to found an organization called The Noble Citizens of Éragny. The very existence of this association highlights the determination of the participants to keep alive the community (or what Bénichou might call the chorus) created by their work.

Conclusion

By developing an original form of participatory performance, rooted in the realities of twenty-first-century life in France, Théâtre du Grabuge aims to achieve two primary objectives. On the one hand, they seek to transform isolated individuals or groups into a tangible community in the here and now; and on the other, they attempt to provide an alternative foundation for a new political community to come. In this respect, the company, as I mentioned in my introduction, is engaged in practice that synthesizes the two different traditions of *théâtre populaire* in France (one, resistant; the other, revolutionary). They try to achieve this double goal by insisting upon the *a priori* emotional bonds and empathetic ties that prefigure the practice of politics itself, and by allowing participants to experience an impossible sense of 'togetherness in difference' through the processes *and* event of theatre.

Notes

1. I should like to thank Théâtre du Grabuge for the right to cite unpublished material. The names of the two young women mentioned in the chapter have been changed to respect their privacy.
2. See http://www.theatredugrabuge.com (accessed October 2009).
3. All the students participated in the *Passerelle*, entitled *Sarah, Agar et les autres*, staged at the Gallo-Roman Museum in Fourvière (October 2005), and several of them took part in the *Passerelle* staged at the homeless shelter at the Riboud Hôtel-Social in Lyon later that year.
3. Unpublished Performance Text.
4. Unpublished Performance Text.
5. Unpublished Performance Text.

Works cited

Duras, Marguerite (1980) 'La perte politique', extract from *Les Yeux verts*, special issue of *Les Cahiers du Cinéma*, 312 (June), 15–16.

Hamidi-Kim, Bérénice (2006) 'Unpublished Interview with Géraldine Bénichou'.

Lingis, Alphonso (1994) *The Community of Those That Have Nothing in Common* (Indianapolis: Indiana University Press).

Nancy, Jean-Luc (1991) *The Inoperative Community*, trans. Peter Connor (Minneapolis: University of Minnesota Press).

Théâtre du Grabuge (2005) *Sarah, Agar et les autres*. Unpublished Performance Text.

—— (2006) *Dis-moi pourquoi dans le secret tu soupires et tu pleures?* Unpublished Performance Text.

9
Amateurism and the 'DIY' Aesthetic: Grand Magasin and Phillipe Quesne

Chloé Déchery

It feels good. It's astonishing. It's a little distressing. It's all around you, you don't really know what's underneath... a shot comes straight at you [...] everything is possible, you know. You don't really know were you are. I like that.[1]

On the margins

The work of Grand Magasin and Philippe Quesne, like that of other contemporary French artists such as Jérôme Bel, Xavier Le Roy, Yves-Noël Genod, Loïc Touzé and Joris Lacoste, is located in an artistic field that defies disciplinary definition. From roughly the start of the 1990s, each of these solo artists and companies has, in turn, abandoned classical dance and text-based theatre in order to create new choreographies and dramaturgies that are no longer centred on perfecting the technique of the dancing body or in creating dramatic conflict. For them, the key is to use the immediacy of performance to undertake an acute observation of reality in all its heterogeneity and brute materiality. This exploratory work which treats reality as an archaeological site discloses the presence of 'things' whose proximity, everydayness and banality usually prevent them from being seen. In *Jérôme Bel* by Jérôme Bel (1995), the body is revealed in its most prosaic form – through the display of skin, folds, orifices and hair; in Xavier Le Roy's *Produit de circonstances* (*Product of Circumstance*, 1999), small-scale biographical anecdotes triumph over spectacular events and moments of crisis; and in *Purgatoire* (*Purgatory*, 2007), Joris Lacoste explores how the sometimes risky co-presence of performer and spectator problematizes the vicarious effects of fiction.

Of course, one can find the same processes and strategies used in Dadaism, Artaud's Theatre of Cruelty, the Happenings of the 1950s and performance art of the 1970s. However, if Grand Magasin refers to Richard Foreman and Stuart Sherman, and Philippe Quesne invokes the ghost of John Cage in *L'Effet de Serge* (*The Serge Effect*, 2007), their shows are primarily designed to engage directly with the facticity of the contemporary world. In keeping with this avant-garde heritage, the performances created by this new generation of French artists are defined by an anti-spectacular aesthetic which gives rise to a non-mimetic theatre, devoid of dramatic characters and story. In the work of Grand Magasin and Philippe Quesne, all the elements common to post-dramatic theatre can be found: the rejection of dramatic illusionism in favour of a theatre of events; the replacement of the fictional character with the presence of the performer; and the replacement of theatre skills and techniques (corporeal and verbal) with everyday actions which remain resolutely non-dramatic and low-key.

Unlike some of their contemporaries, however, Grand Magasin and Vivarium Studio, the company founded by Philippe Quesne, have always been – and still remain – on the margins of conventional theatre in France.[2] After finishing his degree at the École nationale supérieur des arts décoratifs (ENSAD) in Paris, Philippe Quesne, for instance, worked as scenographer in theatre and opera; and Pascale Murtin and François Hiffler, the two founding members of Grand Magasin, initially trained, at the start of the 1980s, as dancers. The third member, Bettina Atala, joined the company in 2001. The two companies work in a craftsman-like way, and always use the same small team of loyal collaborators, honing persistent questions and stubborn obsessions from show to show. The process can be painstakingly slow, and is composed of planning meetings, discussions, debates, background research and workshop/rehearsals. Importantly, there is no pressure to work according to the timetable of 'industrial' theatre making, which demands that a whole show be created within six to eight weeks (see Chapter 6 by Robert Cantarella in this volume).

Although Grand Magasin and Philippe Quesne have been critically acclaimed and their productions programmed in international theatre venues and festivals (notably in Paris, at the Georges Pompidou Centre and the Ménagerie de Verre; in New York at PS122 and at St Ann's Warehouse), they are committed outsiders, proud to engage in what the French art critic Paul Ardenne has called a resistant 'périphérisme' ('peripheralism'). According to Ardenne, this is defined by the attempt 'to reject, at any cost, integration into the art system by remaining on the margins, and by working on the periphery without necessarily seeking to make the latter into a new centre' (Ardenne, 1999: 30). The result of this strategy, Ardenne concludes, is that 'the very notion of the artistic periphery, so cherished by the classical avant-garde, is no longer thought of as the starting point from which to launch the conquest [of society]' (ibid.). In contradistinction, the peripheral artist is now figured as someone who engages in a permanent, but subtle critique of the established order, from a position that is always at odds with dominant trends and accepted ideas. S/he exists as a stubborn outsider.

In line with Ardenne's comments, it comes as no surprise to find Philippe Quesne and Grand Magasin refusing the trappings of authority and rejecting the roles of specialist and expert. Quesne routinely invites amateurs, local rock groups and the general public to participate in his performances, which raucously explode all notions of professionalism and mastery; and Grand Magasin proclaim their amateurism and independence from well-established discourses and faddish schools of thought. According to Pascale Murtin and François Hiffler:

> We don't have any special skills or rely on any particular method of training, we don't come from a theatrical background and we have never been to theatre school. We know a little about dance, and nothing about cinema [...] but all these forms are models and sources that inspire us and which we borrow from, not necessarily naïvely, but clumsily. Yet we are very aware that we will never be able to compete with them. We relate to them in an entirely 'negative' way. It's precisely because theatre exists that it enables us to not care about it; we try to make theatre without being able to really do it properly.
>
> (in Déchery, 2009)

In complete disregard of conventions

If Grand Magasin are reluctant to call their work theatre, it is to escape from the conventions and rules inherent to traditional art forms and established canons. Mixing allusions and quotations, and borrowing as much from fine art practice as from cinema, the company uses a deceptive strategy that allows it to flirt with and subvert the expectations usually associated with the theatrical form: 'The approach we adopt is a little deceptive. For instance, people who come to the shows expecting to see a piece of theatre will only observe performers stuttering and performing blandly. We've never been able to make a piece of theatre, because that requires training and a story to tell' ((in Déchery, 2009). The knowingly naïve discourse and proclaimed amateurism of Grand Magasin are tactics that provide the company with the space to experiment. Not having to justify themselves in relation to a potentially crippling and intimidating list of historical predecessors, they are free to create 'the types of performance that we wanted to experience but were never able to see' (ibid.). The core of Grand Magasin's unique aesthetic is expressed in their refreshingly non-pretentious attitude to performance making:

> From 1982 onwards, thanks to, and in spite of, an almost complete lack of knowledge about theatre, dance and music, we managed to create shows that we only ever dreamt of seeing. Luckily, they were successful and they moved us. Our ambition today still revolves around the possibility that other people might share our enthusiasms.
>
> (ibid.)

But if the stated objective of the company is 'to create something from nothing and in total ignorance of existing models' (ibid.), it is nevertheless true, because of a long experience spanning more than 25 years, that their performances demonstrate a certain *savoir faire* and bear witness to a confident and eclectic scenic practice. And here one arrives at the irresolvable paradox confronting Grand Magasin: how can one continue to make performances and, at the same time, claim to be virtually ignorant about the processes of doing it? According to Grand Magasin, the artist ought to seek to reinvent, constantly, her/his initial state of innocence. The more the artist gains in experience by making shows, the more s/he needs to maintain her/his original sense of not-knowing: 'As time passes, it's difficult to pass yourself off as naïve. But a state of open-minded ignorance is easier to maintain than pretending to be naïve, because all you have to do is not to learn certain things in any depth, and always to leave it a bit vague. You're always looking to learn something, but not enough to be an expert in it' (ibid.). The strategies the company members use in order to maintain this productive amateurism consist essentially in setting themselves impossible tasks and unattainable objectives – for instance, understanding mathematics, learning to play a musical instrument from scratch, or staging a conventional dramatic text in an orthodox manner (which, for Grand Magasin, is not only inconceivable, but also impossible to achieve). In this way, Grand Magasin manage to retain their sense of wonder in the reality that surrounds them, and so 'never grow accustomed to the strangeness of the situations [they] find [them]selves in' (ibid.).

However, this naïvety which Grand Magasin have so assiduously cultivated is currently under threat by the radical changes that have occurred in the habits of French spectators over the past 30 years or so. In these years, contemporary mainstream theatre in France has appropriated and synthesized processes belonging to performance and experimental theatre makers. According to the theatre scholar Frédéric Maurin, these appropriations are characterized by 'the [use of] autofiction, the multi-skilled nature of the performers, and the staging of bodies that refer to themselves and do not serve any other role in the dramaturgy' (Maurin, 2008: 6). As Maurin's comments show all-too-well, a new theatre grammar has been created, and even the type of spectator who attends the productions staged in France's network of Théâtres Nationaux ('National Theatres') is familiar with it:

> The model has evolved over time and it changes at every moment. The idea of contemporary theatre evokes a whole world which is different today from what it was 20 years ago. And spectators are fully versed in its contemporary grammar: soundtracks, silences and gaps, a performance workshop in the style of Pina Bausch, collage, self-reflexivity, all of which sometimes pushes our work in the direction of more traditional theatre making.
>
> (Pascale Murtin and François Hiffler, in Déchery: 2009)

In order to remain on the periphery of a contemporary theatre tradition whose formal heritage they gently refuse, Grand Magasin create performances that allow a more simplistic and more basic level of theatricality to be reactivated. Their shows are characterized, for instance, by the strange appearance of incongruous props, off-beat costumes, dramatic dialogues, direct addresses to the audience, amateurish song and dance moves, and so on. Through the use of such theatrical and metatheatrical devices, the company's work, which often poses complex conceptual questions to do with space, perception and/or language, has an unpretentious and relaxed relationship to philosophical enquiry. Grand Magasin have no interest in psychological introspection or weighty abstraction; instead, they prefer to observe the external world, in an attempt to index reality and to startle the audience into a new awareness of the simple fact of existing. The aim is to 'manipulate knowledge', not to profess expertise (ibid.). In their work, as the name of the company suggests, reality is observed, selected, taken apart and piled up like merchandise displayed on the counter of a general store (*un grand magasin*). This way of grasping the world seeks to collect and order knowledge according to organizational principles that are found in statistics and other forms of data collection. One thinks here of the spreadsheet, designed in the style of Mondrian, which brought the show *Les Déplacements du problème* (*Displacing the Problem*, 2009) to an end. This hands-on approach is very similar to the process described by the French curator and art theorist Nicolas Bourriaud in *Postproduction*:

> Artists today program forms more than they compose them: rather than transfigure a raw element [...], they remix available forms and make use of data. In a universe of products for sale, preexisting forms, signals already emitted, buildings already constructed, paths marked out by their predecessors, artists no longer consider the artistic field (and here one could add television, cinema, or literature) as a museum containing works that must be cited or 'surpassed', as the modernist ideology of originality would have it, but as so many storehouses filled with tools that should be used, stockpiles of data to manipulate and present.
>
> (2005: 17)

Reflecting Bourriaud's ideas, Grand Magasin often borrow terms from *scientific discourses*, playfully massage pre-existing data, engage in non-conclusive experiments, and work with faulty machinery. The objects and gestures that they represent on stage retain their simple, banal and prosaic qualities, and invite the spectator to reconsider the everydayness of the world which surrounds her/him beyond the walls of the theatre. Thus, there are always two levels, two fields of investigation in their work: an existential level, which focuses on everyday objects and encourages spectators to question 'how they might lead their lives' (ibid.); and a theatrical level, which constantly critiques what is being represented on stage.

In direct contact with reality

Philippe Quesne's company Vivarium Studio is equally concerned to highlight the strangeness of everyday existence. Their performances focus on a segment of reality which they scrutinize, pull apart and then reassemble poetically. At all times, the guiding principle is to capture reality in its most prosaic forms: such as the monotonous series of Sundays in *L'Effet de Serge*, where we watch Serge walking about in his apartment, turning on the television, eating crisps and pouring himself a glass of wine. In terms of dramatic action and text, this is theatre at zero degree, a theatre where next to nothing happens and where everything appears random – a car breaks down in a snowy landscape, a man orders a pizza over the telephone, and so on.

To grasp the mundanity of what it means to be in the world, Quesne shapes his dramaturgy from an eclectic mix of found objects and factual documents (anonymous interviews and witness accounts belonging to dentists, model makers or teachers), newspaper articles, poems, popular songs and word lists.

The name of Quesne's company, Vivarium Studio, is apt. In his shows, spectators are encouraged to observe a cross-section of life which he has put under his microscope: 'I assemble scenographic devices which are both theatre sets, and workshops: "vivariums" for the study of human microcosms' (Quesne, 2007b: 5). In *L'Effet de Serge,* for instance, the audience is invited to share the intimacy of Serge's apartment and to gaze, voyeuristically, at the micro-events of his life (someone knocks at the door, Serge hits his head on the wall and suffers from a nose-bleed, and so on). However, at the very back of the stage, an enigmatic off-stage world, glimpsed through a glazed plexiglass window, is hinted at. When a car appears in the performance, it seems as if reality, in all its quotidian beauty, is intruding into the theatre space itself (see the illustration on the front cover of this volume). The rectangular plexiglass window, set into a chipboard wall, frames reality, and so becomes a kind of frame-within-a-frame, magnifying the banality *and* mystery of existence with its unpredictable and enigmatic shifts of matter. At the same time, the window also doubles, discreetly, as a see-through partition which connects the laboratory animal (the performer) with the observer–spectator. Quesne explains: 'My principle of working is to utilize the stage to look at the world sideways on. This obliqueness creates a sense of distance and allows me to question the processes of representation. The spectators are positioned as observers, and invited to act as entomologists' (Quesne [with Pascale Gateau], 2007c).

From bric to brac

In Quesne's performances, worn-out and reassuringly familiar objects such as a ping-pong table, tarpaulin, a remote control helicopter and car headlights are animated with magical properties. In *L'Effet de Serge,* the eponymous character, a kind of minor artist-figure, presents himself as an amateur inventor, a sort of 'conjuror'. Every Sunday, he invites his friends to attend a series of mini-performances that last between one and three minutes, and which provide him with a platform for displaying his most absurd inventions. This device allows Quesne to expose the underside of his own theatrical machine, which is run on a tight

budget, and whose exploration of 'poverty' is based as much on necessity as on political choice.

Despite sharing a similar interest in 'poverty', Quesne's 'do-it-yourself'
aesthetic has little in common with Grotowski's mystical and commu-
nitarian notion of poor theatre. Quesne's performances constantly draw
attention to the financial aspects of producing a show: the same set is
recycled, and objects and elements, such as the smoke machine and
Hermès, a black labrador belonging to a member of the company, turn up
again and again. Each new performance starts with the final image of the
previous one, and together this contributes towards creating a coherent
and largely self-referential theatrical system. By doing this, Quesne subtly
critiques those cultural agendas and policies which simultaneously frame
and condition contemporary art making. His aim is to attack the unethical
and the ecologically dubious logic of a French state-funded system that
invests huge amounts of money and energy into producing avant-garde
spectacles. In this context, it is surely worth pointing out that the title
of the show, *L'Effet de Serge*, is a pun on the French, *l'effet de serre*, which
translates as the 'greenhouse effect'. Quesne explains:

> I think that the apparent poverty of the material we use speaks
> directly about the world we live in. A show is ephemeral, and I can
> never imagine building a set whose costs would be more than our
> wage bill. Besides, recycling scenographic elements is one of my artis-
> tic principles: in *L'Effet de Serge* and in *La Mélancolie des dragons*, there
> is the same smoke machine, tree branches, car, and bay window that
> I used in my previous shows.
>
> (Quesne [with Pascale Gateau], 2007c)

At the same time, Quesne also pokes fun at the lack of ambition and
short-termism which all too often undermine the work of contemporary artists who, in France, are forced to comply with the demands of
government funding. Tellingly, Serge's mini-performances were inspired
by an actual incident relating to the company's attempt to obtain financial backing for the production. In 2007, for its twentieth anniversary,
the Ménagerie de Verre, a performance space in Paris, commissioned
from several artists a series of one-minute shows to be performed in
front of a team of financial backers and producers sent from the Mairie
de Paris and the French Ministry of Culture. By referencing this incident, but in such a way that the process was placed *en abyme*, *L'Effet
de Serge* managed to create a critical but playful distance from its own
funding context.

The artist as explorer

For Philippe Quesne, the artist is, by turns, an inventor, an astronaut, a designer of public parks.[3] He takes samples, wanders about and experiments, in the same way as Serge, who dabbles in pyrotechnics, in order to delight his friends with his weirdly named mini-performances: 'Rolling Effect with Handel' or 'Laser Effect with John Cage'.

The same preoccupation with experimentation and exploration is found in the work of Grand Magasin. The performers adopt the role(s) of enlightened amateurs, curious and enthusiastic philosophers of everyday life who question their perception of the world. In *Panorama commenté (Panorama with Commentary*, 2005) and *Voyez-vous ce que je vois (Can You See What I See*, 2003), the company explored the faculty of sight; and in *Les Déplacements du problème*, the emphasis was on hearing. These performances have a philosophical bias, since they interrogate whether two people can ever see the same thing, or if it is possible to understand each other. In these pieces, the difference between the quest for knowledge and theatrical *savoir faire* is clearly articulated, and the stage becomes a site for pedagogical and poetic experience. In the first instance, the spectator usually learns something that has nothing necessarily to do with the theatrical sphere; in the second, s/he is able to apply that knowledge to the theatre-making process. By questioning what vision means, for instance, the spectator is better equipped to observe what is happening on the stage. By questioning what s/he is hearing, s/he sharpens, in a process of self-reflection, her/his capacities as a spectator. Accordingly, Grand Magasin offer the audience tools to understand and follow their theatre-making process. But by doing this in a theatre, and not in a classroom or in a text book, they encourage the audience to become self-conscious about how it relates to the performance. The audience is invited to reflect on the aesthetic contract that makes theatre possible – that is to say, the mutual pact made between stage and auditorium concerning the supposedly unproblematic and objective reality of what is being represented. By addressing issues around communication and perception, Grand Magasin reassess the conditions that are necessary for a live event to take place.

For Grand Magasin and Philippe Quesne, performance becomes a matrix for a new type of artistic and theatrical pedagogy. This has little to do with using theatre as a vehicle for illustrating pre-existing ideas or concepts; rather, the aim is to create a specific knowledge transaction which takes place in the space between actors and spectators. According to Quesne, 'the public becomes an audience of voyeurs able to spy on the process of art making, observing the artists like "little animals"' (in Sellars, 2007: 42). In Quesne's view, theatre is a dynamic event where mock-scientific questions are raised and tested out in front of an audience. Crucially, however, the results of these experiments are never finalized or simply given – spectators are asked to come to their own conclusions. By dismantling the 'fourth wall' and rejecting dramatic illusionism, Quesne and Grand Magasin allow the spectator to become critically aware, and so to participate actively in the artistic activity represented on stage. There is no pretence at creating a finished product. On the contrary, 'the audience has to put it all together' (ibid.: 39). Tellingly, the research and investigative work which forms a key part of their theatre-making process is put under the spotlight, and imperfections, faults and accidents become the signs of a new sort of artistic integrity. Quesne explains: 'I have always found the theatre completely idiotic in its statuesque conventions of pretending to be something, or to do something. Here, there is a deliberate ambiguity: has the piece begun or not? Are we seeing people rehearse something, or are we watching a series of failed actions? People failing, things not working' (ibid.: 423). The logic of Quesne's aesthetic is visible, too, in Grand Magasin's *Le 5ème forum international du cinéma d'entreprise* (*The 5th International Business/Corporate Film Forum*, 2004), a show where they laid bare the scenic and narrative choices they discarded while devising their show, before recycling them in the final piece. In this production, all the errors and stumblings that invariably inform any devised show were valued as things in themselves and formed part of the performance itself. Nothing was discarded.

This leads me, finally, to address a question that has been haunting this chapter for some time now: what is the political significance of these theatres? Distancing themselves from iconic political theatre makers, such as Armand Gatti and Ariane Mnouchkine, Grand Magasin and Philippe Quesne adopt a deceptive strategy, which abandons a discourse of knowledge for a theatre practice which, little by little, becomes an exercise in personal know how for the audience. By relying on what the philosopher Jacques Rancière calls the 'equality of intelligences' (1991: 38), their performances are not experienced as heavy-handed examples of didacticism; rather, like the work of Xavier Le Roy and Jérôme Bel (see Bojana Cvejic, Chapter 14, and Augusto Corrieri, Chapter 16, in this volume), they establish a concrete relationship with the spectators who witness their explorations. Thus, the theatre event is lived as a moment of common discovery, in which knowledge is shared and developed step-by-step. The time of performance becomes a time for research, a modest apprenticeship in an age of all-too-easy spec-tacular gratification. Because the hierarchical relationship separating actors from spectators has been dismantled, the spectator is figured as someone who postulates, makes mistakes, interprets and corrects her-self/himself. Through her/his silent but attentive presence, the spectator accompanies the unassuming heroes of the show on their hesitant and muddled journeys, and is invited to share their redemptive ignorance and joyous curiosity.

For both Grand Magasin and Quesne, creating and spectating is a question of learning how to produce theatre by watching it unfold. The point is to learn by doing but, at the same time, to maintain a lucid and ultimately emancipatory ignorance. For this reason, the aesthetic poli-tics of Grand Magasin and Philipe Quesne are best described in terms of a politics of gentleness – that is to say, an oblique version of politi-cal theatre that celebrates mild-mannered eccentrics and daydreamers; that hymns the virtues of failure and clumsiness; and that teaches us to question our perception of reality, while distancing itself from all discourses of knowledge and rhetoric(s) of mastery.

Translated by Carl Lavery and Cathy Piquemal

Notes

1. *L'Effet de Serge* (2007a). Unpublished Performance Text.
2. Editors' note: Vivarium Studio performed at the Avignon Festival in 2010 with their most recent show, *Big Bang*. While this might appear to contradict the argument in this chapter by suggesting that they have abandoned the periphery and entered the theatrical mainstream, it is telling that audience reactions were mixed, and many spectators were perplexed and left angered by the work.
3. But what type of park, exactly? The litany which closes *La Mélancolie des Dragons* opens up some poetic possibilities: 'parc des dragons, parc Dürer, parc naturel, parc Citroën, parc Bruegel, parc Melancolia, parc ACDC, parc du rêve' (Unpublished Performance Text).

Works cited

Ardenne, Paul (1999) 'Expérimenter le réel, art et réalité à la fin du XXème siècle', in Paul Ardenne, Laurent Goumarre and Pascal Beausse, *Pratiques contemporai-nes, l'art comme expérience* (Paris: Dis Voir), pp. 9–58.
Bourriaud, Nicolas (2005) *Postproduction*, 2nd edn, trans. Jeanine Herman (New York: Lukas & Sternberg).
Déchery, Chloe (2009) 'Unpublished Interview with Pascale Murtin et François Hiffler'.

Maurin, Frédéric (2008) 'Excéder', *Théâtre/Public*, 190, 68–70.
Quesne, Philipp (2007a) *L'Effet de Serge*. Unpublished Performance Text.
—— (2007b) 'Dossier de presse', *L'Effet de Serge*.
—— (2007c) 'Comédies du réel', Philippe Quesne: entretien avec Pascale
Ganteau', http:// www.mouvement.net (accessed 15 November 2009).
—— (2008) *La Mélancholie des dragons*. Unpublished Performance Text.
Rancière, Jacques (1991) *The Ignorant Schoolmaster: Five Lessons in Intellectual
Emancipation*, trans. Kristin Ross (Stanford, CA: Stanford University Press).
Sellars Tom (2007) '"Flying Paths": Interview with Philippe Quesne', *Theater*,
37:1, 38–45.

Part 2

Contemporary French Performance

10
From Orlan to Bernhardt: Recycling French Feminism, Theatre and Performance

Elaine Aston

The novelist Françoise Sagan, in her experimental biography of Sarah Bernhardt – a fictional correspondence between novelist and actress – gives voice to Bernhardt's lament over the disappearance of the female diva from contemporary French theatre and performance. This is well-illustrated in the following 'letter' from Bernhardt to Sagan:

> Do you mean to say there isn't anyone among your contemporaries who would like to look like no one else on the face of the earth? No one who wants to set himself or herself apart from the common herd? Is there no one who wants to transcend the others, who wants to be adored by them, who wants to distance himself from them and be adored by them precisely because he has distanced himself from them?
>
> (Sagan, 1989: 57)

In response, Sagan confirmed what she referred to as the absence of Bernhardt's 'daughters' from the French stage (ibid.: 58), and did so by positing the 1950s as the period when the Romantic actress lineage died out.[1] It is easy to understand why. The move in France to decentralize theatre (*la décentralisation théâtrale*) in the late 1940s and 1950s, in conjunction with the politically and culturally rebellious shifts in the 1960s, created a climate conducive to the emergence of a feminist generation of theatre and performance makers who eschewed the diva star system of the great French actress tradition. There is, however, one extraordinary exception to this, one *artiste* who has quite literally taken up the idea of 'look[ing] like no one else on the face of the earth': Orlan.

Orlan is arguably the most internationally renowned of French performance artists. Her carnal art, the controversial cosmetic surgery performances that took place in the early 1990s, has been the source and topic of much academic and popular debate in France and elsewhere. Additionally, it has polarized views between those who see her work as a serious, resistant feminist intervention into an idealized Western feminine, and those who dismiss her as a not-to-be-taken-seriously, notorious freak. Looking at the range of the academic responses to Orlan that come from a number of disciplines, including visual, cultural, performance and medical studies, and the many theoretical and critical approaches and discourses through which her work is analysed and framed, I detect a notable and curious absence. While gender-body-technology interests are understandably paramount, given her art of face/body modification, contextualizations of Orlan as a French practitioner are marginal. Introducing her insightful monograph on the artist, Kate Ince writes, 'the issue of Orlan's national identity, and the French context out of which her extensive body of work has arisen, has not so far been discussed in any detail' (2000: 2). While Ince proceeds to address this lack with a brief introduction to the French context, it is, nonetheless, offered 'as a prelude to and non-determining context for' the theoretical engagement which then makes up the body of the study (ibid.). Contributing a chapter to this anthology, explicitly concerned with the political in contemporary French theatre and performance, however, I cannot relegate the French context of Orlan's work to a 'prelude', but rather need to take this up as a matter of some concern.

I propose, therefore, to reflect on the curious phenomenon of Orlan's *déracinement* as a means of complementing the theoretical lines of gender-body-technology enquiry that Orlan's artistry regularly attracts. Relocating Orlan in a French feminist context, I proceed to map an alternative genealogy for the performance of Orlan as a radical reincarnation of the histrionic body of French theatre exemplified by Sarah Bernhardt. Finally, by adopting a critical strategy of recycling French feminism, theatre and performance, I look forward to the past, that is to say, from Orlan back to Bernhardt. In doing so, I intend to focus feminist attention on the dangerous body fascism of a resurgent contemporary feminine that threatens to undermine feminist histories and achievements.

French feminist contexts

Raised in the industrial town of Saint Etienne, Orlan's career began in the post-war climate of youthful rebellion (May 1968 and all that), which heralded a ferment of feminist politics and activism in France, as it did elsewhere in Europe and in the United States. In the 1970s the Mouvement de la libération des femmes (MLF) challenged the social, cultural and political marginalization of women, while feminists working in the arts contested the male domination of cultural production and took up the subject of women's inequality in their artistic practices. Orlan's early body art provides visual registers, traces of issues and concerns that were important to the women's movement in France. The series of body-sculptures that she created in the late 1960s offers an artistic treatment of a feminist psychoanalytical theorizing of subject formation that resonated with the concerns of Psychanalyse et Politique (Psych & Po) – a group that was principally concerned with the question of women's difference and was at the centre of a huge controversy caused by its move to own, legally, the MLF title (see Duchan, 1987: 19–22). Orlan's *trousseaux* works that she began in 1968 objected to a domesticated feminine by stitching bodily and carnal fluids (menstrual blood and sperm) into virginal sheets. Likewise, her series of *MesuRages* from the mid-1970s sought to measure public spaces in Orlan-body measurements by chalking up the lines of her body and by suturing the traces of an *écriture féminine* into the corpus of an architectural masculine.

Throughout the 1980s Orlan performed the character of Saint Orlan in a number of body-multi-media works that folded the desire for women's sexual liberation into the drapery of a baroque-styled Christian iconography of saintliness, in order to refuse the archetypal splitting of the feminine into virgin and whore. While her resistant feminist practice successfully penetrated a number of national and international art institutions, galleries and festivals, Orlan's multi-media body art of the 1980s also had to contend with the mounting backlash against feminism. Although in France feminism was adopted by the State in the short-lived Ministry for Women's Rights (formed after the election of the Socialist President François Mitterand in 1981 and lasting until 1986), the effects of this were limited and problematic (Duchan, 1987: 21). Practical support for professional women artists was poor, while critical interest in their work also remained limited (see Ince, 2000: 4). In Orlan's case, despite managing to find platforms for her work in culturally prestigious venues such as the Georges Pompidou Centre in Paris, she was, as Michelle Hirschhorn observes, effectively written out of the critical and historical contextualizations of contemporary arts practice (1996: 110). The French resistance to Orlan's work can partly be accounted for in terms of the difficulty its feminist approach to and focus on identity creates for the republican modelling of citizenship that France endorses. As Lucille Cairns notes, '[f]eminism in France has never had an easy time', explaining 'that the very notion of gender politics is itself problematic in France, where there is some wariness of any form of identity politics' given the 'faith in the Republic' that enshrines the idea of equality for all citizens, irrespective of gender, race or sexual difference (2000: 85–7).

Within this context, Orlan's strategy of performing her own history, of inserting archival traces, relics of earlier pieces into new works, can be read as a resistance to her early excision from the history of contemporary performance art in France. Her cinema-styled posters of Saint Orlan from the late 1980s that advertise fake films depict images of 'Orlan before St Orlan', while the posters themselves feature later, along with other mementoes from earlier work, in the surgical performance cycle *Reincarnation of Saint Orlan* (1990–93). Equally her aesthetics of recycling constitute, as they do in the work of other French artists such as Agnès Varda and Annette Messager, an important feminist political strategy for keeping open questions of women's equality and liberation, despite the difficulty this presents in France. Concerned with creating feminist futures – 'Remember the Future' is one of Orlan's favourite mottoes (1998: 317) – Orlan is not only self-archivist but also keeper of French feminist histories.

Despite the substantial and varied body of work Orlan has created over the years, it is the relatively short phase of her surgery performances in the early 1990s that marks the ground-swell of international critical interest in her work.[2] In retrospect, this ground-swell is not surprising given the coincidence of the surgery with the 1990s performative gender turn in theory (à la Judith Butler) that seemed to offer the theoretical solution to Orlan's linguistically marked protest from 1968: *JE SUIS UNE HOMME ET UN FEMME (I AM A MAN AND A WOMAN).*[3] Moreover, her staging of an electronic body allowed her to transmit her performance locally and globally. As Ince writes of *Omnipresence*, the seventh of Orlan's surgeries, '[t]he body had become digitally saturated, thoroughly and completely mediatized by the images and electronic signals transmitting the surgery to the world beyond the operating theatre' (2000: 104).

In consequence, Orlan began to appear as an irresistible travelling companion for those critics en route to a rich corpus of postmodern-gender-technology theorizing. There is a risk, however, in the critical fetishization of new technologies, especially when coupled with the grand narrative of anti-essentialist gender theorizing, of eliding the socio-political aesthetics that endure in Orlan's creative practice. Whatever the form her practice takes, Orlan, guardian of French feminist histories, remains attached to the idea of disrobing inequalities. To see the figuring of the Harlequin's multicoloured coat in the fifth surgery, transmitted from a Parisian operating theatre in 1991, as a metaphor for multiculturalism as Orlan advocates (see O'Bryan, 2005: 144), is also to see the challenge this poses in France, where multiculturalism, like feminism, is resisted by the republican view of the social cohesion of individuals irrespective of differences (Cairns, 2000: 86). Similarly, the *Self-Hybridizations* that Orlan began in the late 1990s, in which she remodels her head with representations of pre-Columbian and African women in critically playful interrogations of colonial gazing and beauty-myth making, express the desire for a multicultural model of citizenship while gesturing to the colonial histories of white, French 'othering'. In sum, while Orlan may appear in critical contexts as a de-materialized, technologized 'omnipresence' in a virtual world, her French feminist roots ground her aesthetics as a radical practice that unpicks the fabric of social and cultural inequalities serving to fashion some bodies as stranger than others.

The performance of Orlan

An analysis of Orlan's work in relation to feminism in France can, therefore, be insightful, as these brief reflections suggest, for the ways in which it argues for her art as politicizing rather than sensationalizing. Nonetheless, as a feminist icon operating on 'the beauty myth' (Wolf, 1991),[4] Orlan still remains something of a sensation. Using her body to perform feminist politics in such extreme ways, she runs the risk of not being taken seriously. Tellingly, in the press, Orlan (and the work she embodies) is often treated as a *fait divers,* a sensationalist news story. She attracts media interest and the attention of stars from the music and fashion industry. Fans of Orlan include David Bowie and Peter Gabriel, while Paco Rabanne and Issey Miyake figure among the fashion designers who have collaborated with and been influenced by her. On French television Orlan has been interviewed alongside Madonna 'who eagerly associated her own mild body alterations with Orlan's – at least until Orlan gave her a little bottle containing a piece of her thigh at the end of the show' (Beckett, 1996: 18). Orlan does not, then, eschew media attention, but rather seeks to cultivate 'the cult of personality' that Barbara Rose (1993: 84) argues for as a Duchampian legacy in her work. Star charisma attaches to her performance of Orlan, the artist as the work of art. Interviews she gives are theatrical, while 'aura', to borrow from Walter Benjamin, is something she implicitly claims through 'announcements of her uniqueness' as '"the ultimate work of art"' (Beckett, 1996: 18).

Orlan's concern to lay claim both to 'uniqueness' and to the charismatic star presence of the artist behind and in her work, seem curiously at odds with her academic reception as a postmodern contemporary experimental practitioner. As Ince confesses:

> [O]n a number of occasions when I have discussed her surgical work with people, a kind of puzzlement and wonder has descended on the conversation as a mutual effort is made to describe what we commentators (all too aware of how to be unfashionable in a postmodernist climate) are hesitant to term the 'originality' or 'uniqueness' behind [the *Reincarnation of Saint Orlan*].
>
> (2000: 106)

Similarly, Jill C. O'Bryan observes: 'Orlan's means – elective cosmetic surgery and sensational documentary coverage – may belong to a western, middle-class Hollywood-like aspiration to fame and beauty, but, in using bourgeois means to enact her experimentation, she is deviating from the radical strategies of the avant-garde' (2005: 30)

In consequence, these various factors – 'uniqueness', star charisma, and a practice that operates inside and alongside cultural industries of beauty and fashion – work to queer Orlan's avant-garde belongings to the French performance tradition of bodies that shock 'going back to Dada and the Surrealists' (Beckett, 1996: 18). The performance of Orlan is a genealogical mix of Artaudian-inspired body artist and body art diva.

Demonized for making an (art) exhibition of herself, Orlan decries the value judgements that condone the exhibitionism of the entertainment industry and censure the idea of the artful diva: 'to be a singer or an actor, you have to be very exhibitionist but no one will say that Michael Jackson is too exhibitionist. On the contrary people will say he is extraordinary' (Orlan, 2009). By insisting on her right to become an 'extraordinary' body artist, Orlan hybridizes her theatre of carnal art with the art of the theatrical entertainer. Performance artist performing diva, making a spectacular spectacle of the feminine made strange, Orlan gestures to her carnal art as a contemporary radical reincarnation of the histrionic feminine of *fin de siècle* French theatre whose icon is the most written about actress of all, Sarah Bernhardt.

Critical strategies for reviewing histrionic histories

To view the histrionic French ghosts in Orlan's contemporary carnal art requires a critical strategy that mirrors an important organizational principle of Orlan's art: of bringing opposites together rather than keeping them apart: 'In my work, "And" is an organizing principle that always recurs: "past and present", "public and private", "that which is considered beautiful and that which is considered ugly", "the natural and the artificial"'(quoted in O'Bryan, 2005: 46). The idea of 'And' encourages breaching categories of difference in the interests of seeing differently, and argues for creative-critical ways of looking between or suturing differences. This connects to Orlan's strategy of recycling that looks forward to the past not with nostalgic longing, but as a means of enabling the past to exist differently in the present and of reclaiming the future. Here, recycling and suturing express the desire for a critical porosity that displaces, disturbs and disrupts.

Orlan 'And' Bernhardt conjugates women a century apart separated by different social and cultural contexts, by different points of feminist history, and by seemingly divergent theatre and performance art traditions: 'the Bernhardt' the histrionic face of the nineteenth century 'And' Orlan the 'refacing' icon of the second millennium. Perhaps their iconic, charismatic star status is the only thing that sutures these French *artistes* together? That is almost certainly the case if one accepts the separation between theatre and performance that has been vigorously argued for in late twentieth-century performance scholarship. In her initial discussion of performance and theatricality, for instance, Josette Féral offers Bernhardt as one of her examples of a theatre practice that endorses an idea of 'wholeness' in respect of subject formation. By contrast, Féral argues, 'since it tells of nothing and imitates no one, performance escapes all illusion and representation' and thereafter summarizes: 'It is precisely when it comes to the position of the subject, that performance and theatre would seem to be mutually exclusive and that theatre would perhaps have something to learn from performance' (Féral, 1982: 176–7).[5] In Féral's argument Bernhardt and Orlan would appear as 'mutually exclusive' opposites: the former constrained by the apparatus of 'illusion and representation'; the other escaping through the presentational frame of performance. Some further qualification or modification seems necessary here, however, if one thinks of how Orlan's performance art practice works through the representational, illusion-making apparatus of the 'beauty myth' in order to 'stage' the desire for its disappearance. Equally, while Bernhardt starred in a bourgeois, commercial theatre industry and was an icon of self-produced and mass-produced irresistible femininity, behind the histrionic cult of Bernhardtesque femininity was the art of an illusion perfected by performative means. The actress's capacity for self-construction and re-construction through her histrionic mode of body art acting argued for a femininity that was protean, rather than fixed, while her production of an excess of femininity, on and off the stage, suggested the knowingness of one who masquerades (see Roberts, 2002: 198).

In short, the hold on the theatre and performance distinction is a slippery one and far more porous than one might first suppose, as Philip Auslander's essay collection *From Acting to Performance: Essays in Modernism and Postmodernism* (with a multi-imaged Orlan in her surgical performance on the cover) reveals. As Auslander ghosts theories and traditions of acting (theatre) into the machine of contemporary performance making, it is the body that emerges as 'a central problematic of theatre and performance' (1997: 9).[6] And it is the body where one might begin to make French genealogical connections between the histrionic body of theatre (Bernhardt) and the radical reincarnations of the feminine in performance (Orlan).

Orlan's early body art gestures to Bernhardt's *fin de siècle* French theatre tradition in some interesting ways. Her early body-sculpture photographs from the mid-1960s, for instance, given the contorted poses of her naked body and a face concealed by an abundance of unruly hair, suggest a revisiting of the *hystériques* who starred in Charcot's Salpêtrière clinic/theatre (thought to have influenced Bernhardt's histrionic acting, see Aston, 2007: 157). Moreover, in terms of technique, her *tableaux vivants* point back to the gesturing and posturing of a histrionic, theatrical body. For instance, her 1980s *tableaux* of the baroque-robed Saint Orlan exposing her breast and brandishing easels, crosses or guns, are histrionically marked as spectacular displays of an abjected archetypal femininity, historicizing the 'ageless' cultural reproduction of an objectified feminine.

As Orlan works between the feminine-image-making apparatus of art 'And' performance, her histrionic re-enactments recycle representations of women from art history and the art of the actress/performer as image maker. The same *courtesane*-actress ancestry that Bernhardt inherited, for example, is highlighted in *Le Baiser de l'artiste* (*The Kiss of the Artist*), a *tableau vivant* that had different incarnations between 1976 and 1977:

This work consisted of a photo sculpture of Orlan's naked torso, at throat level of which was written the instruction 'Insert 5F', with an arrow pointing to the nearby slot for coins. Participants in the performance watched their 5F coins fall down a transparent tube into a triangular see-through container attached at the sculpture's crotch. When the coin had descended, Orlan the real-life artist would leap from her nearby position to give the participant a kiss.

(Ince, 2000: 138)

Inviting her 'clients' to deposit their 5 franc coins at her throat, Orlan resurrected the figure of the *mangeuse d'or*, the gold eating *courtisane* in a gestic, in-yer-face tableau that protested at the commerce of art and the (s)exploitation of women.[7] An agit-prop performance of one-to-one intimacy in a public space that foreshadowed the one-to-one performances given by many women practitioners today, the *tableau* invoked the history of the actress as public-prostituted property as the client/ spectator paid for the woman to 'perform'. This was an explicit feminist protest: to be screwed (in French *baiser* means 'to kiss and to fuck') as an artist and as a woman.[8]

Turning to the surgery performances, as many critics have noted, Orlan deploys theatrical conventions to perform the drama of the soon to-be-modified, live body. A rarely made observation, however, is that such conventions are not solely those of the avant-garde theatre where the director is responsible for the *mise en scène*, but those of the Bernhardt's nineteenth-century star tradition where the actress is cast in the starring role and manages the stage/operating theatre. Orlan's surgeon may be in charge of directing the medical operation, but the surgical performance is one that Orlan organizes, choosing the designer costumes, arranging the relics of previous performances, and directing her supporting ensemble of theatre technicians and her film crew. The *mise en scène* is a mix of the theatrical and the presentational: the reading from a philosophical pamphlet rather than the acting out of a role, or the narrative confined to the operating table and a three-act drama of the body before, during and after surgery. In sum, it is through a mixed economy of theatre and performance that Orlan recycles the 'beauty myth' as a site of feminist intervention.

From fin de siècle feminism to millennial body fascism

The radical potential of the surgical performance is, however, by no means secure. As previously mentioned, Orlan's carnal art body practice is frequently treated as a *fait divers*, while criticism for endorsing rather than subverting the idea of a cosmetically enhanced feminine attaches itself to her work. Offering her body as a site of public debate, Orlan invests time in speaking about, lecturing on and framing up her work in order to establish its feminist purpose and reception (see O'Bryan, 2005: ix). By contrast, always ambivalent about feminism, Bernhardt made no explicit political claims for her theatre, and her body-image making was not inherently radical given its production in a bourgeois, commercial theatre industry. Paradoxically, however, as Mary Louise Roberts argues, the actress was seen by aspirant French feminists in the late nineteenth century, such as the *frondeuses* of Marguerite Durand's newspaper, as the icon of the 'freedom and independence' they craved, viewing the actress's refusal to conform to gender norms, roles or behaviour as a 'disruptive act' of female liberation and independence (Roberts, 2002: 199). To these French women Bernhardt was as a symbol of 'the grand feminist future', appearing, as she did, to embody a 'visual image' of the 'New Woman' in *fin de siècle* France: '[h]er uncorseted, malleable torso symbolized a new way of being female – a freedom to play with identity according to the whims of the moment' (ibid.: 198–9).

Conversely, the close of the twentieth century has seen a reclamation of the feminine in the interests of an individualistically styled 'new feminism'. Simply put, this means that feminism has been given a 'new feminine' make-over (see Aston, 2006: 73), in which, ironically, the idea of the 'new woman' has come to signify an investment in, rather than a divestment of, a body-fascist-feminine. Fascism, as Benjamin observed at the beginning of the twentieth century, created opportunities for the 'newly created proletarian masses' to express themselves without conceding any changes to 'property relations': '[F]ascism sees its salvation in giving these masses not their right, but instead a chance to express themselves' (2001: 118). By analogy, what this unorthodox genealogical suturing of French body art divas serves to show is how 'property [body]relations' remain in urgent need of feminist attention and transformation. In brief, despite *fin de siècle* or 1970s feminist efforts to contest and to change the capitalist and patriarchal ownership of women's bodies, as exemplified in Orlan's *Le Baiser de l'artiste*, a millennial intensification of neo-liberalism and global capital has conspired to displace 'the grand feminist future' with the grand illusion of a reclaimed 'new feminine' as the means to, and an expression of, self-empowerment. In an age of cosmetic reproduction, Orlan's unique form of body art is a *MesuRage* of a disenfranchising contemporary feminine.

In French *le corps* is a masculine noun and can mean both 'body' and 'corpse': the living and the dead. Anecdotal theatre history informs us that Bernhardt slept in a coffin because it was the only way she could find a restful 'room of her own'. Visual traces of Orlan's *Le Drapé – le baroque* (*Drapery – The Baroque*, 1979) document the artist's arrival in the Georges Pompidou Centre in a reliquary chest – and to some, it appeared that her living-dead body was carried into the performance space as though in a coffin. As long as the feminine remains interred, sutured or fascistically assigned to the corpse of the masculine, it figures a state of dispossession rather than empowerment. As this critical recycling strategy of looking forward to the past, from Orlan to Bernhardt, attests, in order to resist the death-drive of a contemporary 'new feminine', the reincarnation of a feminist political is urgently required; one in which, mirroring the respective body art of these two French divas, the feminine is released from patriarchal *enterrement*.

Notes

1. See John Stokes (2005) for a further discussion of this.
2. Tanya Augsburg writes: '[p]rior to Barbara Rose's February 1993 *Art in America* article entitled 'Is it Art? On Orlan's Transgressive Acts [sic]' Orlan was virtually unknown in the United States, and she is still best known for the work produced since 1990' (1998: 292).
3. Ince, for instance, describes that it was through working on Judith Butler that she first heard of and became interested in Orlan (2000: 8).
4. With regard to Orlan's feminist iconicity see also Germaine Greer: 'The battered face of the French artist Orlan after surgery, with her stitched and swollen lips and her blood-suffused eyes, is a feminist ikon' (1999: 33).
5. For subsequent revisions to her argument, see Féral (2002).
6. While Auslander looks to continuities between Modernism and Postmodernism in relation to the conjugation of theatre and performance (as does Ince in her study of Orlan), I am arguing for a recycling of theatre/performance histories that reaches further back to the histrionic body.
7. In another of her body-action interventions, *Se vendre sur les marchés en petits morceaux* (*Selling Oneself at Markets in Small Pieces*) that took place between 1976 and 1977, Orlan took herself to market and set up a stall to sell images of her body parts.
8. *Le Baiser* was a critical point in Orlan's career. Not only did the gender divided responses of her 'clients' (women were far more willing to pay than men) attune her to the social and sexual inequalities of a visual economy, but the scandal that her 'French kissing' provoked cost Orlan her teaching position (see Orlan, 2009).

Works cited

Aston, Elaine (2006) '"Bad Girls" and "Sick Boys": New Women Playwrights and the Future of Feminism', in Elaine Aston and Geraldine Harris (eds), *Feminist Futures: Theatre, Performance, Theory* (Basingstoke: Palgrave Macmillan), pp. 71–87.

—— (2007) '"Studies in Hysteria": Actress and Courtesan, Sarah Bernhardt and Mrs Patrick Campbell', in Maggie B. Gale and John Stokes (eds), *The Cambridge Companion to the Actress* (Cambridge: Cambridge University Press), pp. 153–71.

Augsburg, Tanya (1998) 'Orlan's Performative Transformations of Subjectivity', in Peggy Phelan and Jill Lane (eds), *The Ends of Performance* (New York: New York University Press), pp. 285–314.

Auslander, Philip (1997) *From Acting to Performance: Essays in Modernism and Postmodernism* (London: Routledge).

Beckett, Andy (1996) 'Suffering for Her Art', *Independent*, 14 April, pp. 18–21.

Benjamin, Walter (2001) 'The Work of Art in the Age of Mechanical Reproduction', in Vincent B. Leitch (ed), *The Norton Anthology of Theory and Criticism* (London: W. W. Norton), pp. 1166–86.

Cairns, Lucille (2000) 'Sexual Fault Lines: Sex and Gender in the Cultural Context', in William Kidd and Siân Reynolds (eds), *Contemporary French Cultural Studies* (London: Arnold), pp. 81–94.

Duchen, Claire (ed. and trans.) (1987) *French Connections: Voices from the Women's Movement in France* (London: Hutchinson).

Féral, Josette (1982) 'Performance and Theatricality: The Subject Demystified', *Modern Drama*, 25:1, 170–81.

—— (2002) 'Theatricality: the Specificity of Theatrical Language', *Sub-Stance*, 31:2/3, 94–108.

Greer, Germaine (1999) *The Whole Woman* (London: Doubleday).

Hirschhorn, Michelle (1996) 'Orlan: Artist in the Post-Human Age of Mechanical Reincarnation: *body as ready (to be re-) made*', in Griselda Pollock (ed.), *Generations and Geographies in the Visual Arts* (London: Routledge), pp. 110–34.

Ince, Kate (2000) *Orlan: Millennial Female* (Oxford: Berg).

O'Bryan, Jill C. (2005) *Carnal Art: Orlan's Refacing* (Minneapolis: University of Minnesota Press).

Orlan (1998) 'Intervention', in Peggy Phelan and Jill Lane (eds), *The Ends of Performance* (New York: New York University Press), pp. 315–27.

—— (2009) Interview, *Guardian* on-line, 1 July: http://www.guardian.co.uk/artanddesign/2009/jul/01/orlan-performance-artist-carnal-art (accessed 10 July 2009).

Roberts, Mary Louise (2002) *Disruptive Acts: The New Women in Fin-de-Siècle France* (Chicago: The University of Chicago Press).

Rose, Barbara (1993) 'Is it Art? Orlan and the Transgressive Act', *Art in America*, February, 82–7 and 125.

Sagan, Françoise (1989) *Dear Sarah Bernhardt*, trans. Sabine Destrée (London: Macmillan).

Stokes, John (2005) *The French Actress and Her English Audience* (Cambridge: Cambridge University Press).

Wolf, Naomi (1991) *The Beauty Myth* (London: Vintage).

11
Performance and Poetry: Crossed Destinies*

Éric Vautrin

To Henri Chopin, in memoriam

At Harvard in 1955, the philosopher J. L. Austin introduced the notion of the performative utterance to linguistic studies; in the same year, François Dufrêne performed *Crirythmes* at François Maspero's L'Escalier Gallery in Paris. Although initially a Lettrist, Dufrêne broke from the movement by abandoning the 'letter' and by putting the voice and body of the poet at the very centre of his work.[1] His aim was to establish a radically inventive form of poetry that would no longer be merely subservient to discursive or representational language, a gestural and infinitely creative art liberated from all naturalistic pressures to represent reality. Initially, poetry welcomed its encounter with performance, from which it quickly learnt how to manipulate disparate materials stolen from everywhere and anywhere. However, as I show in this essay, a few decades or so later, as a result of its fruitful detour through performance, poetry in France was to reinvest yet again in the text. This allowed it to multiply its compositional strategies, styles of delivery and forms of presentation.

The type of poetry which surged into being in the 1950s in France was nothing new in itself. Already Raoul Hausmann, Hugo Ball, Kurt Schwitters and also Antonin Artaud, amongst others, had experimented with *poésie sonore* (sound poetry) in an attempt to go both beyond and beneath the surface of words. But the emphasis was now very different: in the scores of Dufrêne and then later Henri Chopin and Bernard Heidsieck, the extravagant excesses of Dada, along with the scorching physicality and organic quality of Artaud's language, were mostly absent. Unlike their predecessors, Dufrêne et al. were not interested in inventing an 'infra- or meta-language', or in attacking conventions;

rather, they sought to present written scores, prepared and composed in advance, that aimed to 'get close to [...] our mental mechanisms and our everyday environment' (Heidsieck, 2001: 89). Their relationship with the audience was also very different, with their recitals taking place in art galleries and festivals.

The type of sound poetry created by Heidsieck and Chopin in the 1950s is notable for its enthusiastic embrace of technology, with tape recorders, most famously, offering new possibilities for recording and reworking the voice through editing and mixing. This new mode of mechanical production allowed poetry to escape the confines of the page, and made the breath and the physical 'grain' of the spoken voice just as important as letters and words. At the same time, the willingness of Heidsieck and Chopin to embrace, rather than to reject, modernity held out the possibility that technology could be rescued from the worlds of commerce and the new networks of mass communication that had altered so fundamentally the textures of everyday life. This form of poetry would later become known as 'action poetry', the goal of which, according to Heidsieck, was to produce alternative ways of relating to audiences in order to 'put poetry back on in its feet' (ibid: 9). However, for the sake of accuracy, it is important to note that the defining characteristic of action poetry at this time was not interactivity but materiality. Heidsieck and Chopin wanted spectators and listeners to encounter, immediately and concretely, the very sound and surface of language itself, and so problematize the cognitive qualities of a medium which was (and still is more or less) regarded as a transparent medium for communication (see Figure 2).

In these years, performance poetry sought to renew language by avoiding sentimentalism and dogmatism and by stressing the importance of context (the place or environment in which the poem was articulated). Although this was the common *ethos* for all future experiments in the field, poetic writing in France took two very divergent forms in the alternative directions forged by Heidsieck and Chopin. In general terms, Heidsieck developed a form of 'concrete poetry' that was rooted in reality: his performances were staged in front of a live audience; his texts dealt with contemporary social themes; and the style was minimalist and objective, avoiding both metaphor and narration. In these performances (published initially as *Poème-partition* (*Poem-Partition*, 1955–65) and then later as *Biopsies* (1965–9)), texts and word lists were subjected to accelerations, elongations and vocal distortions. The breathing patterns and unusual rhythms adopted by Heidsieck in his delivery of the poem were intended to bring out the full expressivity of the text.

Figure 2 Bernard Heidsieck reading *Tout autour de Vaduz*, la poésie/nuit, Lyon, 2006 ©Didier Grappe

Heidsieck's experimentation with seriality and predilection for rules and systems, along with his use of pre-recorded texts and voices (captured and edited on tape), meant that language was simultaneously musicalized and made 'strange'. The political significance of Heidsieck's poetic practice was plain for all to see: he was a humanist committed to what might be called 'linguistic materialism'. For him, meaning emerged from the totality of the subject's relationship with and to language, and not solely from the written word, or from more spectacular and abstract modes of communication.

Henri Chopin, by contrast, was more interested in developing a type of pure sound poetry by exploring how microphones and other types of recording devices could disclose the latent possibilities and potentialities of the voice. His ambition was to create an entirely physicalized language, in which the spectator was left to decode the utterances of the speaker. The poet did not speak language; rather s/he existed as a medium for it. In live performance, Chopin's compositions were concerned, uniquely, with the voice and its electronic transmutations; the intention being to question the supposed value of writing as the absolute source of knowledge. Chopin's enthusiasm was boundless.

He travelled the world collecting samples of sonic poetry in order to prove that a revolution was underway, in which human beings would finally be able to communicate the very essence of their humanity in a space beyond nationality and linguistic differences.

In these two examples – which are symptomatic of the aesthetics and politics of poetic practice in France in the 1950s and 1960s – it is important to take into account key social transformations brought about by the onset of globalization. Three points are particularly significant: first, it was much easier to travel the globe (and these poets did it endlessly); second, because of rapid technological innovations, mass communication was experienced as something inescapable and depersonalizing; and third, important shifts in ideological meaning took place – what Heidsieck in 1964 described as the 'dizzying din of values, the annihilation of principles and doctrines that has created the fog in which we currently live and from which we will only emerge with any certitude, from the very fact of their own precariousness and contradictory nature' (2001: 47). Faced with an uncertain society in a seemingly permanent state of flux, poetry became a mode of localized resistance, an attempt to 'allow the [absolute] to be perceived, in the fragility of the instant, in the second, in this matrix of movement, this cogwheel, this mechanized world. This mould. This flux. This wall' (ibid.). Opposing itself to ever increasing levels of social alienation, poetry expressed a desire to re-appropriate technology for human ends and to experiment with new ways of speaking and thinking which openly embraced contradiction. For Heidsieck, Chopin and their contemporaries, poetry was imagined as a new vital space, an alternative site for the recovery of an intimacy and generosity that would resist ideological and economic destabilization, and the oppressive logics that these processes produced and, all too often, sought to obscure.

In the 1960s and 1970s, experimental poetry in France proliferated. Action poetry could be found in theatres and galleries, and was often confounded with performance art (in the expanded sense of the term). In avant-garde circles, artistic practices diversified and crossed over into neighbouring fields to such a degree that existing boundaries between different genres and media were blurred. These years were characterized by an enthusiasm and excitement for interdisciplinary exchange, and it was no surprise that the aesthetic principles of sound poetry were borrowed by theatre makers and composers, and vice versa.[2] As a consequence, performance art became a global practice and old distinctions disappeared. Ironically, at the very moment, when references to the historical avant-garde(s) of the early twentieth century were on the wane in academic scholarship, performance art emerged as a new synthetic and hybrid model for art making.

Conversely, the end of the 1970s reversed this trend; and from the vantage point of the present, these years are perhaps best regarded as a time for reflection and synthesis, caused in no small measure by the many critical studies that started to appear. In 1979, for example, RoseLee Goldberg's *Performance Art: From Futurism to the Present*, Pierre Restany's *L'Autre face de l'art* (*The Other Face of Art*) and Jean Dupuy's *Collective Consciousness: Art Performances In the Seventies* were all published. The same year also saw the appearance of *Poésie sonore internationale* (*Sound Poetry International*), a critical survey, edited by Henri Chopin, which attempted to create an international map of sound poetry. Curiously, in the international debates that followed, little time was spent on thinking about performance as a continually evolving artistic practice; rather, performance was figured mainly as a theoretical object. Everything was declared to be either performative or engaging in some kind of performance or other. In the subsequent analytical and historical accounts that emerged, performance was simultaneously promoted as the archetypal essence of art, a radical gesture aimed at ideology, and a practice that sought to transcend language. According to the new discourses surrounding performance, the body was to be reclaimed from scientific discourse in order to give birth to a new, engaged humanism where technology and globalization would allow greater freedom and equality for human beings, and where the otherness of the 'other' would be respected. A century on from Impressionism and several decades after the transgressive strategies of the historical avant-garde(s) had run out of steam, the ubiquitous practices of performance that Futurism and Dadaism had nonetheless set in motion provided compelling evidence that a second modernity of art was underway. By the late 1970s, the idea of the autonomous masterpiece was well and truly abandoned and art was radically reconfigured as either pure experience (body art) or idea (conceptualism).

Developments in the next decade, however, were to prove very different. In response to the atmosphere of melancholy and depression that reigned in the political realm after the short-lived euphoria of the 1960s and 1970s, and reflecting the conservatism that had triumphed again in painting and photography (both returned to traditional gallery-based formats), performance poetry in the 1980s became better organized and more professionalized. The result was that it oscillated between two extremes: marginalization or institutionalization (spoken word events at Beaubourg, regular programmes on Radio France, a series of international symposia on sound poetry).

A rebirth through text

In the 1990s in France performance poetry found fresh inspiration from an unexpected source: literature. Performance poets started to re-engage with the work of writers who had prepared the way for a new approach to text either by manipulating it as an arbitrary framework (the technique, for instance, of the Oulipo group (Ouvroir de littérature potentielle)), or by privileging the everyday quality of words.[3] In the latter case, poets such as Emmanuel Hocquard, Francis Ponge, Christian Prigent and Denis Roche were particularly influential because of the way in which they stressed the performative (as opposed to metaphori-cal) dimensions of language.

From the end of the 1980s onwards, the return of the literary text in performance circles was augmented by the appearance of new jour-nals, which meant that editing and publishing now played a key role in determining tastes, practices and modes of distribution. Existing publications such as *Action poétique*, *Dock(s)* and *Nioques* were joined by others such as *Java*, *Fusées* (previously *TXT*), *Revue de littérature générale*, and *Revue Perpendiculaire*. Today, this proliferation is being mirrored electronically and there is now a plethora of feed-aggregator sites with good-sized audiences.

As for the poets themselves, some of them were keen to experiment with alternative ways of staging text. In doing so, they re-established a connection with the performance poetry of the 1970s. However, for several reasons, little of which had anything to do with the poets themselves, this new taste for performance was injected with fresh momentum. Theatre managers and producers, for instance, demanded short performances that were inexpensive to produce; artists and pro-grammers in the 1990s (and increasingly in the 2000s) were drawn to new experiments in writing that promised to renew the language and forms of text-based theatre (see Chapter 6 by Robert Cantarella in this volume); and important aesthetic affinities started to appear between writing, choreography and fine art, even though dance had been experimenting with language a little earlier through the work of young French choreographers, Jérôme Bel, Xavier Leroy and Boris Charmatz (see Augusto Corrieri, Chapter 16, and Bojana Cvejic, Chapter 14, in this volume). There were other factors, too. Publishing was in difficulty and sought new ways of gaining an audience; high schools, libraries and bookshops were expanding their public reading programmes; and the development of a so-called alternative scene, located in bohemian squats and alternative theatre venues (initially,

Mains d'œuvres in Paris and Belle de Mai in Marseille, and then later La Générale in Paris and Ground Zero in Lyon) allowed different disciplines to converge.[4] While it is impossible to specify which of these factors carried the greatest weight in this renaissance of performance writing – attention has to be paid to specific circumstances and to individual cases – the radically diverse nature of the field is matched only by the omnipresence of poetry within almost all artistic and performance practices today.

With respect to this point, it is crucial to highlight here the influence that *Revue de littérature générale* (*Review of General Literature,* 1995–6) has had on current thinking. Edited by Olivier Cadiot and Pierre Alferi, this large book, assembled in two thick volumes, compiles the work of an entire generation of writers. In the preface and postface, the authors conceptualize their text as a compendium seeking to establish similarities between apparently disparate forms of writing by way of process rather than theme or style. In the *Revue de littérature générale (RLG)* writing is primarily a matter of technique rather than inspiration, and the poet is someone who compresses, samples and cuts up the materials of language. Cadiot and Alferi argue for a 'mechanical lyric', in which lyricism is a textual phenomenon, produced through the tension created between syntax, grammar and referent. Within a single text, for instance, one might find established literary genres and styles deconstructed and reassembled; different registers of language competing for the same space; and well-known anecdotes and citations juxtaposed to each other. The critical dimension of these writings is found neither in their themes nor expressive form, but rather, as with sound poetry, in the extent to which language is conceived as an experiential space in itself. As Pierre Alferi noted in 1991, writing, like thinking, is a matter of 'finding the correct sentence' (Alferi, 2001: 45).[5] In the *RLG,* every type of writing has a home, including the poetry of objects (Peter Fischli's and David Weiss's famous video installation *Der Lauf der Dinge* (*So Things are Going,* 1987) is mentioned in the second volume); sociological case studies (Pierre Bourdieu transcribing an interview) and philosophical essays (Bernard Steigler, Jean-Luc Nancy, Giorgio Agamben and the like).

I now want to list some of the specific ways in which contemporary performance writing in France, by building on this return to text, has started to proliferate. However, before I proceed, a word of caution is necessary: since the permutations of this work are infinite, it follows that my attempt to provide an exhaustive overview is bound to be problematic and, perhaps, inevitably doomed to failure in advance.

Text as landscape in process

The poet, novelist and playwright Olivier Cadiot remains the most brilliant exponent of the traditional public reading. Cadiot's texts are populated by loners who invent strategies to manipulate language for their own ends. In the novel *Futur, ancien, fugitif* (*Future, Past, Fugitive*,1993), the struggle is against forgetting, and in *Retour définitif et durable de l'être aimé* (*The Definitive and Lasting Return of the Loved One*, 2002), the goal is to survive in spite of the cold. Cadiot's *grands solitaires* wander through landscapes (or textscapes) which accelerate according to the rhythms generated by their inventive syntax, and language is used to transform any thought or situation into a rhythmic device (see David Bradby in Chapter 1, Clare Finburgh in Chapter 4 and Céline Hersant in Chapter 3 in this volume). Where Cadiot's own virtuoso readings highlight the rhythmic and vocal potential inherent in the formalist strategies of the text, the theatrical versions produced by the director Ludovic Lagarde are attempts to adapt these scores to the visual logic of the stage.[6]

Disjunction and accumumlation

In France today, contemporary poets, most notably Jérôme Game, are in the process of revisiting the practices used by sound poets of the 1950s. In Game's montage-like texts, disjunction is exploited in order to speed up the telling of the story and to multiply narrative threads. The point, for Game, is to return language to the body, with its quivers and twitches. In this context, one should also mention Anne-James Chaton and her descriptive lists, even though she is actually closer in spirit to the American Objectivist poets of the 1930s and 1940s who sought to describe, with simplicity and sincerity, their encounter with 'things'; and the work of Thomas Braichet who, in *Conte de F_* (*Tale of F_*2007), re-explored the same terrain as Heidsieck by engaging in performed readings where the live voice was mixed with a pre-recorded narrative.

Logorrhea

However, there are other performance poets in France who prefer to blend pre-prepared scripts with free-form improvisation. By opening her/himself to verbal affect, the poet, in these instances, becomes what s/he speaks, producing, in turn, a dizzying verbal flow. The seemingly endless loops of language create a sense of logorrhoea and *glossolalia*. One of the most exciting of these 'improvisational' poets was Christophe Tarkos, whose notion of the *pâte-mot* – a concept which he developed in his book *Le Signe =* (*The Sign =*, 1999) – is a world composed solely of words. This is a sort of infinite, immanent map in which every linguistic transaction is possible, with all the symbolic, affective and contextual dimensions that this entails. Influenced by the physical performances of Christian Prigent, the contemporary performances of Arno Calleja and Charles Pennequin inscribe themselves within the tradition of Tarkos, who died prematurely in 2004.

Mixing genres: stage and image

Pierre Alferi, Patrick Bouvet, Jérôme Game, Charles Pennequin, Anne Portugal and Nathalie Quintane (to mention only a handful) are poets who collaborate with fine artists, musicians and video-makers to create hybridized forms which are often released later as books, on DVD and video (see Figure 3).[7] In their live performances, readings and improvisations merge with projected images. They sometimes have a critical voice (the work of Berard, Pennequin and Quintane), and, on other occasions, they seek to expand the narrative possibilities of cinema and literature (the practices of Alferi, Bouvet and Game). In both instances, images and words explore the virtuality or potential of the other in a continuous interweaving that expands the possibility of reading and the sites in which it is performed.

Figure 3 Charles Pennequin and the guitarist Jean-François Pauvros, la poésie/ nuit, Lyon, 2007 ©Didier Grappe

Rocking the joint

Different artists exploit more direct and popular performance styles, such as, for instance, pop-singing or rhetorical acts of public speaking, whose formats and convention are then over-exaggerated and mocked. Christophe Fiat, for instance, adopts the persona of a rocker who endlessly strums the same two-chord sequence, and whose rant-like stories, based on a simplistic binary rhythm, are inspired by sci-fi and US detective stories. Here, narration is a kind of endless refrain which deconstructs itself and becomes pure rhythm – Fiat terms this a *ritornello*. Similarly, Manuel Joseph merges news stories with references to popular cinema and literature. Through cut-ups and various kinds of thematic and phonetic allusions, he exposes the violence inherent to everyday speech acts. Here truth is mixed with falsehood to the point that it becomes impossible to separate fiction from reality.

Everyday interventions: the equivocal gesture

If the stage has been swamped by poets interested in exposing the artificial nature of its codes and protocols, there is, conversely, an alternative fascination with placing performance poetry in the non-fictional spaces of everyday life. The emphasis in this practice is on producing ambiguity rather than spectacle. Although Daniel Foucard's performed readings and slideshows are written in a dry, matter-of-fact style and based on PowerPoint presentations and adventure novels, they ultimately lead a life of their own and escape the author's desire to bend them to his will. As a result of the ensuing de-contextualization caused by the tension between formal expectation and actual delivery, they highlight, through the ambiguity provoked, the hidden violence of common utterances.[8]

An alternative trend is evident in the work of writers such as Christophe Hanna, Franck Leibovici and Olivier Quintyn, who seek to construct new forms and situations of and for reading. Influenced by their encounter with the philosophical theories of US Pragmatist philosophers like Richard Rorty, they believe that every type of writing is tied to a concrete situation and ought not to rely on the good will of a reader or spectator to follow a text through from the beginning to the end. Like site-specific installations which merge the artwork with the ambiance of the site in which they are performed (a bar, gallery or street), the performances of Hanna and his contemporaries borrow the formats of newspapers, emails and letters in order to highjack the reading habits associated with them.

New paths: heterogeneous practices

In France today, there is an emergent interest in re-exploring the Actionist art associated with performance poets of the 1970s and 1980s, such as Julien Blaine, Joël Hubaut, Arnaud Labelle-Rejoux and the Boxon group. In their stage work, Xavier Boussiron, Joris Lacoste and Sophie Pérez make work from elaborately constructed visual and narrative material without ever investing in conventional dramatic forms. For them, form is content, and the object of performance is the signifying process itself (narrative, spectacle, etc.). Similarly, Sonia Chiambretto creates theatre texts that analyse the discourses and speech patterns of everyday people – for example, a legionnaire (*Mon képi blanc* (*My White Képi*, 2007)) or an immigrant (*CHTO*, 2006). Others, like Vincent Barras and Jérémie Gindre prefer to use existing performative formats such as lectures and public readings or short sketches. Here, as in the eclectic scores of Frédéric Danos, which insert themselves, invisibly, into social events and cultural gatherings, it is impossible to know if these are 'real' performances or not.[9] Since the extant framework predetermines the type of address used, the performance in question functions as self-destructive virus, critical of the structure in which it is sited and whose effects cannot be determined in advance. Under the name of Das Dingbat, Constantin Alexandrakis and Olivier Nourrisson adopt a related strategy. Their performances are exercises in renaming and recycling, for instance giving titles to absurd photographs found on the internet; or constructing unusual installations from found objects in public spaces – examples include a tree-hut to watch the motorway and an observatory without a lens that was sited in the heart of Paris. In similar vein, Joris Lacoste et Jeanne Revel have experimented in the past few years with 'Méthode W', a methodology which analyses the aesthetic principles of a specific performance and imagines how they might be applied to different shows in an attempt to supply performance with its own generic model of notation.[10]

Poetry and performance: showing the shape of language

In critical, academic and institutional spheres, performance practices and poetic writing start to converge when a specific way of understanding what performance means is placed in proximity to a certain definition of poetry. If poetry truly is, as Cadiot and Alferi define it, 'any form which draws attention to its own outline or shape' (1996: no pagination), that is to say, a type of writing that performs its own processes, and whose mode of enunciation is based on the tensions inherent to the very objects that it calls forth – themes, expressions, codes and formal principles – then it is no different, *in principle*, from performance.[11] This is all the more evident, if we understand performance to be something which is realized in the present. In this case, meaning is located in the experience of the act itself rather than in any attempt to interpret it discursively. Of course, performance and poetry go their separate ways when the former makes a fetish out of the body, political utopianism and the live event, or, inversely, when the latter is regarded as a vehicle for pure lyrical self-expression. But as long as the stakes of performance are centred on the signifying processes that encode representation, then it has much in common with a form of poetry which perceives language as a form of thinking and argumentation, and which experiments with syntax in order to infuse all linguistic codes, both grammatical and iconic, with new life.[12] As modes of thought, performance and poetry are assemblages that share a common heritage, in which composition is preferred to interpretation, and where product gives way to process (research, invention, intensity, hybridization). Both refuse to be confined within fixed limits and seek to blur the boundaries between different media. Their ultimate political objective is to call into question, albeit temporarily and precariously, our capacity to produce a communal perspective on the world by collapsing and merging different languages, vocabularies, utterances and styles that are usually well-policed and kept at a safe distance from each other.

Translated by Carl Lavery and Cathy Piquemal

Notes

*It was not possible because of the sheer list of names cited in this chapter to provide specific information on each poet. We therefore leave it up to the interested reader to make her/his own connections and to do her/his own research. As Vautrin comments, much of this work is now available electronically.

1. Editors' note: Lettrism was a post-Second World War French avant-garde movement, headed by Isidore Issou. Lettrism rejected expressionist and lyrical theories of poetry and sought to base the poem and painting on the acoustic and visual charge of the letter.
2. Henri Chopin, François Dufrêne and Bernard Heidsieck – despite Dufrêne's very different aesthetic viewpoint – all had a fine art practice in this period, which related directly to their sound work, and was in no way intended to resolve their relationship with the written text.
3. Editors' note: The Oulipo group, which included novelists Italo Calvino and Georges Perec, experimented with constrained writing techniques, such as, for instance, using lipograms and palindromes.

4. For details, see Trans Europ Halles network (http://www.teh.net) or Artfactories (http://www.artfactories.net).
5. The full citation is: 'A thought is not an empire in the empire of language, but a march that language steals on itself: a possible language [...] A new sentence is possible in the extent to which it is truly researched. Thinking means: looking for the correct sentence.'
6. Editors' note: Cadiot and Lagarde have collaborated since 1993 and have staged plays and adaptations of Cadiot's novels at the Théâtre nationale de la Colline. For a good reading highlighting the overlap between French performance poetry and theatre, see Clare Finburgh (2007).
7. See Charles Pennequin and Pascal Doury's *Je me jette* (*I Throw Myself*, 2004); Patrick Bouvet's *Big Bright Baby* (2006); Jérôme Game's *Ceci n'est pas une légende ipe pe ce* (*This is not a Legend ipe pe ce*, 2007); and Pierre Alferi and Jacques Julien's *Ça commence à Séoul* (*It Starts in Seoul*, 2007).
8. In his latest novel *Civil* (2008), for example, a police instructor lectures young recruits and the reader is left with no idea at all about what the main protagonist's thoughts on law and order are.
9. In a dance studio, for example, he adopts the persona of a dancer before inviting the other participants to take part in a collective brawl or to join a workshop on invisibility; in a poetry festival, he proposes that each performance has a walk attached to it; and in front of a Parisian museum, he encourages audience members to write their names on the wall in French.
10. See http://www.1110111.org/pratique (accessed 10 January 2010).
11. Editors' note: See the definition of performance we offer in the Introduction to this volume.
12. This includes the way that the signifying process can be hidden, arbitrary, illusory and authoritarian.

Works cited

Alferi, Pierre (2001) *Poems and Monsters: The Language of New Media* (Cambridge, MA: MIT Press, 2001).
Alferi, Pierre (2007) *Chercher une phrase* (Paris: Christian Bourgois).
Alferi, Pierre and Olivier Cadiot (1996) 'Digest', in *Revue de littérature génèrale*, vol. 2 (Paris: P.O. L.), no pagination.
Finburgh, Clare (2007) 'Voix/voie/vie: The Voice in Contemporary French Theatre', *Yale French Studies*, 112, 99–115.
Heidsieck, Bernard (2001) *Notes convergentes* (Paris: Al Dante).

12
Breaking Down the Walls: Interventionist Performance Strategies in French Street Theatre

Susan Haedicke

What in France is today known as *théâtre de rue* (street theatre) exploded on to the urban stage in the 1970s. Although adapted from centuries-old techniques, its immediate aesthetico-political heritage is found in the same anti-establishment impulses that inspired Guy Debord and the Situationists in the 1950s and 1960s, and which led to the student/worker uprisings in May 1968. 'Last May, speech was taken the way, in 1789, the Bastille was taken. The stronghold that was assailed is a knowledge held by the dispensers of culture,' wrote Michel de Certeau in October following the May riots (1998: 11). He argued that while the political regime withstood the assault of 'May '68', the protesters 'created a network of symbols by taking the signs of a society in order to invert their meaning' (ibid.: 7). In this way, they produced what de Certeau calls 'symbolic sites' where seemingly impossible images or events 'modified the tacitly "received" code that separates the possible from the impossible, the licit from the illicit' (ibid.: 8). The dominant discourses – political, social and aesthetic – were thus transformed.

It is easy to see the truth of his claim in the burgeoning street theatre movement in France in the 1970s. Pioneering companies, like Royal de Luxe, Ilotopie, Génerik Vapeur, Transe Express, Oposito and Délices Dada (to name but a few), abandoned traditional theatre buildings for the freedom and populist appeal of the street, offered their shows to the public for free, and insisted on a revolutionary aesthetic of innovation and provocation. These radical French artists launched artistic interventions into the actual life of the city and thereby affected the public's understanding of social life by challenging the demarcation between the *fiction* of the theatre and *reality* of the street. Their productions created 'symbolic sites' that turned aesthetic expectations and socio-political assumptions upside down, thus offering an alternative social

162

experience rooted in performativity (which I understand as the production of reality through symbolic acts).

In the 1960s and 1970s, guerrilla theatre companies experimenting with street theatre were not unique to France. One thinks of groups such as Bread and Puppet Theatre, San Francisco Mime Troupe and El Teatro Campesino in the United States, La Fura dels Baus in Spain, Welfare State International in England and Dogtroep in Holland. But only in France did this art form develop, diversify and enter the mainstream in the 1980s and 1990s. While it is outside the scope of this chapter to analyse the many reasons for the flourishing of street theatre in France, key among them was state support both in terms of funding and innovative populist cultural policies, initiated under François Mitterrand and his Minister of Culture, Jack Lang. National and local government funding of theatre companies made radical experimentation possible, but perhaps more significant was the establishment of numerous funded street theatre festivals.[1] Here, experimental work was shown for free, thus eliminating the need for box-office success. In the 1990s, *centres de création* (creation centres) where theatre companies could devise and construct new shows were set up, and an archive/resource centre for street theatre and circus in Paris (HorsLesMurs) was established. In 2005, Le Temps des arts de la rue, a three-year initiative to promote street theatre, was launched with a starting budget of 2 million euros. While this funding clearly encouraged innovation and proliferation of street theatre, government support alone is insufficient reason for street theatre's success in France. Less tangible, but of equal importance, is the history of protest and other populist activities in public spaces, and the high value placed on the arts in France.[2] It is not surprising, therefore, that street theatre's art-based interruptions in the flow of daily life continue to fascinate the French public.[3]

'The peculiarity of a street performance', writes French scholar Michel Siminot, 'is that it transforms any place, open or closed, into a performance space by a single irruption. It creates in that place a socio-political and an artistic intervention simultaneously' (1999: 6; my translation). That transformation necessarily alters the dynamic between place, actors, audience and context. Street theatre productions superimpose an enacted scene on an actual site and so bridge the gap between the daily activity of the spectator and the aesthetic activity of the performance. For Julie Pellegrin, director of Ferme du Buisson, a centre for contemporary art in France, this 'sustaining [of] a constant tension between art and non-art [...] makes it impossible not to experience the forms politically' (2007–8: 71). Reflecting de Certeau's notion of the 'symbolic site', as the boundaries between art and non-art become porous, the public is presented here with possibilities that previously seemed unimaginable. 'The "exemplary action" that takes place there "opens a breach", not because of its own efficacity [sic], but because it displaces a law that was the more powerful in that it had not been brought to mind; it unveils what was latent and makes it contestable [...]; it creates *possibilities* relative to *impossibilities* that had until then been admitted but not clarified' (de Certeau, 1998: 8; original emphasis). A street theatre performance often functions like this 'exemplary action' and encourages the public to re-imagine everyday life.

Three performance installations, Jeanne Simone's *Le Goudron n'est pas meuble* (*The Tarmac is Not Furniture*, 2006); Le Phun's *La Vengeance des semis* (*The Seedlings' Revenge*, 1986, 1991–2003); and Ilotopie's *Confins* (*Limits*, 2004) create 'symbolic sites' in which the public experience familiar locations and daily activities differently. I use the term 'performance installation' quite deliberately. Claire Bishop argues that installation art 'addresses the viewer directly as a literal presence in the space. Rather than imagining the viewer as a pair of disembodied eyes that survey the work from a distance, installation art presupposes an *embodied* viewer whose senses of touch, smell and sound are as heightened as their sense of vision' (2005: 6; original emphasis). Although the three performance installations I discuss rely on very different performance strategies and offer very different audience experiences, each insists that the spectator must literally enter the performance space. In the case of Jeanne Simone, the performance space, animated by the artists, unexpectedly surrounds the individual, who suddenly realizes that s/he is an audience participant. With Le Phun and Ilotopie, the individual voluntarily steps into the constructed performance space.

While not specific to a particular geographic site, each of these performance installations is specific to a site of public discourse. Art historian Miwon Kwon traces the changes in the concept of site-specificity in the visual arts, and claims that site-specific work is no longer tied to a specific physical location, but rather to the world at large. In this discursive paradigm of site-specificity, the site is a discourse, a field of knowledge that is physicalized, in part, by the place. Kwon explains, site 'is now structured (inter)textually rather than spatially, and its model is not a map but an itinerary, a fragmentary sequence of events and actions *through* spaces, that is, a nomadic narrative whose path is articulated by the passage of the artist [...] the site textualizes spaces and spatializes discourses' (2004: 29; original emphasis). Each of these three productions chooses a 'non-place' as the performance site – a city sidewalk, the median strip in a four-lane boulevard, a train station or the intersection of several busy streets, for example. The French ethnographer Marc Augé defines a 'non-place', characteristic of what he calls supermodernity, as a space of solitude (even in a crowd) where 'the link between individuals and their surroundings in the space of non-place is established through the mediation of words, or even texts' rather than personal interaction (1995: 94). The artists mentioned here seek to overturn the depersonalization of the non-place in which they perform by inserting a performative dimension into daily life, engaging the public directly, transforming the cityscape into scenic décor, and by 'breaking down the walls' between art and non-art: strategies that have the potential to effect social change (for a very different approach to space in French theatre see Chapter 2 by Michel Corvin and Chapter 3 by Céline Hersant in this volume). According to Bishop, interactive performance installations such as these, activate the spectator and 'this activation is [...] regarded as emancipatory, since it is analogous to the viewer's engagement with the world. A transitive relationship therefore comes to be implied between "activated spectatorship" and active engagement in the social-political arena' (2005: 11). Put differently, the audience experiencing installation art can have a corporeal experience of participatory democracy that, in turn, can lead to revised ideas about public space, community involvement and empowerment. Changing the perception, definition, function and possibility of a site through performance is potentially a revolutionary act that can subvert or transform the status quo.

Jeanne Simone, an urban dance company founded in 2004, aesthetically intervenes in a public space, but not through elaborate costumes, loud music or other obvious signals marking the start of a performance. Instead, *Le Goudron n'est pas meuble*[4] begins invisibly with everyday activities as, one-by-one, the six performers enter a public space and read a newspaper, smoke, drink a coffee or lean against a tree. Unless one knows where to look, the performers' entrances are not noticed. The Artistic Dossier for the production (used to sell the show to festivals and city councils) states that a 'key concept is that of porosity between play and reality' (Jeanne Simone, 2007–8: 3). Like the artists who problematize public space, discussed by Pellegrin, these performers begin as '*bricoleurs* who appropriate and manipulate, inventing ways of using or occupying existing forms [...]. Alien to the systems they infiltrate, yet difficult to tell apart, they melt into the scenery the better to subvert it' (Pellegrin, 2007–8: 73). With Jeanne Simone, the studied performance of ordinary activities slowly begins to map the geographic site and its expected spatial practices.

The first time I saw this provocative dance piece was in June 2008 at Les Invites, a festival in Villeurbanne, near Lyon. I noticed a man walking back and forth with a gym bag, but did not know he was one of the actors until he lay down on the pavement and read a newspaper. At another performance in Aurillac in August 2008, the performer who first attracted my attention sat on a bench outside the train station reading a newspaper. She gradually moved closer and closer to the couple sitting next to her on the bench, first sharing her paper with them and then eventually lying sprawled across their laps (see Figure 4). Another performer parked her car in front of the station, opened her door, and listened to music. She slowly slid out of the car and sat on the pavement. The unusual behaviour increased until all six members of the company became visible, and their activities began to dominate the space and change its function. There is no narrative story line although there is a clear arc to the performance, and the performers never develop characters in spite of each one's distinct personality and activities. Each performance is improvised within these parameters and in response to the particular place and the reactions of the public.

Importantly, most of the audience is not expecting to see a show. This unsuspecting public is a crucial element in the performance's transformation of the public space from a 'non-place' into a space that encourages human connection grounded in the senses. The space is no longer a transit point or busy intersection, but a participatory performance site as the performers use stylized and choreographed movements to slow down and play with the people going about their daily activities. In this performance space, it is very hard for the public to remain passive spectators, since they are drawn into the action as their spectatorial role is unexpectedly transformed into unanticipated acting. The performers stop cars and lorries to climb on to them, get into them, decorate them or dance to music blaring from the radio. They lie down in the street, thus forcing traffic to slow down, or put police tape across the entrances to the metro that people must break through or duck under as the escalator carries them to the street level. I was standing on the edge of what had become the performance space, taking pictures – a clear spectating role – when suddenly I felt wads of newspaper being pushed up my trouser legs by an actor who was lying on the ground behind me. I was immediately part of the show, as other spectators took pictures of my reaction. Both performer and spectator inhabit the world of the street and the world of theatre simultaneously. What is experienced in the aesthetic world acquires an uncanny reality, and what is experienced in the actual world develops an imaginative quality. Street theatre does

Figure 4   Montage of images from Jeanne Simone's *Le Goudron n'est pas meuble* at Aurillac, 2008 ©Susan Haedicke

not eliminate the boundary between the fictional world and the actual world. Instead, it constructs an alternative reality.[5] Usually, the unsuspecting spectator laughs as she or he is invited or compelled to become a performer in this artistic intervention, but there are times when some members of the public refuse to play along, and push an actor away or honk while driving dangerously close to an actor in the street. The show ends with each performer slowing down the theatrical activity so much that the audience eventually disperses: 'Once they have breathed new life into this space that, through habit, had become used without being seen, once they have turned it upside down, fleshed and sounded it out, they settle down and allow the normal flux of reality to reappear' (Jeanne Simone, 2007–8: 3).

When asked about the starting point of the performance, Laure Terrier, the artistic director of the company, responded without hesitation, 'le lieu' – 'the place'. But for her, 'place' is not just geographic location. Rather, it is a blend of de Certeau's 'practised place' where connection is established between a physical and auditory site and a corporeal perception and sensation (de Certeau, 1988: 117–22), and American art historian Grant Kester's 'conversation pieces' which he identifies as 'community + communication' artworks that begin as a dialogue and find their artistic practice and form in the interpersonal relations experienced during the event: 'parting from the traditions of object-making, these artists have adopted a performative, process-based approach. They are "context-providers" rather than "content-providers"' (Kester, 2004: 1). Trained as a dancer, Terrier uses dance as a response to the place – the heat, the damp, the noise, all stimulate her body. It is not the dance itself that interests her, however. She uses 'dance to reveal and to enter into discussion with the bodies next to me in a particular place: the non-dancing body, the spectator, the passer-by' (Terrier in Haedicke, 2008a; my translation). Her moving body, she believes, overturns the public's expectations of movement and interaction in the space and gives permission for other bodies who just happen to be there to re-inhabit and take over the public space – 'a transgression, certainly, but also an authorization' (ibid.).

Whereas the performers in *Le Goudron n'est pas meuble* swirl the action around the unsuspecting public, in the performance installations by Le Phun and Ilotopie, on the other hand, the audience is invited to enter the clearly demarcated performance space. In these works, the intentional theatricalization of the world makes its performed idiosyncrasies and trivialities more *real* (or at least more transparent) than 'real life'. This, in turn, draws attention to the spaces themselves and the socio-political contexts that determine their meaning, identity and function. Like hyperrealist art, they put the image being interrogated in unusually sharp focus so that things taken for granted or overlooked seem to be surprisingly vivid. The environment creates a 'symbolic site' of heightened reality that challenges the public's unexamined assumptions.

Several years ago, Le Phun developed *La Vengeance des semis*,[6] a piece constructed as a simulacrum of a French farm, with a cottage, gardens of flowers and vegetables, sheds and livestock. They placed it incongruously in an urban centre, and since it was not advertised, its appearance in spaces where it did not belong – the platform at a train station, a city square, along a main road – was startling and unsettling. The farm is set up during the night so that it is in place and 'running' by the time people begin going to work. For three days or more, Le Phun live and work the farm. They cook, eat, sleep, garden, harvest their crops, and tend the animals as the public wanders through the space. The small Phun farm (a pun on the English 'fun farm') is clearly out of place in its surroundings, hemmed in on all sides by the urban setting – a rural oasis amidst concrete. Here, the vegetables must grow quickly, not even waiting for the plants. The tomatoes, aubergines, cabbages, and other fruits and vegetables that appear in artistic patterns right on the soil, get bigger and bigger each day, until they are ready to be harvested. In a video of the performance in Australia, a spectator asked an apparent farmer, 'Are you artists?' He responded, 'We're farmers – see our crops, our animals. Would you like some soup made from the vegetables in our garden?' To which the Australian answered, 'I grow vegetables and mine never look like that.' The actor just shrugged and offered him a shovel.

Creating an intentional performance of the quotidian, Le Phun offer a reality that mimics everyday life on a farm, but in a troubling way that defies logic. The work challenges the audience with a unique proposition: to accept the lie as the truth. It is this apparent disconnection between what the spectators see to be real and what they know must be real that shakes the security and stability of their everyday world. And, just as suddenly as the farm appears, it disappears. The actors dismantle the cottage, gardens, sheds and pastures overnight, so in the morning, the farm is a public memory that has forever altered the cityscape for those who saw it. The disappearance of this performative family farm also draws attention to the plight of the small independent farmer and the increasing number of family farm closures in France – an important issue as farm subsidies are being debated in the European Union.

In *Confins*,[7] Ilotopie drew attention to the obvious theatricality of a public space by building an imaginative community on urban sidewalks: a self-contained 'village-spectacle' that imposed itself on the life of the city. *Confins* was the fourth creation in a series of *champs d'expériences* that the company's co-director, Françoise Léger, describes as 'a process of wide open explorations in the social "field" [or arena], the field of ways of life, of questions of engagement, of the place and role of the artist in society' (Heilmann et al., 2008: 87; my translation). These works, she writes, were artistic forays into the 'continuum between life and its representation, between text and context, between spectators and actors. The fragility, the uncertainty, the unpredictability of the experiences, the doubts are the ingredients with which to weave new connections, seminal routes where one doesn't know who initiates what!' (ibid.). Léger admits that *Confins* was the result of an enduring dream to create 'a total spectacle, a show that would blend life, perform-ance, the quotidian, the extraordinary, and the prosaic; a show where the involvement of the actors would be without cessation, a show that would put us definitively in the game, and force us to invent life that works with that game' (ibid: 102).

The 12 actors arrive and begin construction of their space-age-looking village. Narrow orange tubes connect the many elliptical pods, pointed at each end. The pods are either green and blue or green and orange. Slides or slopes create an easy way to descend from the pods several meters above the pavement. Every section of the village is connected to the parts around it, so nothing is free-standing (almost like a tinker-toy creation with pods replacing the circular wooden connectors). The actors talk with passers-by, share food, answer questions and play with children as they build their habitat. Unlike Le Phun's performers, the Ilotopie performers openly acknowledge that the construction is a per-formance project, when asked by the public.

The performance installation is 'an ephemeral site that develops forms of the future and offers itself to passers-by, the public, spectators – porous spaces, both interior and exterior, welded together, architecture for men and women, conceived like enormous clothing' (Heilmann et al., 2008: 103). The actors live in their overcrowded village of open and exposed living spaces for six to nine days and nights and invite the public to join them. They shower in a suspended pod, sleep in other pods, eat, dance and play cards in the open air with the public walking through the habitat, stopping to chat or stare, or joining in the activi-ties. Inspired by the myth of Sisyphus, the artists transform the endless pushing of the boulder uphill only to watch it roll back down, into recognizable and yet iconic ordinary activities. They play a game with children, who are encouraged to sort black and white pebbles into two separate piles, only to see them put back into one jar once they have finished. In another example, a man dressed in a suit and carrying a briefcase walks up a ramp and slides back down over and over, offering a vivid visual metaphor of the monotony of a traditional nine-to-five job. The pace is slow, the text is improvised, and there are no narrative builds. Ilotopie put ordinary life on display and encourage the urban inhabitants to see city life with new eyes. 'To work with the real is essentially political,' claims Léger. 'To choose a public space for a décor, to reintroduce both the myth [of Sisyphus] and utopia into this space of ordinary life, signals that we can alter our daily life, our way of living together' (ibid.: 104). Although the activities in the performance event seem to move at a recognizably realistic pace, in actuality life here is in hyper-drive as the village is constructed, inhabited and dismantled in about a week.

Long-time photographer and chronicler of street theatre, Christophe Renaud de Lage, writes:

> To break the established rapport between stage and auditorium, to leave the beaten path created by institutions, to transform the rapport with the public, to rediscover a taste for risk and innovation, to invent new modes of production, to refuse the tyranny of money and its submission to mass appeal, to imagine other ways of living, to look for new connections with objects, things and people, to shift the focus from 'me' to the collective, all that, yes, is really revolutionary. It is true that in order to change life, we must begin by transforming, each at her/his own pace, our rapport with the world.
>
> (2000: 16; my translation)

The utopian rhetoric that de Lage uses to describe street theatre (and this is sometimes echoed in work by scholars in theatre, sociology and human geography) may seem out of place in France today. Tensions over issues of immigration and national identity, and the attendant racial hostilities, have increased in the last few decades. These are vividly demonstrated in incidents such as the 1989 *l'affaire des foulards* (the headscarf affair); the closure of the Sangatte refugee camp in 2003; rioting in several major French cities in response to the death of two teenagers of North-African and African descent who were chased by the police in 2005; and the 2009 bulldozing of the 'Jungle', a refugee camp near Calais.[8] In addition to this, the current economic crisis, high unemployment, President Sarkozy's aggressive right-wing government, and the growing popularity of the far Right, continue to enflame the population.[9]

French street theatre at its best holds on to its original revolutionary fervour to expose or counteract societal injustices and tensions over volatile social issues, thus performatively maintaining the radical thread in French culture and urban theory eloquently espoused by thinkers like Lefebvre, Debord and de Certeau. Street theatre's innovative performance practices not only transgress aesthetic boundaries as they overlap the worlds of art and non-art, they also intervene in official and popular discourses on a range of socio-political concerns. While the performances certainly entertain the public, they also create 'symbolic sites' and, to adopt Pellegrin's term, 'recolonize' public space. And regardless of the difficult present in which France is mired, taking back the streets just might lead to radical social change.

Notes

1. See Sue Harris (2004) and Floriane Gaber (2009a and 2009b).
2. In addition, some of the major theorists on public space have been based in France. I am thinking particularly of Michel de Certeau, Guy Debord, Michel Foucault and Henri Lefebvre.
3. 250 street theatre festivals occur in France alone, and some of the oldest, like those in Aurillac, Chalon-sur-Saône and Sotteville-lès-Rouen, have celebrated their twentieth anniversary.
4. Two video clips of performances of *Le Goudron n'est pas meuble* are available on Dailymotion. One took place in Paris in June 2007 (www.dailymotion.com/video/x36yqq_compagnie-jeanne-simone_fun). A longer clip of the production in Aurillac in August 2008 reveals the start of the show as the actors and their actions blend into the surroundings at first, and it continues as the performers gradually exaggerate ordinary activities to signal performance (www.dailymotion.pl/video/x7j67z_le-goudron-nest-pas-meublecie-jeann_creation).
5. Unlike Augusto Boal's 'invisible theatre', which acts as a powerful theatrical tool to affect social change by creating the theatrical interventions that are experienced as real by an unsuspecting audience, here the public must understand that the actions are performed.
6. Photographs and a video clip of *The Seedlings' Revenge on Manchester* (Manchester, July 2003) are available on Le Phun's website: www.lephun.net.
7. Photographs of *Confins* are available on Ilotopie's website: www.ilotopie.com. A video of *Confins* is available at HorsLesMurs.
8. *L'affaire des foulards* refers to an infamous incident in recent French history when the headmaster of a school in the Parisian *banlieues* prohibited three Maghrebi girls from attending if they wore headscarves. This eventually resulted in a 2004 law banning the wearing of all 'ostentatious' religious symbols in public schools.
9. See Alec Hargreaves (1995) and Andrew Hussey (2008) for good discussions of racial tensions in France today. In my article, 'The Outsider Outside: Performing Immigration in French Street Theatre,' (2008b), I look at issues of immigration in France, and French attitudes towards the perceived threat to national identity that migrants pose, as a way to examine the potential for the efficacy of street theatre productions that theatricalize the outsider.

Works cited

Augé, Marc (1995) *Non-Places: Introduction to an Anthropology of Supermodernity*, trans. John Howe (London: Verso).

Bishop, Claire (2005) *Installation Art* (London: Routledge).

de Certeau, Michel (1988) *The Practice of Everyday Life*, trans. Steven Rendall (Berkeley: University of California Press).

—— (1998) *The Capture of Speech and Other Political Writings*, trans. Tom Conley (Minneapolis: University of Minnesota Press).

de Lage, Christophe Renaud (2000) *Intérieur rue: 10 ans de théâtre de rue (1989–1999)* (Paris: Éditions Théâtrales).

Delfour, Jean-Jacques (1997) 'Rue et théâtre de rue: habitation de l'espace urbain et spectacle théâtral', in *Espaces et Sociétés 90/91: Les Langages de la rue* (Paris: L'Harmattan), pp. 145–66.

Gaber, Floriane (2009a) *40 Years of Street Arts*, trans. Kate Merrill (Paris: Editions Ici & Là).

—— (2009b) *How It All Started: Street Arts in the Context of the 1970s*, trans. Kate Merrill (Paris: Éditions Ici & Là).

Haedicke, Susan (2008a) 'Unpublished Interview with Laure Terrier'.

—— (2008b) 'The Outsider Outside: Performing Immigration in French Street Theatre', in Patrick Anderson and Jisha Menon (eds), *Performance and Violence: Local Roots and Global Routes of Conflict* (Basingstoke: Palgrave Macmillan), pp. 31–53.

Hargreaves, Alec G. (1995) *Immigration, 'Race' and Ethnicity in Contemporary France* (London: Routledge).

Harris, Sue (2004) '"Dancing in the Streets": The Aurillac Festival of Street Theatre', *Contemporary Theatre Review*, 14:2, 57–71.

Heilmann, Éric, et al. (2008) *Les Utopies à l'épreuve de l'art: Ilotopie* (Montpellier: L'Entretemps Éditions).

HorsLesMurs (2008) *Le Goliath 2008–2010: L'Annuaire des professionnels* (Fontenay-sous-Bois: HorsLesMurs).

Hussey, Andrew (2008) 'The Paris Intifada: The Long War in the Banlieue', *Granta*, 101, 41–59.

Jeanne Simone (2007–8) *Le Goudron n'est pas meuble. Artistic Dossier* (unpublished), (English translation by the company).

Kester, Grant H. (2004) *Conversation Pieces: Community + Communication in Modern Art* (Los Angeles: University of California Press).

Kwon, Miwon (2004) *One Place after Another: Site-Specific Art and Locational Identity* (Cambridge, MA: MIT Press).

Pellegrin, Julie (2007–8) 'Recolonizing Public Space: Direct Action and Delinquency', *Art Press 2*, 7:3, 69–77.

Siminot, Michel (1999) 'L'Art de la rue. Scène urbaine – scène commune?', *Rue de la Folie*, 3:1, 1–15.

14
Xavier le Roy: The Dissenting Choreography of One Frenchman Less

Bojana Cvejic

Xavier Le Roy has conceived and presented his work as contemporary dance signed by a French choreographer, as opposed to disseminating it under the banner of French dance *per se*. As a contemporary French artist, Le Roy is inclined towards the themes and methods of French theory, such as, for instance, its critique of spectacle, exploration of alternative forms of spectatorship and interest in how the body is represented. But in his attitude towards the material conditions of dance and its modes of production (both in terms of institution and dissemination), he has consciously sought to distance himself from the authorship model of choreography that dominates the French dance scene. More often that not, this positions the choreographer as the director of a given dance company, and also places her/him at the head of a Centre chorégraphique national (CNN). Le Roy's work has remained steadfastly independent and internationally orientated, and his attempt to experiment with alternative ways of working has, by implication, real aesthetic and political significance. This fact is critical because it determines the specific form of Le Roy's *dissent* from the majority of French *nouvelle danse* practitioners like Maguy Marin, Régine Chopinot, Angelin Preljocaj or Mathilde Monnier. In this mode of production, the existence of a stable company and well-funded infrastructure subsidized by the French State has resulted in a distinctive choreographic style and 'signature' that is perpetuated from one choreography to another.

   Le Roy's work is also dissensual within the larger, international framework of contemporary dance *per se*. His performances choreograph bodies and movements, as well as inviting heterogeneous forms of spectatorial attention, that usually have no 'part' in dance work today. My use of the word 'part' is intentional – it refers to Jacques Rancière's notion of 'the distribution of the sensible', which might be understood as the disciplinary management of actions, movements, gestures, bodies and patterns of perception by the established order (2006:12). By drawing on Rancière's ideas, I want to show in this chapter how Le Roy dissents from dominant conceptions of choreography and performance in France and elsewhere.

Choreographing *dispositifs*

In dance criticism, Le Roy's background in molecular biology has provided a convenient rationale for understanding his research-oriented work. Since he had to produce his biography in a programme note for the first time in 1994, Le Roy has been designated as a 'scientist *cum* dancer'. This moniker has meant that Le Roy, like his friend and fellow French choreographer Jérôme Bel, has often been criticized (sometimes quite violently) by some dance scholars for his supposedly 'conceptualist' approach to dance.[1] Here the word 'conceptualist' is synonymous with a critical form of choreography that draws, in Le Roy's case, on the thinking of philosophers such as (amongst others) Gilles Deleuze, Donna Haraway, Bruno Latour and Jacques Rancière. However, if Le Roy's performances, and the writings that accompany them, are examined in greater detail, a conceptual or theoretical orientation does certainly emerge, but only as a technique for sharpening thought, which operates in and through the performance event itself.[2] Ultimately, it is not theory that supplies Le Roy with ideas to choreograph on the stage; his ideas stem from a concern with issues that are specific to the representation of human and non-human bodies in movement, and to the types of spectatorship that these engage.

A more accurate way of approaching Le Roy's choreography is to see it in terms of the famous *politique des auteurs* (politics of authorship) that emerged in French cinema in the 1950s and 1960s.[3] Le Roy's politics of authorship lie in the way that he purposefully attempts to rupture the Modernist view of dance as the continuous flow of motion in and through body, and which necessarily takes place within a specific medium.[4] Instead, his work proposes a radically heteronomous view of choreography as the organization of any movement whatever.[5] The focus of his research does not target the medium of dance itself, but rather aims at a much wider *dispositif* that one might refer to, in broad terms, as 'theatrical performance'. In line with Michel Foucault's articulation of the concept, the word *dispositif,* as I use it, is more than a spatial or architectural arrangement of stage space; it is an apparatus that shapes spectatorial attention by organizing its modes of perception in an ideological fashion.

Le Roy's preoccupation with the theatrical *dispositif* resides in his two-fold critique of representation. The first object of critique concerns the notion of spectatorship and deals with questions of perception, recognition and identity. The second tackles the issue of authorship, a problem that Le Roy explicitly critiqued when he exchanged authorial positions with Jérôme Bel in the performance, *Xavier Le Roy* (1999). Whereas Bel signed the performance as its author, Le Roy 'realized' it, thus separating the function of 'authoring' from the labour of making. In a 2003 interview, Le Roy explained:

> I was trying to affirm a certain kind of movement, a 'language' or signature as the first step usually needed to develop a career as a choreographer. If this is accepted the next step is to extend and transmit this 'language' to others in order to make group choreography, like some kind of clone of yourself that allows your signature to establish itself and gain recognition. Having accomplished that, you then have access to larger means of production (from solo to company director in a Stadttheater for example).
>
> (Le Roy, 2003)

For Le Roy, 'signature' epitomizes the distinctive aesthetic traits of an individual dance style that is translated from one work to another in order to represent the choreographer in the entirety of her/his *œuvre*. Aesthetic continuity of this sort is politically conservative, since it tends to ignore, if not wilfully repress, the questions that a more singular working practice might uncover. For Le Roy, by contrast, to choreograph is ostensibly to pose a series of specific problems that can only be solved by adopting a strikingly different *dispositif* for each new performance. In the following analytical accounts of his three major works – *Self-Unfinished* (1998), *Untitled* (2005) and *Le Sacre du printemps (The Rite of Spring, 2007)* – I shall describe how Le Roy disrupts the dominant Western tradition of choreography.

Beyond recognition: *Self-Unfinished*

The format of the performance solo in the piece *Self-Unfinished* marked a conscious effort, on Le Roy's part, to break with the protocol of the 'signature'. The objective was not only to perform on the stage alone, but to take responsibility for every aspect of the work in a test of artistic self-reliance. Le Roy was concerned to explore what happens in a situation where to ask *anything* from *anybody* is untenable. This experiment was conducive with his on-going interest in fragmenting, dismembering and disfiguring the body in and through movement. However, unlike earlier work, such as *Narcisse flip* (*Narcissus Flip,* 1997), which had brought to mind the image of a schizophrenic body by separating and isolating body parts, *Self-Unfinished* was driven by an attempt to prevent audiences from reading metaphors into his choreography. Le Roy wanted to short-circuit the process of 'recognition', and his performance was determined by the following question: if metaphor is the product of recognition, is recognition the dominant, if not the only, mode of spectatorial reception?

Self-Unfinished opens with Le Roy sitting at a table, observing the audience entering the space. The moment the performance begins, he looks away. During the course of the performance, he hides his head in various 'headless' bodily configurations deviating as far as possible from any recognizably human figure. After a loop of slow walks in which endless combinations of movements on stage are exhausted to the point of disorientation, Le Roy turns his shirt inside-out, while still walking. He flips his costume and bends, splitting his body in two. The result is that two pairs of 'legs' seem to appear – one masculine; the other feminine – even though the audience is always aware that these 'legs' are, in actual fact, two arms and two legs belonging to the same male body. The 'legs' are entangled and move in parallel, yet always face opposite directions. Once 'undressed' and mangled up in this way, the body appears to proliferate as a multiplicity of beings or monsters that exist on a borderline between male/ female and human/non-human. Beyond its conventional meaning as a terrifying creature, monstrosity here takes on its more archaic etymology of demonstrating, exhibiting and pointing to what normally remains hidden. If Le Roy's performance were to be captured in a series of snapshots, the multiple photographs would surely exhibit – or show – a body in transition, on its way to becoming other, that is to say, non-human.

In *Self-Unfinished,* Le Roy's strategy for avoiding metaphor was to create a game of choices for the spectator. Faced with a series of paradoxes, the spectator was challenged to see a non-human body in a human one. However, since no shape or configuration established itself long enough to become a recognizable image, recognition was inevitably frustrated. As such, the spectator was constantly invited to think about what the monstrous body in front of it was supposed to be representing, while being forced to accept that no answer was forthcoming. Le Roy explains *à propos* of *Self-Unfinished*:

I wasn't interested in producing the question, 'who is that?', even though I knew the question was a plausible one. As far as possible,

I wanted the question to be 'what is that?', and so invite the audience to ponder the meaning of these things placed in front of it. And I thought that the richness of the performance was found in the way that the spectator could attribute different meanings to the same object (or same movement), and that each individual spectator would regularly remind herself/himself that the body s/he was gazing at was both human and inhuman at the same time. As if s/he were to say to herself/himself 'that's just a person there' and then straight afterwards 'but no, it's not possible, it can't be...'.

(in Cvejic, 2009)

Encounter with indiscernibility: *Untitled*

In *Untitled* (2005), Le Roy continued in his attempts to break with the *dispositif* associated with the 'theatre of representation'. The performance was both nameless (hence, the title of the piece) and authorless (at the time of the performance, the authorship of *Untitled* could only be speculated about).[6] This conceptual intervention weakened the logic of representational theatre in what is arguably its major register – the nominal framework that allows audiences to attribute their judgement of artworks to an author. Since there was neither an author to refer back to, nor a title to associate with a definite subject or theme, the audience was confronted with a void, an emptiness. Yet, for all the politics involved in Le Roy's act of resistance, his decision was guided by much more than a straightforward desire to partake in a simple form of institutional critique; his refusal to 'sign' and title the piece was meant to reinforce the work's facticity.[7] A short description will clarify why.

As they entered the auditorium, spectators were given small battery-powered torches to find their seats, just as if they were being ushered into the cinema. However, it soon became clear that the stage itself would remain dark. From their seats, spectators began to inspect the stage, searching for the action. As they adjusted their vision to the space, they began to see objects – indiscernible objects – emerging from the obscurity, but they could barely determine whether these shapes were puppets or live (human) bodies. While the spectators shone their lights on the void of the stage, a white fog slowly covered the space, reflecting the light rays of the lamps. Vision as a faculty of perception was not denied as such; it was simply that its objects were missing.

In the performance, there was little to observe unless the spectator was prepared to search for it, and to try and discern movement from stillness and figure from background. It was often easier for the spectators to see each other than to watch the performers. As a consequence, the power of the spectacle was redirected from the stage to the audience. In so doing, *Untitled* clearly marked the dissipation of the object of performance as something that is gazed at by spectators. Rather, the performance was governed by the audience, that is to say, by their reactions to what they could and could not perceive. In *Untitled* the act of not-seeing was just as significant as the action that was occurring on stage.

But why the puppets? Le Roy admits that this investigation was inspired by Michel Serres's notion of the 'quasi-object' that he encountered in Bruno Latour's *We Have Never Been Modern* (1991). In *Untitled*, Le Roy was specifically interested in exploring how everyday objects, such as clothes and furniture, modify the ergonomics and behaviour of the body, giving it a different weight, elasticity and fluidity. Puppets attracted him because they involve human beings in a prosthetic relationship with and to an inanimate object. To move a puppet either indirectly by manipulating strings, or by engaging with it physically, also requires the human body to move. For Le Roy, as I deduced from my long affiliation with him, the idea of using 'real' puppets and mixing them with human performers disguised as puppets was triggered by the following question: how can one dispense with those forms of movement, which, no matter how unfixed, transformative and evanescent, still enable us to recognize a subject or object, even if this recognition is only fleeting?[8] The strategy of undecidability that Le Roy had used in *Self-Unfinished* was unable to answer this specific question, and so his focus turned accordingly in *Untitled* to the notion and experience of indiscernability. In the latter piece, Le Roy's choreography of dissent is characterized by a heterogeneous encounter between spectators who are forced to act because they are unable to see, and a blind stage that cannot look back.

Recasting *Le Sacre du printemps*

In his solo *Le Sacre du printemps* a man comes on stage, and turns his back on an audience bathed in brilliant light. On the downbeat of his first move (which seems to resemble the gesture made by a musical conductor), the opening bars of Stravinsky's *Le Sacre du printemps* are heard. A few minutes later, the man turns to face the audience directly and starts to 'conduct' them, calling on individual spectators to 'play' their 'instruments', as and when the music requires it. Things are immediately complicated, however, because the movements that would normally produce sound are instigated, in advance, by the music itself. The impression one has is of a mechanical karaoke. It appears that if the man were to leave the stage, the music would simply continue on its own.

The 'conductor' in this strange concert is, of course, Le Roy, who is performing in front of, and crucially *with*, an audience. The latter is seated in a conventional theatre auditorium that mimics the spatial design of a symphonic orchestra in a concert hall, with each place corresponding to a given instrument, the sound of which emerges, as if by magic, from a speaker placed beneath the seats of the spectators. But Le Roy, of course, is neither a conductor nor musician. Rather, choreography serves him in *Le Sacre du printemps* as a heuristic device: by learning the movements of conducting, he begins to listen to the music as a musician or conductor might do. Le Roy's venture into conducting can be seen as an exercise in emancipation, the pedagogical principle that Rancière developed in his seminal parable *The Ignorant Schoolmaster: Five Lessons in Intellectual Emancipation*. In that text, Rancière opposes 'emancipation' to 'instruction' (1991: 17). Whereas instruction implies an unequal and stultifying relationship rooted in the knowledge/authority of the teacher, emancipation takes place in a learning environment where both master and student are equally ignorant. Here, learning rests on the assumption of what Rancière calls the 'equality of intelligences', as well as on the existence of a third or mediating term that both connects and disconnects master and student (ibid.: 38). In *The Ignorant Schoolmaster*, this link is embodied by the book (the text) that verifies the acts of learning and teaching (see ibid.: 20–5). In Le Roy's performance, by contrast, Stravinsky's music takes the place of the book and works as an emancipatory device linking the ignorant 'conductor' to his equally ignorant 'orchestra-audience'.

Le Roy's conducting gestures are encoded in a particular way that some might recognize as belonging to those of the conductor Simon Rattle. They seem like hieroglyphs whose function is to signify and announce the music to come. Like Rattle, Le Roy, 'the dancing conductor', mimes how the music is supposed to feel, or more precisely, he represents the emotion that the musicians will subsequently interpret musically. But in doing this, Le Roy sometimes stumbles, falls behind, and fails to master his task; at other times, he deliberately lets the music continue so that he can dance on it. The performance appears untimely. Deprived of their capacity to synchronize, perfectly, sound and image, spectators sometimes laugh at this performance. They laugh at a lapse of control on the part of the conductor, and then experience that laughter as a relief from the uneasiness they feel at being asked to do what they are ordinarily not capable of: playing music.

Yet beyond the comedy, there is a serious intention behind Le Roy's's venture. His aim is to encourage the audience to join him in a performative task of which they are both ignorant. All they have in common is Stravinsky's music as a link to emancipate them from their respective roles. By sharing in the illusion of co-creating *Le Sacre du printemps* with the dancing conductor in front of them, the spectators are potentially endowed with a new capacity: the ability to listen to and perceive music as musicians. Le Roy rejects a pedagogical choreography. Instead of showing the spectators what the music could mean choreographically, he asks them to pretend to create it. In this way, Le Roy configures *Le Sacre du printemps* as yet another dissensual form that redistributes the competences and roles of those who are performing, in addition to those who are watching and listening. The spectators are emancipated in the extent to which they are invited to reinvent their own roles. As Rancière explains: 'The collective power shared by spectators does not stem from the fact that they are members of a collective body or from some specific form of interactivity. It is the power each of them has to translate what she perceives in her own way [...]. It is in this power of associating and dissociating that the emancipation of the spectator occurs' (2009: 19).

Choreographies of dissent

With *Le Sacre du printemps*, both the focus and function of Le Roy's choreography has undergone a major, if imperceptible shift. In *Self-Unfinished*, the object, for Le Roy, was still the body, the construction of which was intended to reconfigure the perspective of the audience by encouraging it to reconsider what could be seen, heard, felt and thought. In that work, Le Roy looked for forms of movement that would make the body unrecognizable and so dissociate it from conventional tropes related to gender and even accepted notions of what constitutes a human figure. According to Le Roy, the open-ended nature of the work invited the audience to use its imagination: 'There is a process for each spectator. It's your imagination creating this... I don't decide what is to be seen. There are a few proposals and then things appear and disappear in a *va-et-vient*. It's about oscillating between contrary perceptions' (2003).

Whereas *Self-Unfinished* directed the spectator's gaze away from the traditional object of performance, *Untitled* used choreography to reconfigure the entirety of the theatrical spectacle. The indiscernability of bodies, objects and movements reversed the habitual focus of attention.

Not only was the audience suddenly made aware of itself as hand-held torches picked out faces and body parts of fellow spectators in the darkness, but it no longer knew what to look at, or how to respond to the objects and shapes that it could barely see on the stage. The disorientating *sensorium* of the event, caused by diminished visibility, interfered with the traditional parameters of audience reception – the capacity to feel, understand and judge. In the process, the behaviour of the audience, which was now louder and more visible than the on-stage action, hijacked the event and became the focus of the spectacle.

At first glance, the choreography in *Le Sacre du printemps* seems to be less aggressively dissensual than the two performances mentioned above. Its function is no longer to disrupt a regime of spectatorship, but rather to translate musical performance into a contemporary dance event. Yet despite this, Le Roy posed a fundamental question that is related to the notion of emancipation: how can a dancer become a conductor? In the extent to which he identifies performing with movement and thus suggests that *everything is choreography*, Le Roy transposed the act of conducting into a form of dance, and deployed choreography as a tool for autonomous, self-directed learning. The same principle of learning without instruction allowed the spectators to enter a musical work *as if* they were creating it themselves. From being used primarily as a critical device, choreography in *Le Sacre du printemps* was intended as an experiment in emancipation, both for the dancer becoming a conductor and for the audience becoming an 'orchestra'. Arguably, the most significant aspect of the performance was found in the way that spectators were provided with the possibility of undergoing a process of what Rancière calls 'subjectification'. As Rancière explains it, subjectification occurs when through 'a series of actions of a body', 'a capacity for enunciation not previously identifiable within a given field of experience' is produced. Embracing this capacity is, Rancière argues, intimately connected with 'the reconfiguration of the field of experience' (1999: 35), for it is this that allows subjects to escape from the places they are meant to occupy and to disidentify with the people they are supposed to be.

Postscript

Having selected three performances for discussion, I have left a significant part of Le Roy's work out of consideration.[9] This includes projects such as *E.X.T.E.N.S.I.O.N.S.* (1999) and *6M1L* (Six Months One Location) (2008). In these project-platforms, Le Roy's attention is focused specifically on organizing the conditions of research and collaboration for freelance artists outside of the institutional structures currently existing in Europe. In these events, experimentation lies in drastically changing the economic and political conditions of free-lance project-based work. For instance, during *6M1L* a group of choreographers temporarily left the network of venues and festivals that have rendered their work nomadic, intermittent and spectacle-oriented, and instead gathered to share their projects and to collaborate together while working continuously in one place over a long period of time. In this regard, Le Roy's reconfiguration of the French and European dance landscape is an experiment to see if these conditions will engender other research methods, performance formats and ways of working and being together than the ones currently practised in the field. By seeking yet another *politique des auteurs* in self-organized structures today, Le Roy's work begins to grow and multiply with that of other *auteurs*. It remains to be seen how this politics will play out aesthetically, and where, and, of course, if at all in new performances.

Notes

1. See Cvejic (2006) for a detailed discussion of this point.
2. This is where Le Roy's work departs from Bel's conceptual operations. For instance, in *The Last Performance* in 1998, Bel 'rehearses' Roland Barthes' death of the author thesis, and the show is more concerned to critique theatre as a form of spectacle than to explore dance for its own sake. By contrast, Le Roy engages with the spectator more experientially than critically, as I will show in the main text. See Chapter 16 by Augusto Corrieri in this volume.
3. *La politique des auteurs* is a mode of film criticism developed by a group of young filmmakers in France – Eric Rohmer, Jean-Luc Godard, Jacques Rivette and François Truffaut – in the pages of the *Cahiers du Cinéma* and *Arts* between 1951 and 1958. They sought to assert the status of the film maker as artist, an *auteur* who, for them, was the equivalent of a novelist, poet, painter or composer. This claim led to the development of a new paradigm, the *cinéma des auteurs* or 'art cinema', where film is considered as a medium which reflects the poetics of the author, and not simply as a product of mass entertainment. In comparing Le Roy's politics of authorship with Godard's *politique des auteurs*, I am stressing a self-reflexive concern with the art of choreography, as opposed to choreographic craftsmanship in dance.
4. André Lepecki shows that dance as an autonomous art form in the West has been aligned with the 'kinetic project of modernity', which predicates movement as a mode of being. In the 1930s, the advent of modern dance in the US reasserted the ontology of dance as motility or uninterrupted movement (Lepecki, 2006: 3). 'Modern dance' is the term for a historical style of dance practices that developed in the US and Europe between the wars by choreographers Isadora Duncan, Mary Wigman, Doris Humphrey, Martha Graham et al. Another use of the term implies the strict ontological identification of dance with a moving body.

5. Le Roy's answer to the question of how to define choreography posed by the Viennese online journal *CORPUS* was: 'Choreography is (an) artificially staged action(s) and/or situation(s).' In place of movement and organization, Le Roy's definition uses terms such as 'artificial action(s)' and 'situation(s)' and 'staging'. By 'staging' Le Roy insists on theatre as a site of choreography and as a *dispositif* governing the situation of a show for an audience. See: http://www.corpusweb.net/index.php?option=com_content&task=view&id=663&Itemid=35 (accessed 1 February 2009).
6. During the period of its performance, the author of *Untitled* was only known to the show's producers and performers.
7. The performance ended by turning into an artist's talk with the audience, in which one of the performers stepped out of his puppet costume, and took on the role of spokesperson for the performance. In many of the talks held after the performance of *Untitled* the spectators repeatedly behaved as if they had been hoaxed. They persisted in trying to discover the motivations of the author and in understanding her/his reasons for concealment, as well as protesting about the situation in which they were put.
8. Essays and reviews, as well as reports from spectators, all evidence the need to name, and therefore designate the 'bodies' that Le Roy 'passes through' in *Self-Unfinished*. For instance, the German dance theorist Gerald Siegmund writes on the occasion of Tanzplatform Germany 2000: 'Le Roy walks on his shoulders, his arms flapping like chicken wings, his naked back to the audience... Le Roy evoked images of sculptured bodies and of bizarre animals that propel themselves forward in the most imaginative way' (Unknown source, courtesy of Xavier Le Roy).
9. Le Roy's works include 20 performances and projects, created since 1994. One of them, *E.X.T.E.N.S.I.O.N.S.* which ran between 1999 and 2001, was explicitly conceived and framed as a research project. Le Roy invited 20 artists to explore games and rules (as generators of choreography), working processes, and the notion of rehearsal as product and performance. Since 2004, Le Roy has been exploring a field that was completely unknown to him – twentieth-century and contemporary music. See: http://www.insituproductions.net/_eng/frameset.html.

Works cited

Cvejic, Bojana (2006), 'To End With Judgment by Way of Clarification', in Martina Hochmuth, Krassimira Kruschkova and Georg Schollhammer (eds), *It Takes Place When It Doesn't: On Dance and Performance* (Frankfurt: Revolve), pp. 49–58.
—— (2009) 'Unpublished Interview with Xavier Le Roy'.
Le Roy, Xavier (2003) 'Interview with Dorothea von Hantelmann', http://www.insituproductions.net/eng/frameset.html (accessed 1 February 2010).
Lepecki, André (2006) *Exhausting Dance: Performance and the Politics of Movement* (London: Routledge).
Rancière, Jacques (1991) *The Ignorant Schoolmaster: Five Lessons in Intellectual Emancipation*, trans. Kristin Ross (Stanford, CA: Stanford University Press).

—— (1999) *Disagreement: Politics and Philosophy*, trans. Julie Rose (Minneapolis: University of Minnesota Press).

—— (2006) *The Politics of Aesthetics*, trans. Gabriel Rockill (London: Verso).

—— (2009) 'The Emancipated Spectator', in *The Emancipated Spectator*, trans. Gregory Elliot (London: Verso), pp. 1–21.

15
A Theological Turn? French Postmodern Dance and Herman Diephuis's *D'Après J.-C.*

Nigel Stewart

Unlike other authors in this collection who have viewed French post-modern dance through the political ideas of Jacques Rancière and Guy Debord (see Bojana Cvejic (Chapter 14) and Augusto Corrieri (Chapter 16) in this volume), I intend to reflect on how it can embody and articulate the theological idea of grace as a gift given through the suffering of the flesh and the sensible intuition of life. I do this in the following stages. First, with reference to choreographic works by Jérôme Bel and Mathilde Monnier, I explore French postmodern dance in terms of the distinction that Jacques Derrida makes between a 'theological stage' of representation and a 'nontheological' theatre of unrepresentable life. Second, I contest that distinction by reading *D'après J.-C.* (*After JC*, 2004), a work by French-based choreographer Herman Diephuis, through Jean-Luc Marion's phenomenology of revelation. Finally, I suggest that *D'après J.-C.* reverberates with a much neglected Catholic tradition in French thought and theatre, and at the same time challenges French republican secularism not because of its differences from French postmodern dance, but rather because of what it has in common with the latter.

Modelling his argument on Derrida's well-known essay on Antonin Artaud, the dance theorist André Lepecki claims that the work of Jérôme Bel, and by implication French postmodern dance in general, 'displays [an ...] antitheological force' that counters the 'theological stage' (Lepecki, 2006: 54). Just as, for Roland Barthes, a 'text' has 'a single "theological" meaning' when it is mistaken for 'a line of words releasing [...] the "message" of the Author-God' (Barthes, 1977: 146), so, for Derrida:

> [t]he stage is theological for as long as its structure [...] comports the following elements: an author-creator who, absent and from afar,

is armed with a text and keeps watch over, assembles, regulates the time or the meaning of representation, letting this latter represent him as concerns what is called the content of his thoughts, his intentions, his ideas. He lets representation represent him through representatives, directors or actors, enslaved interpreters who represent characters who, primarily through what they say, more or less directly represent the thought of the 'creator'. Interpretive slaves who faithfully execute the providential designs of the 'master'.

(Derrida, 1978: 235)

To follow Derrida, a 'theological' choreography would be one in which dancer-representatives slavishly represent the auteur-choreographer's 'word' (signified idea, intention, concept), and, by extension, where spectators slavishly interpret the metaphysical meaning of this 'word' without distortion caused by the anarchic play of the physical signifier. From this perspective, French postmodern dance is decisively 'non-theological' since it calls representation itself into question. It has three major strategies for doing this. The first is to break the bond between material things and the linguistic means we have of understanding them. For instance, Jérôme Bel's *Jérôme Bel* (1995) tests the extent of language's power to author-ize physical things (see also Augusto Corrieri's chapter in this volume). Four completely naked performers are on an eight-by-ten metre stage running up to a back wall. Two of them, Claire Haenni and Frédéric Seguette, use chalk to write their personal details (names, age, bank balance, telephone numbers, weight and height) on the wall. Impassively, they then stand under what they have written. However, another performer, Gisèle Temey, chalks up 'Thomas Edison' and stands underneath this title holding an illuminated light bulb. The fourth performer, Yseult Roch, writes and positions herself below the title 'Stravinsky, Igor'; she will spend most of the show singing *Le Sacre du printemps* (see Lepecki, 2006: 49). As a result of this kind of bathetic overdetermination, *Jérôme Bel* undoes the homology between the biological identity of the physical body, cultural identity and the linguistic referent which glues the two together, and thus exposes the process in which individual subjectivities are composed through the subjectification of bodies to cultural codes and linguistic inscriptions. Moreover, in citing canonical texts (*Le Sacre du printemps*) Bel both acknowledges and troubles the determination of a professional identity by an historical tradition, a matter taken up in Xavier Le Roy's solo *Le Sacre du printemps* (2007), in which Le Roy conducts a recording of Stravinsky's ballet (see Bojana Cvejic, Chapter 14 in this volume).

Secondly, French postmodern dance is 'nontheological' since it undercuts representation by avoiding a totalizing choreographic structure that would fuse style and substance, and form and meaning. It does that by foregrounding the metonymic contingency of its constitutive elements, rather than by blending those elements into metaphors of a metaphysical reality. The choreographer Mathilde Monnier's *Déroutes* (*Diversions*, 2004) exemplifies this strategy. Not only do we see a plethora of elements in random juxtaposition but they criss-cross the stage with divergent rhythms and tempi, creating multiple foci, 'de-routing' the spectator's attention, and thus contesting the perspectival power of the proscenium arch's upstage-centre focal point. In one sequence a man in blue sleepwalks from upstage left to downstage right; a woman in orange urgently skips backwards; a large woman in grey waddles from upstage right to downstage centre; the man in blue, now upstage left, slides large blocks of ice till they smash into a fridge downstage right, the ice just missing a man in yellow lunging stage centre. Later the man in blue staggers with a five-aside football net over his head, whilst a young woman stretches and slips on the ice now melting stage centre. Throughout, one of the performers – Herman Diephuis no less – has a peculiar regularity: 'I'm changing costumes every ten minutes and I do the same tour of the stage with each new costume (I'm like the clock of the piece)'. Yet 'small changes are included to create [...] surprise. I end in the fridge' (Diephuis, 2009). The disorientating effect provoked by this contingent, value-free collage of equally important elements is radically democratic: it is now the spectator who produces meaning, and not the Author-God.

The third 'nontheological' aspect of French postmodern dance is visceral excess. In Jérôme Bel's *Jérôme Bel* the naked performers calmly stare at, draw and write on each other, dividing up the body like an animal carcass; they pull at their own loose flesh, one of them folding his scrotum over his penis; and two, Frédéric Seguette and Claire Haenni, urinate on the floor. Ladling up their urine with their hands, they then erase their personal details on the wall, but in such a way that a new sentence is formed: 'Éric chante Sting'. Sure enough, the four performers exit and in the dark a fully-dressed man, Éric Affergan, sings Sting's song 'An Englishman in New York' (Lepecki, 2006: 56–7). This goes beyond the aforementioned ways in which language is complicated at a conceptual level at the start of this show as, indeed, it also does in Bel's later work *The Last Performance* (1998). It also involves, yet ultimately transcends, a state of 'abjection' that 'pulverizes the subject', and thus abrogates the symbolic order of language through which the subject is constituted (Kristeva, 1982: 5). Of course, language here loses its meta-physical power to preside over, categorize and determine who bodies are and what bodies do, but it is retained as a material practice that evolves amongst the other things that bodies can do.

What is left once French postmodern dance has dismantled the representational structures of the 'theological stage' through bathetic overdetermination, metonymic contingency and visceral excess? The answer is beauty, as Tim Etchells finds witnessing Bel's *The Show Must Go On* (2000):

> I find myself looking at the people, my eyes scanning left to right and back again at whim. The way that one moves her wrist, the way that one dips his eyes. [...] I start to think that everyone looks beautiful in Jérôme's shows. [...] Perhaps this beauty arises because everyone here is [...] present in a mode that is resolutely without drama. [...] Where drama might demand or force my attention on a moment-by-moment basis, the gift of [...] Bel's work, is that it gives me the [...] time to look [...]. The [...] slowness of change in the piece and the simplicity of movement, all [...] occasion a wealth of vivid, amazing detail.
>
> (Etchells, 2000: 2)

Thus if French postmodern dance rejects the way in which 'the theo-logical stage comports a passive, seated public [...] of consumers [...] attending a production [...] offered to their voyeuristic scrutiny' (Derrida, 1978: 235), it does so not only so that those consumers can be 'reborn' as active readers of 'obtuse meaning' by virtue of 'signifiant' performance texts (Barthes, 1977: 54–5, 148), but, as Bel's work dem-onstrates, so that spectators may bear witness to performers as human beings by virtue of their vulnerability and ipseity.[1]

So what then of *D'après J-C.*? In the terms set out by Lepecki and Derrida, Diephuis's 50-minute work appears to be the very opposite of the anti-theological impulse dominating French postmodern dance. There are two 'theological' reasons for this, both of which guide the spectator to understand the show in particular ways. Firstly, the mac-rostructure of the work creates a coherent representational framework. The piece consists, in effect, of a montage of *tableaux vivants* based on paintings of different stages of the life of Christ by Bellini, Botticelli, Caravaggio, Da Vinci, Durer, Memling, Michelangelo, Raphael and other Renaissance artists. In each tableau, two dancers explicitly rec-reate poses depicted in those paintings. Christ is danced by Julien

Gallée-Ferré; Mary by Claire Haenni, veteran of Jérôme Bel's company. He is dressed in a white T-shirt and track-suit trousers; she in blue track-suit trousers, a white T-shirt and a white 'hoody' with black and blue horizontal stripes (see Figure 6). Their poses are organized to form an obvious linear narrative. The first section recreates paintings of the Madonna and Child, the second of Christ's ministry, the third the Deposition from the Cross, the fourth *Pietàs*, the last Christ in the tomb. This linear progression is made emphatic by the fact that each section occurs downstage of the point where the previous section has just occurred. Thus images concerning Madonna and Child are located far upstage centre, the Depositions occur stage centre, and Christ in the tomb the furthest point downstage centre. Unlike Monnier's *Déroutes*, the show works with the laws of perspective that are obtained in the proscenium arch theatre.

This untroubled perspective allows the spectator to become absorbed with carefully worked representational effects. One of the most striking is at the start: in pitch dark Bach's *Cantata for Alto* (BWV 170) is blasted, Mary hovers in mid-air and the dark is riven by a long thin bright white slit. Christ crawls out from the slit's end. Creation has taken place *ex nihilo*. The effect depends on optical tricks. Before the show starts, Haenni stands on a masked plinth placed on a black table covered in a black cloth. She is wrapped in a long white apron and then concealed head to foot by a large black cape. Furthermore, all exit signs are turned off whilst lights are trained into the auditorium; when those lights fade to blackout at the show's start spectators struggle to see anything at all. Haenni's face is then picked out by a tightly focused profile. Carefully she opens the cape to expose a strip of the white apron subtly illuminated by low level floods and stage-right rectangular arrangements of mid-height Svobodas (low-voltage lamps wired in series). So, unlike the 'nontheological' choreographies I have mentioned, the opening illusion, reinforced by the drama of Bach's music, is not broken down into the elements through which it is cunningly constructed. At this point, spectators drift into the illusion itself: the stage provides metaphors of a metaphysical reality which it does not dispel.

The second main 'theological' characteristic of *D'après J.-C.* is dynamic expressivity. This is especially the case with Haenni who has been trained in the Expressionist technique of Hans Züllig, which provided the basis for company dance class at Pina Bausch's Wuppertal Tanztheater. The company joke that the end of the second section, in which Haenni fluidly changes plane whilst carving through space, is the 'Bausch bit'. Indeed, Haenni's ability to modulate the tensional

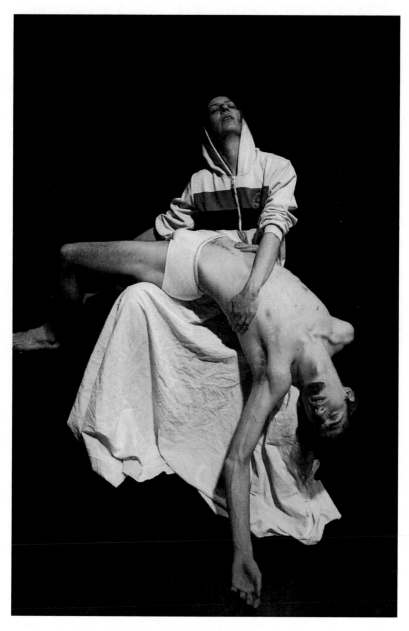

Figure 6 Julien Gallée-Ferré (Christ) and Claire Haenni (Mary) in Herman Diephuis's *D'après J.-C.*, 2006 Photo: Marco Barbon

qualities of her own body in a manner reminiscent of Expressionist dance is remarkable. This is everywhere evident in the second section in which, by turns, her hands can be clawed or slack, her face grimaced or sunken, but dynamic modulation is easier to contemplate in the central Deposition scene. For the third tableau, based on a Deposition fresco of around 1325 by Pietro Lorenzetti, Haenni hollows her cheeks and torso with abrupt centripetal force in opposition to her lips which pout towards the back of Gallée-Ferré's limp right hand. Yet in the next tableau, based on a 1435 Deposition by Rogier van der Weyden, Haenni's head and arms flop but her body widens with freer outward flow than the depiction of Mary in the original altar panel. In fact, Diephuis is willing to make some of the lesser known originals more dynamic. For instance, in the sixth tableau Gallée-Ferré's right arm is pulled diagonally forward by Haenni and her gaze lifts to create more line, depth and volume than in Dieric Bouts's rather flat *Passion Altarpiece* (*circa* 1455) from which this tableau is derived.

From my account of this Expressionist tendency we could infer that *behind* Haenni's movements is an intending self that is expressed through what is represented *by* those movements. If, in turn, this representation is compliant with what Diephuis intends, Haenni's dynamic expressivity would typify a 'theological' choreography as defined in Derrida's terms. Indeed, if the spectator of *D'après J.-C.* then merely interprets what the dancer intends, it could also be said that the spectator's interpretation is the last in a hierarchy of slavish interpretations: from actual events (the life of Jesus, a first-century Nazarene Jew) to their retelling (the Gospels); to liturgical schema (the Nativity, the Deposition, the Tomb, etc.) which distil the Gospel narratives; to painterly representations of those schema; to Diephuis's choreographic representations of those paintings; to the horizon of the intending 'I' of the dancer who animates that choreography according to the choreographer's intentions; and so finally to the horizon of the spectator's understanding of the dancer.

And yet ultimately *D'après J.-C.* cannot be categorized accordingly to this 'theological' versus 'nontheological' binary logic. Partly this is because there are too many so-called 'nontheological' goings-on. For a start, things drop. When Gallée-Ferré sits on Haenni's knees in a series of Madonna and Child tableaux, he picks up a different object – a book, an apple, a toy bird, a pear – for each pose, but when the pose ends he lets the object fall. Later a large plastic fish and many bread buns plummet from the flies, the clutter of which brings the second section, that most climatic of all sections, to an abrupt and bathetic end. It is not just the sound of these objects as they smack the ground that disturbs contemplation of the otherwise exquisite tenderness of the first section or the exhilarating speed of the second; rather it is the fact that the sacred illusion of a meticulously composed representation, which gains its dynamic agency through some kind of resistance to gravity, has suddenly been interrupted by the real weight of things, and thus of things *qua* things: things as profane or concrete.

The same is true of bodies. The exemplary case of the profane intruding within the sacred is the central third section in which Gallée-Ferré and Haenni are augmented by an ensemble of between 10 and 12 volunteers of different ages who help create the Deposition tableaux. Diephuis's rule is that these persons must be non-dancers. Although exactly the same tableaux are efficiently rehearsed with each new ensemble, and although the 'profane' ensemble of non-dancers and the 'sacred' trained dancers are integrated in each stage picture, the spectator is always aware of the difference between the two, a difference registered not simply because the ensemble wear their own casual clothes but the 'daily' way in which they hold their bodies in contradistinction to the sophisticated 'extra-daily' organization of weight manifest in the bodies of the two dancers (for instance, Haenni's subtle play of tensions). Certainly, the obligation placed upon the ensemble to lift and manipulate Gallée-Ferré and Haenni demands physical application, but such demands would be within the capabilities of anyone who, like Simon of Cyrene, was cajoled from the street to fulfil the same task. Aware of this and that a different ensemble will be used elsewhere, the spectator is all the more attentive to the peculiarity of each person in the present ensemble. Moreover, each tableau is weighed long enough for the spectator to behold each person with a care and fascination that matches Etchells' discovery of beauty and vivid detail in the performers he witnesses in Bel's *The Show Must Go On*.

In fact, the weight of things is also felt within the two dancers' work. At the end of the first section, Haenni lets Gallée-Ferré drop to the floor. In between each of the four loops of the second section, both dancers 'drop' the shapes they momentarily hold and then walk matter of factly back to their starting positions for the next loop. This rift between starting and dropping has an even more critical function in the fastest passage of the show that bursts forth after the fourth loop. Here the dissolving from one pose to the next is so swift that these poses marvellously coalesce into an illusion of animate life – yet even here each pose is weighed for just long enough to prevent those dissolvings from becoming entirely seamless and the illusion entirely complete. It is like watching an early film or a cartoon flip-book: attention is drawn both to the flow of time *and* to the flicker of the void between each temporal instant. Here what can be said about choreography is the same as what the film theorist Mary Ann Doane, summarizing Gilles Deleuze, says about 'cinematography': namely, that it makes 'possible the synthesis through the projection of [separate and instantaneous] moments, but nevertheless depend[s] upon their spacing and separate articulation. [...T]ime is a series of equivalent and equidistant instants [...] subjected to no hierarchy whatsoever' (Doanne, 2002:179). This is precisely the feature which I noted in the 'nontheological' presentification of elements as contingent and contiguous.

But to acknowledge properly this contingency and the feeling of weight intrinsic to the experience of contingency, I must step beyond Derrida to his sometime student, the phenomenologist Jean-Luc Marion. For Marion, contingency and gravity are intimately allied, for 'contingent says what touches me, what [...] arrives to me (according to the Latin) or (according to the German) what [...] "falls upon me from above"' (Marion, 2002: 125). But for Diephuis as for Marion this goes beyond the obvious – the objects and bodies that fall to the floor, the fish and buns that fall from the flies – to the ethical implications of witnessing this performance. To grasp the contingency of a phenomenon we must allow it to fall upon us in the sense that 'it must first be endured, borne, suffered' (ibid.). This is precisely what happens to Haenni when she holds Gallée-Ferré in the first and final sections, and what happens to the ensemble when they hold both performers: they literally endure, bear, suffer (in the fuller and older sense of being open to and vulnerable before) the weight of these bodies (see Figure 6). If Diephuis, like the Renaissance artists he copies, emphasizes the compositional clarity of each tableau and avoids visceral excess (say, afterbirth in the nativity tableaux, or blood and water in the Deposition tableaux), he does so to clarify (kin)aesthetically the primary structure of care as a be-holding of the other (in this double sense). And the audience too, is implicated in this structure: we behold them holding. Indeed, if, as I have indicated, we are given the full weight of time to care for the other upon whom we gaze, we can no longer be an observer of 'a constituted spectacle'; rather, this other casts *me* as her/his witness, 'weighs on my gaze like a weight, a burden' so that I 'learn of myself from what the gaze of the Other says to me in silence' (ibid.: 232–3).

What is said and learnt in this case? Diephuis told me that the Depositions and *Pietàs* bear down on him with the memory of caring for a close friend with AIDS, a friend who uncomplainingly gave his body to be lifted and shifted when he could no longer move himself. Yet the explication of such meanings, even those held by the choreographer, does not account for the (kin)aesthetic idea of those *Pietàs* in performance. Certainly, the meanings that we receive from a performance can be enduring, or they might be as fleeting as meanings that rise with the vapours of perfume (Marion, 2008: 132) – but, again, all such meanings are spoken in silence from within the 'carnal texture' of the performance itself: 'The explication does not give us the idea itself; it is but a second version of it, a more manageable derivative' (Merleau-Ponty, 1968: 150). In this sense, *D'après J.-C.* is not an *exposable* representation – exposed by and reducible to a ruling concept that regulates how that work should be understood, tells us what it is 'about', and is itself independent of that representation. Rather, as Marion, quoting Immanuel Kant, says of the 'aesthetic idea' in general, *D'après J.-C.* is an 'inexposable representation of the imagination' in which concepts are born within, contingent upon and 'saturated' by the spectator's sensible intuition of the kinaesthetic idea given in each experience of that work in performance (Marion, 2000: 196, 197). This, then, troubles the earlier suggestion that any spectator of *D'après J.-C.* is the last in a hierarchy of 'enslaved interpreters', each of whom reduces their lived experience of what they receive from above to an interpretation that slavishly represents what has been supposedly intended in what they receive.

As an 'inexposable representation of the imagination', *D'après J.-C.* also deconstructs Derrida's opposition between a 'theological stage' of 'total representation' and a 'nontheological' Artaudian theatre presentifying 'unrepresentable' life (Derrida, 1978: 234). For here the different ways in which time is given for the spectator to bear witness to movement is such that the emphasis in performance is not on what each movement represents, but on the presentification in movement of different appearances of what is represented. This is supremely evident in that passage following the fourth loop of the second section. I wanted to write this chapter because I once thought that this passage exemplified a transmutation of static visuality into kinetic temporality, but I now see it, and the show in general, as a profound mediation on visibility itself. I see the visible bursting. Here the tension between a synthesis of movements and the spacing and separate articulation of each contingent movement ensures that as a spectator I achieve not an accumulative synthesis of the whole but rather an 'instantaneous synthesis' of each movement as it occurs (Marion, 2000: 199). Here dancing works like a cubist painting, for I see neither the original paintings as such, nor even different facets of those paintings, but rather a 'continual proliferat[ion]' of different appearances of each painting's different facets within the ever-evolving texture of moving bodies. The choreographer and dancer, like the cubist painter, 'exhaust [themselves] in the endless race toward the impossible and ever elusive summation of the visible bursting' (Marion, 2002: 201, 202). For Marion, this 'visible bursting' speaks of the grace, gift or givenness of life itself which gives itself most fully in revelation. And, crucially, for Marion, speaking as a phenomenologist, the 'paradigm' case of the phenomenon of revelation is 'the manifestation of Jesus Christ' (ibid.: 236) – or, I might add, a revelation that is *d'après J.-C.* ('after' or 'according to' Jesus Christ). This is because 'the phenomenon of Christ gives itself intuitively', first, 'as an event that is perfectly unforeseeable because radically heterogeneous to what it nevertheless completes (the prophecies)'; second, as an event that is 'unbearable' in that he is revealed 'by an excess of intuition, a 'vision' that, as on the Damascus Road, I 'no longer see by dint of seeing'; and third as an event that is 'irregardable [...] because [...] he regards me in such a way that he constitutes me as his witness rather than some transcendental I, constituting him to [my] own liking' (Marion, 2000: 236, 238–40).

Experienced in these ways, *D'après J.-C.* not only presents a theological turn, albeit of an unorthodox kind, in French dance (and it is important to remember here that France is a country where *laïcité* has been an integral part of the republican constitution since the 1870s); it also resonates with the concerns of French Catholic humanist thinkers such as Charles Péguy and Paul Claudel, and later Maurice Blondel and Emmanuel Mounier, as well as with those French phenomenologists – including Gabriel Marcel, Michel Henry and Marion himself – who have taken a 'theological turn' (Marion, 2000). Unlike the monarchist and proto-fascist Catholicism of Charles Maurras and Action française, Catholic humanism stressed that, through the revelation of God within human experience, we can realize the degree to which we are existentially bound to each other. Equally, it argued that in realizing the conditions of existence through suffering in the flesh with and for others, we can experience God. This was a largely existentialist spirituality which, by necessity, flowered into an inclusive and transcendent form of Socialism in which to suffer for and with others was to experience grace. As Alexander Dru puts it in relation to Péguy – and as audiences might experience in the instantaneous synthesis of contingent movement in *D'après J.-C.* – grace is experienced at the 'junction of the temporal and the eternal, not in some theory or metaphysic but, as with Kierkegaard, in the instant of existence, which is the meeting-point of time and eternity' (Dru, 1970: 134).

Diephuis is not the only performance maker in France whose work can be grasped in terms of an ethics and politics of grace and revelation. According to David Bradby, influential directors and playwrights like Eric-Emmanuel Schmitt, Valère Novarina and Olivier Py propose 'a new kind of relationship with [the] audience not unlike that sought by Bill Viola: a space for reflection and contemplation' in which we may 'glimpse' a 'moment of eternity' that 'may reconcile us' to 'the suffering that is everywhere around and within' (Bradby, 2005: 244).

To conclude, I will finish where I began and note that, in deconstructing the Derridean opposition between theological and anti-theological theatre(s), *D'après J.-C.* claims many of the so-called 'nontheological' characteristics of French postmodern dance (contingency, presentification, witnessing) as part of this turn. In this respect, *D'après J.-C.* is indeed a revelation *d'après J.-C.*

Notes

1. Editors' note: For Barthes, the function of obtuse meaning is to multiply the possibility of meaning(s), while remaining, itself, beyond description: 'the obtuse meaning is a signifier without a signified, hence the difficulty in naming it' (1977: 61). This notion of obtuse meaning is comparable with the notion of the '(kin)aesthetic idea' developed later in the essay.

Works cited

Barthes, Roland (1977) *Image-Music-Text*, ed. and trans. Stephen Heath (London: Fontana).

Bradby, David (2005) 'Olivier Py: A Poet of the Stage: Analysis and Interview', *Contemporary Theatre Review*, 15: 2, 234–45.

Derrida, Jacques (1978) 'The Theatre of Cruelty and the Closure of Representation', in *Writing and Difference*, trans. Alan Bass (London: Routledge & Kegan Paul), pp. 232–50.

Diephuis, Herman (2009) '*D'après J.-C.*', e-mail correspondence with the author, 14 July.

Doane, Mary Ann (2002) *The Emergence of Cinematic Time: Modernity, Contingency, The Archive* (Cambridge, MA: Harvard University Press).

Dru, Alexander (1970) 'Catholic Humanism', in John Cruickshank (ed.), *French Literature and its Background, 6: The Twentieth Century* (Oxford: Oxford University Press), pp. 128–42.

Etchells, Tim (2000) 'The Show Must Go On', *R B Jérôme Bel* [Online] Available at: http://82.238.77.78/jeromebel/eng/jeromebel.asp?m=4&t=11 (accessed 8 July 2009).

Kristeva, Julia (1982) *Powers of Horror: An Essay on Abjection*, trans. Leon S. Roudiez (New York: Columbia University Press).

Lepecki, André (2004) *Exhausting Dance: Performance and the Politics of Movement* (London: Routledge).

Marion, Jean-Luc (2000) 'The Saturated Phenomenon', in Dominique Janicaud et al. (eds), *Phenomenology and the 'Theological Turn': The French Debate* (New York: Fordham University Press), pp. 176–216.

—— (2002) *Being Given: Towards a Phenomenology of Givenness*, trans. Jeffrey L. Kosky (Stanford, CA: Stanford University Press).

—— (2008) *The Visible and the Revealed*, trans. Christina M. Gschwandtner (New York: Fordham University Press).

Merleau-Ponty, Maurice (1968) *The Visible and The Invisible*, ed. Claude Lefort, trans. Alphonso Lingis (Evanston, IL: Northwestern University Press).

16
Watching People in the Light: Jérôme Bel and the Classical Theatre

Augusto Corrieri

In a 2001 interview, when asked 'What is a show for you?' the French choreographer Jérôme Bel replied rather simply: 'It is live people in the dark who watch other living ones in the light' (Bel, 2001).

This is a disarmingly conventional answer, something we might expect to read in an old-fashioned children's book entitled *What is Theatre?* In its evocation of a darkened auditorium, a stage and silent spectators, this rather classical depiction of theatre sounds decidedly anachronistic, especially when considering the manifold ruptures and provocations so characteristic of the histories of performance in the twentieth and twenty-first centuries. What is more perplexing is the fact that Bel is often associated, in France and abroad, with ideas of rupture and provocation, earning him a string of labels such as the *enfant terrible* of choreography, the 'anti-dance' artist and 'radical avant-garde conceptualist'.

However misled and misleading these labels may be, the term 'radical' might be useful if we consider the word's etymology, meaning 'roots'. Bel's aesthetic and critical project continues to provoke thought, delight and infuriate because it probes the roots of Western theatre and spectacle. His performances operate through a series of subtle yet disarmingly simple definitions and re-definitions of the terminology of theatre: basic questions – what is theatre? what is dance? what is an audience? what is a performer? – are asked, again and again, from one show to the next, with the awareness (and hope) that only by insisting on these fundamental questions can we uncover the inevitable links that bind theatre to larger concerns of language, representation and ethics.

If, as the Italian philosopher Giorgio Agamben has suggested, 'terminology is the poetic moment of thought' (2009: 1), the way in which Bel pays heed to the basic terminology of theatre – its constituent parts and mechanisms – has produced a series of performances which invite and crystallize poetic moments of thought. Moments of thought on the body and its representation, on the layers of cultural signification that engulf the subject, on navigating the media-saturated landscape of the twenty-first century, and, more recently, on the knowledge held by dancers and its transmission through documentary-style performances.

In order to best describe Bel's practice and its excavation of the theatrical event, I will focus on two works that have had the strongest impact on my own performance practice: his first, *Nom donné par l'auteur* (*Name Given by the Author*, 1994), and his best known, *The Show Must Go On* (2001). As a UK-based performance maker versed in devised and physical theatre at the Devon-based Dartington College of Arts, coming across Bel's *The Show Must Go On*, by chance, one night in Milan in 2002, was pivotal in making me question the silent assumptions that much UK experimental performance rests on, and in determining what kind of work I would then go on to make. One of the great novelties lay in the disarming clarity and legibility with which the actions were presented and arranged in time. Whereas my peers and I had consistently aimed for a complex mode of performance composition that resisted naming and recognizable imagery, opting for a dramaturgy of the ambiguous, the multi-layered, the organic, the juxtaposed and the multiple, here in this large Milan theatre was a seemingly flat, linear, almost banal dramaturgy in which everyday discrete elements were presented one after the other, often following a clear and available rule.

It is not uncommon for spectators at a Jérôme Bel performance to experience a similar capsizing of assumptions, and this might be part of the reason he has achieved a certain cult status, comparable perhaps to that of the late German choreographer Pina Bausch. What one faces in Bel's works is a radically innovative stage language, not because he fashions new images and actions, but rather because he renounces doing so in favour of re-arranging existing ones into new combinations. As if poetry might be found precisely by staying within the obvious, the banal and the clichéd.[1]

Critiquing the theatre

A very important detail for beginning to approach Bel's work, and a feature that has remained unchanged throughout his whole practice, is the placing of his works within theatres as opposed to alternative, found or dance spaces. Indeed, his project might be described as a critical dialogue with the limitations offered by the traditional theatre space and its social, political and aesthetic conventions. The minimalist aesthetic of the shows, which typically feature a bare stage and performers dressed in everyday clothes executing ordinary tasks, acquires its charge and urgency only because it is framed by red velvet curtains, gold scrollwork and the proscenium arch. As Bel says, 'I can't imagine my work outside of the theatre. If what I do on stage were to be moved out to a public space, no one would notice it. [...] Only the black box of the theatre, with lighting and the immobile position of the audience, allows showing these things' (Bel, 2008).

At this point one might ask: why choose the theatre as an institution to be deconstructed? Does it not belong to a bygone epoch, and therefore reflect values and ideologies that are no longer relevant to ours? Bel states:

> This deliberate decision to work 'within' the theatre is difficult to explain. My artistic idea is to work on theatrical structures, as I am certain that if theatre still exists, it is because it is representative of society's psychical, social and political structures. There must be parallels between theatrical structure and the structure of the city, the history of theatre and the history of humanity. To work within theatre makes it possible to reveal hidden problems of society.
>
> (Bel, 2002a)

The word *theatre*, in Bel's work, acquires two different if co-dependent meanings. The first meaning is decidedly tied to its tradition and etymology: in the West, theatre is by definition 'the place of seeing', a 2500-year mechanism with specific codes and systems, that posits the existence of a stage on which performers move, speak or sing and are observed by an audience.

The second meaning is especially relevant to our epoch, and might be best conveyed by one of its synonyms: *spectacle*. In 1967, the year before the students' and workers' uprisings in Paris, the Situationist artist and Marxist theorist Guy Debord published *The Society of the Spectacle*, portraying and condemning an age dominated by an all pervading capitalist order in which social relations are mediated by images. Besieged by an 'eternal present' (Debord, 1990: 12), the individual is, according to Debord, reduced to the state of a drugged and passive spectator, overpowered by the 'ponderous stage-management of diversionary thought' (ibid.: 54). Cut off from her/his communal and critical faculties, 'the spectator feels at home nowhere, because the spectacle is everywhere' (Debord, 1995: 23).

Debord's theatrical language is useful for linking an otherwise anachronistic notion of theatre to the spectacular excesses of our contemporary global culture. Across Jérôme Bel's performance works, theatre is probed as a prototype of the spectacular, establishing a metonymic relation between the mechanisms of the stage and those of mainstream capitalist media. Theatre matters not to the extent that it directly contests the society of the spectacle, but rather as a place and an activity that, given its avowed mission to create spectacle, might offer us a laboratory of sorts for considering the very processes that hold us captive.

However, unlike Debord's incendiary life and writings, Bel's stance is rarely oppositional. In place of a desire to outplay spectacle and arrest its seemingly inevitable flow once and for all, Bel's intention is to examine what fascinates and seduces us. Like other French artists and companies such as Philippe Quesne, Grand Magasin and Philippe Parreno (see Chapter 9 by Chloé Déchery and Chapter 13 by Carl Lavery in this volume), Bel is concerned to resist the dizzying rhythms of spectacular affect, patiently preferring to re-orient our desires towards a slower pace of existence. By making us aware of the theatrical mechanism and our place within it, he invites us to observe ourselves observing, and to understand what is taking place before us.

1994: *Nom donné par l'auteur*

Bel's account of how he came to make his first work, *Nom donné par l'auteur*, is in itself a curiosity, a tale which has gained mythical status within the French and European dance scene(s). Originally trained at the Centre national de danse contemporaine (CNDC) at Angers, one of several national centres in France, Bel went on to dance for a number of emerging European choreographers of the late 1980s (including Angelin Preljocaj and Caterina Sagna). His experiences as a dancer in France and Italy proved disappointing, given dance's deeply ingrained high modernist tendencies which are centred on the unshakable idea that to move is to express some kind of inner organic truth (see Chapter 14 by Bojana Cvejic in this volume). Bel paused his career as a dancer and, thanks to the fact that a public library had recently opened on his street, began reading the works of various (French) philosophers, including Roland Barthes, Michel Foucault, Gilles Deleuze and Louis Althusser. These readings gave him the tools for questioning the foundations of performance itself, resulting in the making of *Nom donné par l'auteur*, a piece devoid of a single dance step, favouring instead a slow, silent and contemplative series of arrangements of objects.

Despite the 'mythical' quality of this biographical narrative, it never-theless enables us to identify two of Bel's aims: first, his attempt to still the dancing body of high modernism; second, his concern to reconfig-ure the time and space of dance performance through concepts deriving from contemporary French philosophers, especially those paying heed to language and discourse as matrices of human thought and action.

In *Nom donné par l'auteur*, we see a bare stage, fully lit. In silence, the two performers (Bel and Frédéric Seguette) walk on wearing casual everyday clothes; they gradually introduce on stage the elements of this reduced spectacle, which consist of ten household objects such as a hairdryer, torch, a pair of ice-skating boots, a football, vacuum cleaner, and others. Throughout the show the performers' attitude might be described as that of impassive workers: they carry out each action as if it were the most ordinary of tasks, on a par with non-theatrical everyday activities.[2]

Over the 60 minutes of the performance we witness a choreography stripped of dance (as we might conventionally understand the word 'dance'). Instead, following clear and exact rules and procedures, the two performers arrange the household objects in different signifying combinations, allowing comical puns and sets of ideas to emerge as if of their own accord. For example, in the opening section, the perform-ers sit opposite each other with the objects placed at their feet. For the first ten minutes, they repeatedly pick up one object each and hold it next to the other, giving the audience ample time to observe the effect of that proximity. It is a game we might compare to taking two words at random from a book, and pairing them up to see what meanings they suggest. The result is in turn mysterious and comical, as we find ourselves elaborating on the physical and semantic effects produced by the various pairs: a dictionary and a football, a football and a lit torch, two ice-skating boots, the mouth of a vacuum cleaner (on) and the lit torch, an open dictionary and a hair dryer, the vacuum cleaner (on) and the hair dryer (on).

The show continues by exploring further permutations in which the objects and their associated uses are combined and recombined, like words in a sentence whose meaning is never stable. The perform-ers' bodies are used as if they too were objects, entities that partake in the same chains of signification. In one notable sequence, Seguette drops the dictionary and football to the floor whilst simultaneously lowering himself flatly to the ground, thereby re-inventing his own body as just one more fallen object among others. Everything here is shown to function according to systems of meaning: the mass-produced everyday objects, the performers' male bodies, directions, positions, and even less graspable entities such as light, shadows and air. Signs are moved around, swapped for one another, rotated, turned upside down, switched on and off. As if echoing a slogan of deconstructive philosophy, there is nothing in Bel's performance that is 'outside the text' (see Nigel Stewart, Chapter 15 in this volume).[3] Our role, as spectators, is to engage in continuous active interpretation: the sequences taking place on stage only acquire meaning (and therefore substance) through our process of reading. We could even say that the show 'happens' in our minds as much as it does on stage.

By Bel's own admission, the writings of philosopher and literary theorist Roland Barthes had a direct influence on *Nom donné par l'auteur*. In his own words, Bel took Barthes' reflections on signs, literature and writing, and adapted them to the space and time of live performance.[4] We can very briefly attempt to map this relationship by showing the obvious correspondences between Barthes' much cited essay 'The Death of the Author' and Bel's performance.

First, in this essay Barthes argues that the author of a text can no longer be considered a point of origin for the work. Barthes advocates a 'removal of the Author', specifying that 'one could talk here with Brecht of a veritable "distancing", the Author diminishing like a figurine at the far end of the literary stage' (Barthes, 1977: 145). We find this echoed in Bel's performance in the extent to which the performers function on a par with the objects and their significations, reframing the place of human authorial agency as one element amongst others. Furthermore, the title of the show draws a peculiar self-reflexive attention to, as well as interrogating, the causal relation between artist and work, author and text.

Second, Barthes argues that the text possesses no interiority, that there is no secret to discover behind it: 'In the multiplicity of writing [...] there is nothing beneath' (ibid.: 147). This is put into practice by Bel through the clarity and meticulousness with which the two performers arrange and combine the objects-signs, always spelling out a sentence-idea which the spectators are encouraged to read flatly. Bel's dramaturgy resists all depth, everything happens on the surface and is shared with the audience in the most transparent way possible.

Perhaps most importantly, Barthes' claim that 'a text's unity lies not in its origin but in its destination' (ibid.: 148) finds its fullest embodiment in Bel's self-professed activation of the spectator. This is a theatre that is always completed, if not made, by the viewer. As an audience member, one is happy to realize that to spectate is to do. Without ever resorting to any form of audience participation (which, by definition, violates the spectator's position through the pretence of 'involvement'), Bel invites us to pay attention to how we pay attention – the active processes by which we perceive, notice and interpret – and to consider how these processes are inevitably (and problematically) tied to pre-existing structures of language, meaning and culture.

2001: *The Show Must Go On*

Picture the beginning of a typical theatre-going experience. We arrive at the theatre and take our seats. The auditorium grows dark, the stage lights fade up, and the actors or dancers appear. It goes without saying that this is how most theatrical performances begin. *The Show Must Go On*, which is a kind of ode to and a portrait of theatrical performance, pays special to attention to this particular ritual of commencement.

The lights go dark in the auditorium. A man sitting by a CD player, off stage, is seen inserting a CD. The song 'Tonight' from *West Side Story* plays, while the audience sits in the dark, listening. Once the song is over another CD is inserted, and we hear 'Let the Sunshine In' from the musical *Hair*. Over the four minutes of the track, we are presented with the theatre lights gradually fading up, revealing an empty stage. Then it is 'Come Together' by the Beatles: nothing visibly happens until the song's chorus kicks in ('Come together'), which prompts 20 performers to walk casually on stage and stand there facing us. The next song is 'Let's Dance' by David Bowie. The performers don't move from their positions, but every time the song's chorus announces 'Let's dance' they start dancing energetically, each person on her/his own, before returning to stillness.

The songs lay bare the score that underlies the whole show, simultaneously describing the archetypal arc through which theatre happens, and commenting metatheatrically on the performance we are now watching. There is a stripping down here of theatre to its basic operational units, which openly invites the audience to partake in its evolution and demands. From start to finish, we are made playfully aware of the rules of the particular game that is theatre, and our place within those rules. In one notable sequence halfway through the show, the stage is bare and instead the auditorium is filled with pink light, while Edith Piaf's 'La vie en rose' is played. Then the lights fade to black, and in darkness we listen to 'Imagine' by John Lennon. With nothing to see, we are asked to imagine, which is the basic task required of a spectator at a show. Then, in a move reminiscent of John Cage's notorious piece *4'33"* (1952), we listen to 'The Sound of Silence' by Simon and Garfunkel. When the strains of the chorus are heard, the track is muted, leaving us in the dark, listening to the sound of silence. What are we doing here, in the theatre, when the thing we have come to witness is nothing but ourselves, in the silence and the darkness? Can we still call this a 'show', given that it has been (almost) reduced to nothing?

This is a reduction that seeks to get as close as possible to the end of theatre, its aim and its fall, shining a light on the very mechanism designed for spectacle, only to return to its joys and possibilities. The show invites us to consider the various lines that demarcate the moments and spaces of theatre: we approach those lines and dwell in the strange logic of separation that theatre is built on. But those lines are never erased, and theatre remains intact. As critic Gerald Siegmund has noted:

> Jérôme Bel does not set up somewhere new to take the place of the old theatre. [...] His tactic is to pass through and cross out a well-known place so as to perturb its order. [...] Thus the row of footlights, which separates the theatre hall from the stage, in *The Show Must Go On* remains a central element of the show. Equally this assures the distance of reflection in relation to the stage, without which the show could not effectively continue.
>
> (2002)

As we sit in the theatre we are given ample time to observe the effect that the songs have on us: their hold on us, the fact that we can relate 'personally' to these mass-distributed global sound tracks, because they capture our own private thoughts and feelings.[5] There is no business like our emotions, our sorrows and joys, and it is at these feelings that capitalism's images and sounds take their aim and succeed so spectacularly in piercing. If it is therefore harder and harder to think our desire apart from the contemporary capitalist environment that presses around us, it goes without saying that any contemporary staging of emotions (which could be another way of describing *The Show Must Go On*) must necessarily embrace pop images and sounds.

This embrace, however, is not uncritical, and it becomes each spectator's job to navigate her or his own path through the show, just as we do in our everyday lives. In other words, if there is a critique here, this is not found in what the show supposedly *says*, but rather in what it *does*: it is here, in the performative space of doubt where any stable position, idea, or message is made untenable, that *The Show Must Go On* can be understood as operating a critique of spectacle.

Let us take the 'Titanic' scene. The 20 performers stand in pairs, one person behind the other. As the Céline Dion ballad plays, we see each pair of performers enact the iconic image from the film, in which the Hollywood star Leonardo DiCaprio holds Kate Winslet at the front of the ship, James Cameron's camera swooping dramatically from one side to the other (on this stage, the swooping was achieved by each performer holding the other by the armpits and gently inching them to the side).

What does a scene like this do in its literal re-enactment of the iconic film scene? As I remember during that night in Milan in 2002, many spectators gasped and giggled as the song started playing, in recognition of the film that everyone there had probably seen, or at least encountered through word of mouth and advertising. And yet, something else was at stake here, too. Beyond this first moment of recognition, as an audience member I started to project that sentimental love story on to the couples on stage. This could not be helped, for it is exactly what the scene was telling me to do. And yet my projection remained somewhat ineffective: there was a certain ironic distance, produced by the fact that the performers were dressed in everyday clothes and were in no way pretending to be the film characters. I was therefore made aware of a gap between the song's dramatic pathos and the actual individuals on stage. I reflected that the people in front of me could not be reduced to cheap Hollywood narratives, for these performers, just like me and every other audience member there, had complex lives and feelings. This recognition of a shared humanity generated a curious surge of emotional empathy on my part, which coupled together with soaring lyrics such as 'Near, far, wherever you are, I believe that the heart does go on', pushed me closer and closer to tears.

In other words, there was an emotive quality to this scene's complex interplay of fictions and realities, and the Dion song, with its synthesized guitar riffs and impossibly devotional love lyrics, was undoubtedly at the heart of it. If we cannot stage love without recurring to certain Hollywood clichés, then we can use those clichés for our own ends. If our imagination is colonized by a received imagery, it might be futile to try and resist it, because we will almost inevitably reproduce its effects. The best strategy, as Bel suggests, might be to do exactly what the songs and images tell us to do, in the hope that through this literal performance of instructions and expressions something might be found that necessarily escapes commodity and regulation.

Pop songs, spectacle, theatre conventions, language and culture are the mechanisms that simultaneously enable us to live, and constrain our lives. We can never escape their linguistic codes, for the simple reason that they are what we use to articulate our very escapes. It is this critical approach that places Jérôme Bel within a lineage of artists and thinkers who, within (and without) France, have attempted to outwit the spectacle's inevitable flooding of everyday life. Only by placing the accent on the act of performance itself, as opposed to its supposed content or political message, can we engage a politics of perception. In the 'here' and 'now' of theatre we can then attempt to scrutinize, outplay, and perhaps laugh at the codes which we endlessly write and which in turn write us.

Notes

1. The insistence with which Bel utilizes 'ready mades' from pop culture and the history of dance stands in almost diametrical opposition to Xavier Le Roy's pursuit of misrecognition and fragmentation of the body-image. Whilst both artists are constantly coupled, as if in a common pursit to challenge the politics of spectacle and dance, I suggest that Bel's work is firmly rooted *within* the legible signs and codes of the theatre, whereas Le Roy aims at their transcendence. (See Chapter 14 by Bojana Cvejic in this volume.)
2. The two performers' task-like mode of performance is haunted by the ongoing legacy of Happenings in the 1960s and Performance Art in the 1970s, as well as that of the group known as Judson Dance Theatre (1962–4). From that group, choreographer Yvonne Rainer's 1965 'No Manifesto', which begins with 'No to spectacle no to virtuosity no to transformations and magic and make-believe' (in Wood, 2007: 20), finds new definition in the two performers' quiet operations.
3. The reference is to philosopher Jacques Derrida's statement, '*il n'y a pas de hors-texte*', 'there is nothing outside of the text' (Derrida, 1997: 158; original italics).
4. For Bel's own account of just how closely his practice has taken its cue from core concepts developed by Barthes, see Bel (2002b).
5. For a compelling account of *The Show Must Go On*'s use of pop songs, see Tim Etchells (2004).

Works cited

Agamben, Giorgio (2009) *What is an Apparatus? And Other Essays* (Stanford, CA: Stanford University Press).

Bel, Jérôme (2001) 'Interview with Fabienne Arvers', http://82.238.77.78/jeromebel/eng/jeromebel.asp?m=4&t=1 (accessed September 2010).

—— (2002a) 'Interview with Gerald Siegmund', http://82.238.77.78/jeromebel/eng/jeromebel.asp?m=4&t=4 (accessed September 2010).

—— (2002b) 'Interview with Marianne Alphant', http://82.238.77.78/jeromebel/eng/jeromebel.asp?m=4&t=13 (accessed September 2010).

—— (2008) 'Interview with Daniel Buren', http://82.238.77.78/jeromebel/eng/jeromebel.asp?m=4&t=36 (accessed September 2010).

Barthes, Roland (1977) 'The Death of the Author', in ed. and trans. Stephen Heath, *Image-Music-Text* (London: Fontana).

Debord, Guy (1990) *Comments on the Society of the Spectacle*, trans. Malcolm Imrie (London: Verso).

—— (1995) *Society of the Spectacle*, trans. Donald Nicholson-Smith (New York: Zone Books).

Derrida, Jacques (1997) *Of Grammatology*, trans. Gayatri Chakravorty Spivak (Baltimore, MD: Johns Hopkins University Press).

Etchells, Tim (2004) 'More and More Clever Watching More and More Stupid: Some Thoughts Around Rules, Games and The Show Must Go On', *Dance Theatre Journal*, 20:2, 10–20.

Siegmund, Gerald (2002) 'Singing Life with Bodies', http://82.238.77.78/jeromebel/eng/jeromebel.asp?m=4&t=8 (accessed September 2010).

Wood, Catherine (2007) *Yvonne Rainer: The Mind is a Muscle* (London: Afterall).

Après toutes ces elles/After All this Else: 'New' French Feminisms Translated to the British Scene[1]

Geraldine Harris

> So: this history cannot be written; it would have to be collective, multiple; it would be of contradictions. But still [...] I'll have a go, prefacing everything with the reminder of what I say has no authority but that of my own authorship.
>
> (Ward Jouve, 1991: 66)

This chapter is a consideration of the impact on British theatre and performance of what in the 1980s and early 1990s was often termed 'New French Feminisms'. This is an enormous topic for a short essay so Carl and Clare, the editors of this volume, have encouraged me to take something of an autobiographical approach. This means that this account is largely written from the perspective of British feminist theatre criticism...but not entirely – since in this area above all, 'theory' and 'practice' (should in theory) be as inseparable as the layers of a *mille feuille*.

In the long wake of (mostly French) poststructuralist theory, within the academic sphere it has become axiomatic that an autobiographical strategy signals an understanding of history, and of the subject who writes, as contingent, multiple and contradictory. The cynic might observe that this gives it the status of a 'get out of jail free' card in regard to incoherence, error or omission. Despite the drift of the quote above (referring to the history of the famous/notorious French feminist collective Psychanalyse et Politique, Psych & Po), this is not Nicole Ward Jouve's position in her collection of essays written between 1985 and 1990 and published as *White Woman Speaks with Forked Tongue, Criticism as Autobiography* (1991). A bilingual Frenchwoman living in England, in 1991 Ward Jouve was a Professor of English and Related Literature at York University, publishing both academic and creative writing. Amongst other things *White Woman* explores ways of translating certain strands of French feminist thought and in particular the work of Hélène Cixous for a British context. This on the understanding that translation is always 'a necessary betrayal' yet 'a productive one' which 'distorts' but also 'gives new life' (ibid.: 92). The back cover indicates that this is part of an exploration of 'how it might be possible to intervene in academic discourse to establish a feminist critical voice?'. Twenty years ago I thought I had grasped the threads joining this aim: the theme of translation, Ward Jouve's mixing of the critical and the autobiographical, and precisely how all of this related to Cixous. Now I am not sure I truly followed Ward Jouve's direction. Nevertheless, I was influenced by this book, not least in my own attempts to interpret Cixous, as detailed in an issue of the *Contemporary Theatre Review* on the theme of 'Spectacle, Silence and Subversion: Women's Performance Language and Strategies'(see Harris, 1994).

I am running ahead of myself but I wanted to start with *White Woman* because it remains the most illuminating and downright *enjoyable* work of literary criticism I have ever read. In line with Cixous's warning against turning 'theory into an idol' (Cixous, 1988: 144), and operating on the understanding that *all* writing, including criticism, is a construction of the self 'through process and relationship' (Ward Jouve, 1991: 10), Ward Jouve avoids treating 'New French Feminisms' as 'theory' to be simply 'applied' to texts, or to be 'imitated' to 'make more in the same vein' (ibid.: 9). Ward Jouve argues that such methods reduce criticism to 'fantasy' divorced from situated material realities, which as a consequence cannot do justice *either to* the particularity of the text being read *or* to that of the self under construction (ibid.: 8). Instead, Ward Jouve takes up Cixous's challenge to women to write themselves, as a practice of *écriture féminine* that attempts to subvert the regulatory scripts of the phallic symbolic (see Cixous, 1981). In Cixous's writing this aim informed a blurring of the traditional distinctions between academic, creative and personal writing and the same applies to Ward Jouve's approach in *White Woman*. Yet Ward Jouve is clearly writing *herself* rather than imitating pre-existing examples of *écriture féminine* produced or identified by Cixous, or other critics; and it is her distinctive down-to-earth voice, as well as the often humorous connections she makes between her everyday life and the texts and histories she is interpreting, that renders this book so illuminating and so pleasurable. The same factors paradoxically convey a flavour of the playfulness said to characterize the work of some of the more literary French thinkers (like Cixous) that seldom comes across in direct translation. In short, Ward Jouve (re)interprets 'French

Feminisms' *through* her own (bi-culturally/geographically/personally) situated political practice(s), and in doing so honours something crucial to their spirit (although, perhaps not that which provoked the fire bombing of the premises of Psych & Po *by other feminists* (see Ward Jouve, 1991: 69–70)).

In terms of direct translation, my first encounter with 'New French Feminisms' was through the anthology of that name edited by Elaine Marks and Isabelle de Courtivron. Published in Britain in 1981, this book offers a selection of writings from between 40 and 50 women. There is not much playfulness in evidence in most of these pieces. Rather, there is indeed an incendiary revolutionary fervour, so gloriously liberating in its excessiveness that it just seemed too dull, too tame, to knuckle down to the three introductions that place these ideas, historically, culturally and politically *as* French.

It was apparent that these feminisms, like their British counterparts, could be loosely grouped in relation to various theoretico-political dynamics. Sometimes these harden into factions but usually *as* dynamics – to quote Cixous on theory again, they were clearly 'instruments [to be used as] means of advancing further', which could be substituted and hybridized at will (Cixous, 1988: 144). In *New French Feminisms* the two dynamics that emerged most strongly were informed by Marxist-Socialism and by poststructuralist linguistic theory, specifically deconstruction and psychoanalysis. For British readers it was, of course, this latter which justified the 'New' in the title. This was also Toril Moi's justification, in *Sexual/Textual Politics* (1985), for picking out Cixous, Luce Irigaray and Julia Kristeva from the host of voices offered by Marks and de Courtivron. Moi argues that these three are 'the most representative of the main trends in French feminist theory' yet in contradictory fashion also, 'more closely concerned with the specific problems raised by women's relation to writing and language than many other feminist theorists in France' (Moi, 1985: 97). Either way, in Britain Moi's 'Holy Trinity' came to stand for all 'New French Feminisms' (Ward Jouve, 1991: 48), and Moi also opened the debate as to whether or not some of this thinking (specifically that of Cixous and Irigaray) was essentialist, in its tendency to privilege sexual difference above other differences. This judgement was complicated by ambiguity over whether the *féminine* in *écriture féminine* (a concept that all three had, inaccurately, become associated with) should be translated as 'female', which for English-speaking feminists refers to biological sex, or as 'feminine' which we understand to refer to socially constructed gender (see Moi, 1985: 97 and 112–13).[2] Moi suggests that this political distinction did not exist in France (ibid.: 97). This situation was further complicated by the fact that many so-called 'New French Feminists' including Cixous, and on occasion Kristeva, refused the title 'feminist' (see Greenstein Burke, 1978: 846).

Nevertheless, of Moi's front runners Cixous was the obvious favourite for Theatre Studies in the United Kingdom, although in the1980s only two pieces of her writing relating to this field were available in translation: the essay 'Aller à la mer' ('Going to the Sea', 1977, translated 1984), a scorching critique of the representation of female characters in classical drama, and the playtext *Portrait of Dora* (1976, translated 1979). Cixous was also the most utopian and creative of the three, and practised as she preached so that other writings such as 'Le Rire de la Meduse' ('The Laugh of Medusa') ('Medusa') first published in 1975, were as, if not more, inspirational than *Dora*. Yet, it is worth noting in terms of *Dora*'s possible theatrical influence that it was staged at the New End Theatre in London in May 1979 and available in translation in advance of any of Cixous's critical works.

This was the scene as set when I stumbled upon it, because although my early research was on French popular performance, I did not knowingly encounter 'New French Feminisms' before 1987, 12 years after the initial publication of 'Medusa'. This is not so long as regards the dissemination and absorption of radical ideas in the academic sphere, especially when as theory, they require a grasp of the two Big Jacques, Derrida and Lacan, hard going if, for your first degree, the 'Holy Trinity' was Aristotle, Stanislavski and Brecht. However, within the realm of politics 12 years is a very long time indeed. All else aside, during this period even the most hard-line Marxist had been forced to admit the failures of Communism. This cut the ground from under Socialist feminism which had previously been a major dynamic in British theatre, creating a vacuum for 'New French Feminisms' to fill. However, by 1987 Ward Jouve notes that in France people were saying that feminism was 'finished', '*pas fameux*', 'old' (1991: 102). Still, let's face it, at any given moment in its history, someone, somewhere, has been declaring feminism to be 'finished' and she goes on to say 'Anglo- Saxon countries' were 'holding out better', partly due to 'the curious phenomenon' that '[i]n the past two or three years, so-called French Feminism(s) *as theory*, has become immensely fashionable and the debates it is spawning are buoying up Anglo-Saxon critical debates' (ibid.: original emphasis).

In context then, my own discovery of 'New French Feminisms' was not so behindhand particularly within the field of Theatre Studies. As Elaine Aston has indicated, due to the struggles to establish the autonomy of this 'relatively young' discipline, there was a 'time lag' between 'feminism as a social movement' [and within British theatre] in the 1970s and 'its coming to have an impact on Theatre Studies in the 1980s' (Aston, 2008: x).

As late as 1989, in the first (of only two editions of) *Women and Theatre Newsletter*, the editors Maggie Gale and Susan Bassnett described the publication as aimed at those 'who previously felt that they were working in isolation or that women's theatre was a minority interest', but added that this area was 'growing and developing at enormous speed' (1989: 1). Indeed, this newsletter portended an explosion of events and publications in the United Kingdom covering an enormous variety of women's practices and feminist theories. In 1989, however, the newsletter's list of research interests and courses suggest an understandable focus on recovering the lost history of women in theatre. Amongst those working on the contemporary, only two people, Nike Imoru and Pete Mathers, indicate research interests in 'French Feminisms' (specifically Cixous), and only my own module on Feminist Theatre at Lancaster, appears to be teaching this topic. Actually, this was suggested by a colleague who offered to teach it, but instead left me in the (I retrospectively realize as happy) position of learning about it with the students, a viable possibility when for each third-year module, contact hours were six per week. Also (at a time when PCs were still rare and for many, email and the web still science fiction) Gale and Bassnett acknowledge that their information was probably incomplete. It certainly misses many who became familiar faces at events concerned with *écriture feminine*, or rather a 'women's/female/feminine/ feminist language' within theatre, with all the potential slippages between sex, gender and political identification that my backslashes imply.

What *is* evident in this newsletter is that this slippery territory had already been broached by professional practitioners via the Magdalena project. The brainchild of Jill Greenhalgh, the Magdalena officially started in Cardiff in 1986 with an International Festival of Women in Experimental Theatre, featuring artists from 15 countries.[3] In her 1989 book documenting this event, Susan Bassnett frames the project with quotes from Cixous's 'Medusa' and although primarily dedicated to exploring its concerns as *practice*, amongst other activities, in 1987 the Magdalena mounted two conference/workshops both entitled 'A Women's Language in Theatre?' (see Bassnett, 1989; and Fry, 2007). I missed these events but did attend the week-long Magdalena workshop series on 'Process: The Devising of Original Material' in Cardiff in 1988, where the opening ceremony included Imuro speaking on Cixous. However, responses to Imuro were mixed because the (international) participants represented a broad spectrum of performance cultures, understandings of and attitudes towards feminism and to academic discourse. For example, I worked under Annie Griffin (originally from Canada) who performed her solo show *Almost Persuaded* (1987) during the event. Although like most of the workshop leaders Griffin had trained in physical theatre, she had done so with Philippe Gaulier, whereas many of the others, such as Greenhalgh herself, came from backgrounds influenced by Jerzy Grotowski, or Eugenio Barba and Odin Theatret. If Griffin's practice could be related to 'French Feminisms', it had more in common with Irigaray's concept of 'feminine mimicry' than the Cixous of the 'Medusa' period and was distinctly postmodern in style (Irigaray, 1985).[4] This was evinced by *Almost Persuaded* which used country and western music as a starting point, and employed theatrical self-reflexivity, parody and pastiche. While particular inflections of these latter strategies did occur in the work of core Magdalena participants and that of Cixous and Irigaray, this was rarely, if ever, achieved with reference to contemporary popular forms. Other performances shown at 'Process' included Bobby Baker's now celebrated piece *Drawing on a Mother's Experience* (1988). Baker's work has always touched on key tropes for 'French Feminisms' such as the female hysteric as figure of resistance and the abject maternal, and has been analysed with reference to all three of Moi's 'Holy Trinity' (see Barrett and Baker, 2007). Yet there is no evidence of Baker herself having any awareness of these ideas, although intriguingly, her style chimes with Ward Jouve's. In short, at the more public Magdalena events, women were 'creating their tongues plural' but not necessarily due to the influence of 'French Feminisms' (Cixous and Clement, 1985: 136). However, the Magdalena also produced two devised touring shows: *Nominatae Filiea* (1988) and *Midnight Level Six* (1991) (see Bassnett, 1989; and Fry, 2007). I only saw the latter piece but as far as I can tell both shows contained echoes of the classical and religious references found in 'Medusa' and of the sort of aesthetic that in the United Kingdom came to be associated with French poststructuralism, which essentially operated within the vocabularies established within European (high) Modernist avant-garde practice. Reflecting Cixous's early writing, how far the representations of woman/women in these shows were actually deconstructive and how far essentialist remains in contention. Yet, as with Cixous herself, this does not cancel out the importance of the Magdalena's contribution in encouraging women from numerous countries to explore their own creativity.

Further, if Cixous was a source of inspiration for the Magdalena, this was always an interpretation and transformation. While playwrights

were occasionally connected with the project, attention was over-
whelmingly focused on performer training and the embodied, visual
and non-verbal languages of performance, and hence devising. In contrast, despite her many references to the body, Cixous was not being
metaphorical in 'Medusa' and elsewhere when she spoke of *writing*, and
her (early) interests like those of Irigaray and Kristeva were decidedly
literary. Indeed, while Cixous is ascribed authorship of *Dora*, the published text is based on director Simone Benmussa's devised adaptation
for the stage of a radio play by Cixous and, for some of us, the innovative nature of this work lay more in Benmussa's notes on the processes
of production than in Cixous's text.

   Even so, it was disappointing when at the colloquium in her honour
at Liverpool University in 1989, Cixous talked for two and a half hours
about novels, which as she ascertained before commencing, none of
us had read. At a 1992 'Glass Ceiling' discussion at the Institute of
Contemporary Arts in London, organized by Sphinx Theatre, Cixous
did discuss theatre and naturally her focus was on her recent col-
laborations with Arianne Mnouchkine at the Théâtre du Soleil. It was
rapidly apparent how far she had moved on from the Cixous of the
1970s, although she *did* reiterate her rejection of the term feminist.
Prompted by this talk, back in Lancaster I tackled (in French) Cixous's
epic history play *L'Indiade ou L'Inde de leurs rêves* (*The Indiade or India of
Their Dreams*, 1987) written for Mnouchkine. My laboriously achieved
understanding of the play and the accompanying essays revealed that
just as I was first reading it, she had recanted her critique of classical
drama in 'Aller à la mer' and had now embraced Shakespeare and Grand
Opera as sources of inspiration. While the play indicates a continuing
preoccupation with the writer and writing (literal), the essays demonstrate Cixous incorporating ideas from Artaud, Grotowski and the type
of theatrical interculturalism associated with them and championed
by Mnouchkine. As a result, in the *Indiade* a concern for differences in
general has displaced sexual difference, but critically, this is less a matter of cultural and historical specificity and more of a 'universal human
condition' for which India and Indians function as poetic metaphors.
Combined with Mnouchkine's spectacular staging, this led to the
production being accused of 'Orientalism' and 'cultural colonialism'
(see Dobson, 2002: 88–103). Interestingly, although Théâtre du Soleil
was now relatively mainstream, in the late 1960s Mnouchkine had
embraced the same 'third theatre' paradigm as defined by Barba and
often marked by interculturalism, from which many founder members
of the Magdalena also emerged (see Bassnett, 1989: 16–19). As such, it

seems that Cixous and the Magdalena were always in the same dance, just never quite in time.

Far clearer in the 1994 'Strategies' issue of the *Contemporary Theatre Review* cited above, than in the 1989 newsletter, is that the Magdalena's emphasis on practice was shared by many of us teaching and researching women's theatre. Seven of eight essays in this volume including my own, are concerned with the documentation and analysis of 'experimental' productions undertaken with students or in a professional capacity. In her editorial Margaret Llewellyn-Jones describes five of them as struggling with the 'nature and possibility of a theatrical *écriture féminine*' (1994: 6), and variously they make references to Cixous, Kristeva or Irigaray but, notably, translated through Artaud, Benmussa, Mnouchkine or Peter Brook. Some are devised productions, others are based on playtexts yet, despite the fact that by then it featured on most British University feminist theatre courses, none of these are of *Dora* – and following the professional production in London in 1979, I have never heard again of a staging of a full-length version of this play in the United Kingdom.

It has often been remarked that so few of Cixous's plays have been translated and staged in Britain. My experience of work-shopping *Dora*, reading *L'Indiade* and seeing *Black Sail/White Sail* in the 1994 Sphinx touring production, suggests that in the absence of a director of the brilliance of Benmussa or Mnouchkine, from a British theatrical perspective, these works do indeed appear literary rather than dramatic, or to be blunt, extremely wordy and rather abstract. Significantly, even though in this country in the 1980s and early 1990s women playwrights were at the forefront of theatrical experimentation, it was hard to identify contemporary British playtexts, as opposed to productions, that might have been directly or indirectly influenced by 'New French Feminisms'. It was through the search for examples that the notion of a theatrical *écriture féminine* started to solidify into theory or rather, to be more precise, into a checklist of characteristics drawn from all three of the 'Holy Trinity' which could then be applied to playtexts. Typically, these included non-linear or fragmented narrative structures that resisted closure; temporal and/or spatial disruption; poetic polyvocal language; silences, gaps, hesitations and repetitions; the representation of (female) subjectivity as abjected and/or multiple and contradictory; the hysteric as a figure for female resistance; and the deconstruction of classical myth or religious and secular archetypes. Ignoring Cixous's injunction as to the impossibility of defining *écriture féminine* (Cixous, 1981: 253–4), the danger of this game is immediately apparent. In terms of formal properties and even some 'themes' this list might be applied to any number of texts, including works like (arguably misogynist) August Strindberg's *Dream Play* (1901). Indeed, in 1991 John Fiske famously drew second hand on 'French Feminisms' to describe television soap opera as demonstrating a 'feminine aesthetic' that corresponds to a model of female sexuality/ subjectivity (Fiske, 1991: 197).

There were a few female authored British playtexts which did demonstrate many of the above properties and seemed to be influenced by 'French Feminisms'. Amongst these were *Heresies* (1986) by Deborah Levy who was associated with the Magdalena and attended one of the 1987 'Women's Language in Theatre' events, and *Augustine: Big Hysteria* (1991) by Anna Furse, who emerged from the same Grotowskian influenced 'third theatre' as that project. Although, a distinctive work in its own right (not least that it is far less wordy) as a production, *Augustine* had striking commonalities with Cixous's/Benmussa's *Dora,* and in 1996 Geraldine Cousin asserted that it takes *The Newly Born Woman* (Cixous and Clement, 1985) as 'one of its reference points' (Cousin, 1996: 12). Yet in her own essay on *Augustine* in 'Strategies', while Furse quotes Cixous and acknowledges that it might be discussed in terms of a 'Feminine Theatre Language', she put its genesis down solely to her practical experiments since 1980 with the feminist company Blood Group. She states '[...] practice preceded theory at all levels of my work. I simply wouldn't know how to make a piece of theatre theoretically, whilst it is tremendously heartening to discover a critical vocabulary which echoes one's own creative practice' (1994: 33). Ward Jouve might affirm that this suggests a closer sympathy between Furse and Cixous than had the reverse been the case. If there ever was/is/ could be such a thing as *écriture féminine* to challenge, genuinely, the regulatory forces of the phallic symbolic, it must be a practice that precedes *any* discourse, or, at the very least, is simultaneous with it.

Personally, I *like* theory, not as a beginning, nor as an end but as an 'instrument' and one which can blunt from use. By the time 'Strategies' was published in 1994, while 'French Feminisms' still featured in my teaching, like many, I was less interested in Cixous and more in Irigaray and Kristeva. Yet, impatient of the limitations of *all* this thinking in relation to issues of racism and sexuality, I was also drawn to the accumulating body of postmodern feminist, postcolonial and queer theory (largely but not entirely) emerging from the United States which was transforming contemporary theatre and performance criticism. This in turn generated interest in US practitioners such as Split Britches, whose work I had fallen in love with on seeing *Dress Suits for Hire* at the Drill Hall in London in 1987. 'French Feminisms' also had a significant impact in the United States, although initially with greater interest in the lesbian feminist theorist Monique Wittig, and *Dress Suits for Hire*, devised around a witty, startling and poetic text by Holly Hughes, could be discussed in such terms. However, this was French Feminisms translated through US culture and its contemporary popular forms as well as its queer sub-culture and specifically lesbian butch/fem play. Inevitably, in the 1990s the favoured paradigm in discussing Split Britches (and much other prac-tice) derived from Judith Butler's articulation of gender as performative. Amongst other things, Butler's rigorous feminist *and* queer deconstruc-tion of Lacan drew extensively on Kristeva and Irigaray (see Butler, 1990 and 1993). Split Britches' work, like Ward Jouve's in *White Woman* has always been rooted in their own everyday lives. By contrast, unfortu-nately, Butler's early work supported tendencies to a formalism divorced from material realities that was always problematic not just within 'New French Feminisms' (as theory) but within so much criticism derived from poststructuralism and postmodernism. I cannot help feel that, alongside a deadening emphasis on subversion and resistance (as opposed to good, old fashioned *rebellion*), this formalism (so very close to form*ula*) has significantly contributed to a widespread insistence that feminisms are 'finished' in the Anglo-Saxon countries. Yet it seems to me that so many of us women (and marginalized 'others'), in theatre as elsewhere, have not even *begun* to write themselves, 'to speak, to steal/to fly' (Cixous, 1981: 258). Nor 'to recover back the bod[ies] that ha[ve] been more than confiscated from them' (ibid.: 250). It would still be a mistake to approach Old/New French Feminisms seeking models for these processes to be imitated or applied critically to the results, not least because many of these ideas are of a place and a moment now long passed. However, in the field of women's theatre and performance in 1980s and early 1990s Britain, these *Elles* (multiple, collective) were *always* being translated through time, space, cultures, theatre and performance vocabularies, per-sonal and political histories. On such terms, and after all (this) else, they might still offer some beautiful, witty and gloriously excessive sparks of inspiration.

Notes

1. At the time of writing (summer 2009), there is a major retrospective of the work of women artists at the Georges Pompidou Centre, entitled *Elles*.
2. Irigaray's notion of *parler femme* is not dissimilar to Cixous's *écriture féminine* (see Moi, 1985: 144–5). However, Kristeva rejected such concepts entirely (ibid.: 163–4).
3. The Magdalena continues to this day, see http://www.the magdalenaproject. org.

4. Irigaray's 'feminine mimicry' denotes a deliberate and exaggerated assumption of femininity by a woman as a resistant political strategy, a concept that clearly influenced Judith Butler's thinking in *Gender Trouble* (1990). See also Irigaray (1985: 44–7).

Works cited

Aston, Elaine (2008) 'Foreword', in Sue Ellen Case, *Feminism and Theatre*, rev. edn (Basingstoke: Palgrave Macmillan).

Barrett Michèle and Bobby Baker (eds) (2007) *Bobby Baker: Redeeming Features of Daily Life* (London: Routledge).

Bassnett, Susan (1989) *Magdalena International Women's Experimental Theatre* (Oxford: Berg).

Butler, Judith (1990) *Gender Trouble: Feminism and the Subversion of Identity* (London and New York: Routledge).

—— (1993) *Bodies That Matter: On the Discursive Limits of 'Sex'* (London and New York: Routledge).

Cixous, Hélène (1979) *Portrait of Dora*, trans. Anita Barrows, in *Benmussa Directs: Portrait of Dora and the Singular Life of Albert Nobbs* (London: John Calder).

—— (1981) 'The Laugh of Medusa', in Elaine Marks and Isabelle de Courtivron (eds), *New French Feminisms, An Anthology* (Brighton: Harvester Press), pp. 245–64.

—— (1984) 'Aller à la mer', trans. Barbara Kerslake, *Modern Drama*, 27:4, 546–8.

—— (1987) *L'Indiade ou L'Inde de leurs rêves et quelques écrits sur le theatre* (Paris: Théâtre du Soleil).

—— (1988), in Susan Sellars (ed.), *Writing Differences: Readings from the Seminar of Hélène Cixous* (Milton Keynes: Open University Press).

Cixous, Hélène and Catherine Clement (1985) *The Newly Born Woman*, trans. Betsy Wing (Manchester, Manchester University Press).

Cousin, Geraldine (1996) *Women in Dramatic Place and Time* (London: Routledge).

Dobson, Julia (2002) *Hélène Cixous and the Theatre: The Scene of Writing* (Oxford: Peter Lang).

Fiske, John (1991) *Television Culture* (London: Routledge).

Fry, Chris (2007) *The Way of the Magdalena* (Hostelbro: Open Page).

Furse, Anna (1994) '*Augustine: Big Hysteria*, Writing the Body', in Margaret Llewellyn-Jones (ed.), 'Spectacle, Silence and Subversion: Women's Performance Language and Strategies', *Contemporary Theatre Review*, 2:1, 25–34.

Gale, Maggie, and Susan Bassnett (1989) *Women and Theatre Newsletter* (Coventry: Warwick University).

Greenstein Burke, Carolyn (1978) 'Report from Paris: Women's Writing and the Women's Movement', *Signs*, 3:4, 843–55.

Harris, Geraldine (1994) 'Confusions of Identity in Theory and Practice', in Margaret Llewellyn-Jones (ed.), 'Spectacle, Silence and Subversion: Women's Performance Language and Strategies', *Contemporary Theatre Review*, 2:1, 11–24.

Irigaray, Luce (1985) *This Sex Which is Not One*, trans. Carolyn Burke and Catherine Porter (Ithica, NY: Cornell University Press).

Marks, Elaine, and Isabelle de Courtivron (eds) (1981) *New French Feminisms, An Anthology* (Brighton: Harvester Press).

Moi, Toril (1985) *Sexual Textual Politics: Feminist Literary Theory* (London Routledge).

Ward Jouve, Nicole (1991) *White Woman Speaks with Forked Tongue, Criticism as Autobiography* (London: Routledge).

Index